THE NATURE OF THOUGHT
Essays in Honor of D. O. Hebb

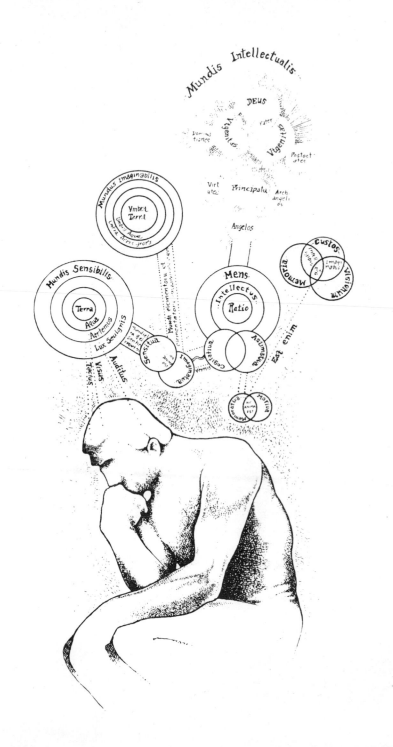

It might be argued that the task of the psychologist, the task of understanding behavior and reducing the vagaries of human thought to a mechanical process of cause and effect, is a more difficult one than that of any other scientist.

—D. O. Hebb

THE NATURE
OF THOUGHT

Essays in Honor of D. O. Hebb

Edited by
PETER W. JUSCZYK
RAYMOND M. KLEIN
Dalhousie University

 LAWRENCE ERLBAUM ASSOCIATES, PUBLISHERS
1980   Hillsdale, New Jersey

Lawrence Erlbaum Associates, Inc., Publishers
365 Broadway
Hillsdale, New Jersey 07642

Library of Congress Cataloging in Publication Data

Main entry under title:

The Nature of thought.

Includes bibliographies and index.
1. Thought and thinking—Addresses, essays,
lectures.   2. Hebb, Donald Olding,
I. Jusczyk, Peter W.   II. Klein,
Raymond M.
BF455.N35   153.4   80-18697
ISBN 0-89859-034-5

Printed in the United States of America

To our parents—
Walter, Eleanor, Max, and Edith

Contents

Preface

Early in 1977, Dalhousie University was honored by the return of one of its most illustrious alumni, D. O. Hebb. After a long and distinguished career at McGill University, Hebb joined the psychology department as Professor Emeritus. In celebration of this happy event the editors decided to dedicate a special lecture series in his honor and chose as a topic a subject of great interest to him—the nature of thought. In planning our lecture series, we attempted to put together a list of North American scholars of diverse backgrounds whose positions on thought seemed to be having a great impact on cognitive psychology. When most of the eminent scholars we had invited agreed to participate, we thought it would be a fitting tribute to Don to put together a book in his honor, which would be based on the lectures. Accordingly, this volume includes papers from the lectures in our series, plus four additional chapters by members of our department, (Klein, Jusczyk and Earhard, Nadel, and Goddard). Because of prior commitments, one of the original participants in the lecture series, Jerry Fodor, was unable to contribute a chapter. We believe that scholars and advanced students interested in the study of thought will find the papers in this volume useful in understanding some of the major trends in cognitive psychology.

The book begins with a short essay by Klein that provides some insights into the origins of Hebb's ideas and an overview of the impact that Hebb's thinking has had on current psychological theorizing.

Hebb's latest views on the subject of thought follow in his chapter, aptly titled, "The Structure of Thought." In his essay, Hebb addresses two issues concerning thought, namely, what are its constituent parts and how is thought directed. Within the framework of his cell-assembly theory, he argues that the main structure of thought is nonverbal, although it may have some verbal components as well. Hebb contrasts his view with what he sees as the traditional view that images cannot serve as the primary vehicle of thought. With respect to the second issue—the directedness of thought—he grapples with the problem of how one is able to maintain concentration until a conclusion is reached. He speculates that the answer may lie in the exceptionally high number of inhibitory neurons found in the human brain.

The remaining essays have been organized under broad headings. The papers included in the section entitled "Information-Processing Analysis" are indicative of the fruitful influence that research in artificial intelligence has had on cognitive psychology. For example, important insights into human problem solving have been gained by attempting to simulate this behavior on computers. Professor Simon has been outstanding in these efforts, and in his chapter he suggests ways in which computer simulation may illuminate the phenomena of human understanding. It is Simon's contention that processes that mediate understanding are represented in information-processing models of human thinking. In a similar spirit, Bever, Straub, Terrace, and Townsend suggest that information-processing models may provide a basis for explaining serially integrated behavior in people *and in animals*. Bever and his colleagues show that serial constraints in language have analogues in the performance of nonlinguistic tasks, both by humans and pigeons. In their chapter, they argue that "humans and animals alike utilize sequence representations and scanning procedures that are similar and similarly dependent on environmental contingencies."

The next section of the book focuses on issues in "Attention and Performance." Two contrasting views are presented. Posner argues that the information-processing framework, in general, and the reaction time methodology, in particular, can bridge the gap between physiology and subjective experience. In his essay he insists that chronometric studies of performance have begun to provide anwers to questions about the nature of consciousness—questions hitherto thought to be exclusively the province of those specialists who alter the mind and brain via drugs, surgery, and other means. By contrast, Neisser challenges the validity of the analogy between the way in which people and computers process information. In particular, he argues that findings from studies of dual task performance are incompatible with the notion, prevalent in information-processing theories, that the mind has a central processor of limited capacity.

Each of the papers in the section on "Mental Representation" deals with some aspect of the way in which concepts are represented in thought. Paivio examines recent studies of mental comparison for clues as to the nature of mental representation. On the basis of the pattern of results from these studies, he argues strongly in favor of the view that the underlying system of mental representation is modality-specific. Jusczyk and Earhard also address the question of the nature of the underlying system of mental representation. However, in contrast to Paivio, their examination of the literature leads them to the conclusion that not only must such a system necessarily be propositionally based, but also that a propositional base is presupposed by modality-specific models of representation. In their essay, they also devote some attention to what the basic elements, structure, and operations of such a propositional system might be. Krueger and Osherson explore another dimension of mental representaion, viz. how can one segregate from the set of all possible concepts those which are natural for humans. In their essay they examine one condition on conceptual naturalness: structural simplicity. They hypothesize the existence of a mental mechanism that computes the structural simplicity of sets and present evidence in favor of one theory (Goodman's) that describes its behavior.

A major theme in Hebb's work is that "the problem of understanding behavior is the problem of understanding the total action of the nervous system and vice versa." This theme is the focal point for the final section of the book, "Mind and Brain," which includes papers by two of Hebb's former students. In his chapter, Nadel asserts that there are cognitive maps in the brains of rats and men. He develops a model of how the hippocampus of the brain performs the cognitive mapping function, presenting fascinating evidence from clinical, neurophysiological, and behavioral studies in its support. In the final chapter, Goddard updates Hebb's cell-assembly theory in light of developments in neuroscience over the past three decades. He describes discoveries made in his laboratory and elsewhere and explores theoretical implications with significance for cognitive psychology that are generated by viewing this new knowledge from a Hebbian perspective.

We would like to acknowledge the support of a number of individuals who made this tribute to Dr. Hebb possible. Dr. Guy MacLean, Vice President (Academic & Research) at Dalhousie, provided additional funds through his office that made the lecture series possible. Bruce Earhard read and commented on a number of the chapters in this volume. Nancy Beattie and the departmental secretarial staff contributed their talents (and exhibited great patience) in the preparation of several of the manuscripts and other numerous clerical chores, and the assistance of Anne Ferguson in the preparation of the Subject Index was invaluable. Our wives, Ann Marie and Marilyn, were understanding throughout this whole period. Finally, we would express our sincere thanks to Don Hebb for returning to his alma mater, and by so doing, enriching the intellectual milieu at Dalhousie.

PETER W. JUSCZYK
RAYMOND M. KLEIN

THE NATURE OF THOUGHT
Essays in Honor of D. O. Hebb

I INTRODUCTION

1 D. O. Hebb: An Appreciation

Raymond M. Klein
Dalhousie University

Donald Olding Hebb was born in Chester, Nova Scotia on July 22, 1904. He attended Dalhousie University in Halifax, Novia Scotia, and in 1925 received his Bachelor's degree.[1] Today, Don Hebb is again living in Chester and has returned to Dalhousie as Professor Emeritus in the Department of Psychology. In the intervening years he became a major force in international psychology and major architect of modern psychological theory.

Hebb is perhaps best known for his neuropsychological cell-assembly theory, which was described in *The Organization of Behavior* in 1949. A central tenet of his theory is that one's previous experiences leave structural traces that exert an enduring influence on one's later perceptions and thoughts. Therefore, it would seem appropriate to examine Hebb's illustrious career in light of some of the prior experiences that shaped his thinking.[2]

GRADUATE WORK

On graduating from Dalhousie, Hebb aspired to write novels but chose instead to earn a living in the field of education. He spent several years as a teacher in the public schools and later as a public school principal. During this

---

[1]Although Hebb's undergraduate performance was not exceptional, it was also not as poor as he later made it out to be (1959). Hebb's best subjects were mathematics and physics. Interestingly, in 1925, psychology was taught within the Philosophy Department at Dalhousie, which did not have a separate Department of Psychology until 1948.

[2]For more thorough treatments of the influential experiences in Hebb's career, and more personal ones, see Hebb, 1959; 1980.

time he became interested in psychology chiefly through exposure to the writings of William James, Sigmund Freud, and James Watson. He managed to get accepted on a part-time basis by the McGill graduate program. Impressed at that time by Pavlov's work, which had been recently translated into English, Hebb considered himself fortunate to get a research assistant-ship with Dr. L. A. Andreyev, a visiting scholar from Pavlov's laboratory. On closer examination, Hebb lost his enthusiasm for Pavlov's program, and as he puts it (1959), "was softened up for my encounter with Köhler's Gestalt psychology and Lashley's critique of reflexology [p. 624]." Thus, after receiving his Master's degree from McGill in 1934, Hebb decided that full-time graduate work in physiological psychology was called for—if possible, under Lashley. By dint of great determination, Hebb gained entrance into Lashey's laboratory at the University of Chicago in 1934 and in the next year moved with Lashey to Harvard. Hebb acquired knowledge and skills he was lacking in anatomy and physiology and in 1936 completed his doctoral thesis on the effects of early visual deprivation and brain lesions on visual perception in the rat.

POSTGRADUATE WORK

Hebb attaches great significance to two postdoctoral experiences. After receiving his Ph. D., he was appointed a Fellow at the Montreal Neurological Institute (then often referred to as Penfield's clinic, now as simply MNI). There Hebb explored the impact of brain injury or surgery, particularly lesions of the frontal lobes on human intelligence and behavior. Hebb's observations that removal of large amounts of some cortical tissue might have little effect on memory and intelligence (see Hebb, 1945, for a review) was an important basis for his cell-assembly theory.

A few years later, Hebb began a second postdoctoral appointment, this time at the Yerkes Laboratories of Primate Biology. Lashley had just been appointed director, and together with Henry Nissen and Hebb, planned to explore the effects of various brain lesions on the behavior (performance and temperament) of adult chimpanzees. Although neither the opportunity to interact again with Lashley nor the research program materialized, Hebb still learned a great deal from the chimpanzees and his fellow researchers. Instead of brain lesions, he explored fear, anger, and other emotional processes in the chimpanzee. Hebb found this experience to be very broadening:

> I am accustomed to say that I learned more about human beings during that time than in any other five year period of my life except the first. After two or three months of daily observation the thirty adults of the colony were as distinctive in personality as one would expect of thirty human beings assembled

more or less at random. The personalities were human personalities, too, combinations of attitudes and motives and sensitivities that are quite familiar in human society [Hebb, 1980].

During this time, Hebb also began working out the details of his neuropsychological theory and in this effort he found the intellectual climate at the Yerkes Lab invaluable. In the preface to *The Organization of Behavior* (1949) Hebb guesses that his "greatest debt . . . is to the weekly colloquium and the persistent theoretical debate at the Yerkes Laboratories of Primate Biology between 1942 and 1947 [p. viii]."

In 1947 Hebb returned to McGill as Professor of Psychology and in 1948 was appointed Chairman of the Department. Under Hebb's leadership, the McGill department was to become one of the foremost psychology departments in North America and one of the most stimulating.

HEBB'S PROGRAM:
THE ORGANIZATION OF BEHAVIOR

In 1949 Hebb published *The Organization of Behavior: A Neuropsychological Theory*. It was an ambitious undertaking. In the preface Hebb notes: "In this book I have tried to bring together a number of different lines of research, in a general theory of behavior that attempts to bridge the gap between neurophysiology and psychology, as well as that between laboratory psychology and the problems of the clinic [Hebb, 1949, p. vii]." Considering the breadth of knowledge and experience Hebb brought into the enterprise, it is not surprising that he was so successful. Hebb (1959) himself was unhappy about the "misleading degree of specificity in some places, the vagueness in others [p. 624]" and expected the book to meet with a complete lack of interest. He was wrong. The book attracted extremely favorable international attention and was to have a profound impact upon the course of modern psychological science.

To appreciate why Hebb's ideas were so well received, it is necessary to understand the state of psychological science in 1949 and to have a feeling for the growing dissatisfaction with the ideas that dominated psychology at that time. Two early reviewers of Hebb's book emphasized the contrast between Hebb's program and those of his contemporaries:

In this lively and intelligent book, Dr. Hebb has tried to develop some broad principles of nervous organization which might have explanatory value in psychology. His aim throughout is to find conceptions "which will be valid physiologically and at the same time 'molar' enough to be useful in the analysis of behavior (p. 11)." If the task is difficult, Hebb has nonetheless made an original and exciting beginning. In the stagnant atmosphere of contemporary psychological discussion this little book comes like a breath of fresh air [Zangwill, 1950, p. 142].

I believe *The Organization of Behavior* to be the most important contribution to psychological theory in recent years. Unlike those of his contemporaries who are less interested in psychology than in some restricted aspect thereof to which their principles confine them, Hebb has made a noteworthy attempt to take the experimentally determined facts of behavior, as they are, and account for them in terms of events within the central nervous system [Attneave, 1950, p. 633].

In 1949, Gestalt theory was ascendant in the realm of perception, whereas S–R connectionism, principally Hull's, was ascendant in the realm of learning. Progress in psychology was hampered by the extreme polarization between adherents of these two frameworks. Although each claimed to be a comprehensive theory of behavior, neither theory was very successful in accounting for those aspects of behavior upon which the other focused. Concepts of attention, imagery, and expectancy were avoided, and explanations of thought were simplistic (e.g., Watson's subvocal speech) or more usually just not attempted. Both theoretical frameworks emphasized the stimulus, implied prompt transmission of sensory excitation to the motor side, and played down the role of motor responses in learning and perception.[3] Furthermore, treatment of the physiological level within these frameworks was either naive or absent. Learnng theorists tended to treat the brain as a switchboard with connections between stimuli and responses rigidly determining what an organism does. Gestalt psychologists proposed a "field theory" in which the cortex is regarded as a statistically homogenous medium with fields or waves of excitation in particular patterns determining the sensory control of motor centers. Neither of these viewpoints was fruitful from the point of view of understanding how the nervous systems controls behavior. An alternative and increasingly popular strategy was the avoidance of physiological hypotheses altogether (Skinner, 1938).

From Hebb's point of view, these ideas were leading psychology into blind alleys, and in *The Organization of Behavior* (1949) he cogently explains why. At the same time, he offers in their place an integrative, interdisciplinary approach and a single conceptual framework for dealing with thinking, perception, and learning in "terms of events within the central nervous system."

---

[3]A minimal role was accorded to motor processes by Hebb's learning theorist contemporaries: Feedback from one response can serve as the stimulus for the next response, thus allowing the formation of S–R chains. The bankruptcy of this explanation of sequential behavior was noted by Hebb (1949), and by Lashley in his classic paper "The Problem of Serial Order in Behavior" (1951). See Bever et al., Chapter 4, this volume, for a new approach to this enduring problem.

The nature and impact of Hebb's program can be understood in terms of four interlocking themes:

1. His belief in the necessity for an interdisciplinary approach to brain and behavior, one in which psychologist, neurophysiologist, clinician, and anatomist share ideas and findings and consider knowledge in the others' realms when building models to account for the evidence generated in their own.
2. His emphasis on the central problem of thought and the importance of internal mental processes such as attention, imagery, expectancy, hypotheses, etc.
3. His critique of the reigning theories of learning and perception for insufficient breadth (including the failure to handle thought adequately), physiological naivete, and in Hebb's view, several incorrect assumptions.
4. His proposal of an imaginative neuropsychological theory that was interdisciplinary in conception and broad in scope. A theory that made concrete predictions about real world variables and kindled the imagination of a generation of scientists.

Although scholars may differ on how to weigh the importance of these themes, in my view Hebb's impact on the course of psychology stems from the confluence of all four. It is to a brief discussion of each that I now turn.

Brain and Behavior

The importance of reciprocal assistance between psychologist and neurophysiologist is the most general theme developed by Hebb: "Psychologist and neurophysiologist thus chart the same bay together—working perhaps from opposite shores, sometimes overlapping and duplicating one another, but using some of the same fixed points and continually with the opportunity of contributing to each other's results. The problem of understanding behavior is the problem of understanding the total action of the nervous system, and *vice versa* [Hebb, 1949, p. xiv]." However, as Hebb points out, the value of this interdisciplinary approach was not universally acknowledged: "A vigorous movement has appeared in psychology and psychiatry to be rid of "physiologizing," that is to stop using physiological hypotheses. This point of view has been clearly and effectively put by Skinner (1938) . . . and is related to logical positivism. . . . This book is written in profound disagreement with such a program for psychology [Hebb, 1949, p. xiv]." Because of Hebb's advocacy of an interdisciplinary approach and his exciting and noteworthy exploitation of it in *The Organization of Behavior,* the book became a rallying point for those interested in bridging the gap between brain and behavior, and a vantage point from which to oppose Skinner's radical behaviorism. The recent proliferation of journals devoted to bridging this gap (Brain, Behavior & Evolution; Brain & Behavioral Sciences; Behavioral & Neural Biology, to mention a few) and the great progress in recent years in what has come to be called the neurosciences are noteworthy indications of the fruitfulness of the interdisciplinary approach advocated by Hebb. Chapters 10 and 11 in this volume by Nadel and Goddard, both McGill students who admit to Hebb's influence, provide skillful examples of the fertility of this approach.

Thinking

Having argued forcefully for an interdisciplinary approach to brain and behavior, Hebb outlines what for him is the central problems to be tackled by such an approach:

> Psychologically, it is the problem of thought: some sort of process that is not fully controlled by environmental stimulation and yet cooperates closely with that stimulation. From another point of view, physiologically, the problem is that of the transmission of excitation from sensory to motor cortex.... The failure of psychology to handle thought adequately... has been the essential weakness of modern psychological theory [Hebb, 1949, p. xvi].

Hebb points out that proponents of switchboard, field, and other approaches to the sensorimotor interface had not "made any serious attempt to elaborate ideas of a central mechanism to account for the delay, between stimulation and response, that seems so characteristic of thought [p. xvii]."[4]

In his later work Hebb repeatedly chides his fellow psychologists, past and present, for their inadequate treatment of this central and most difficult problem. In his 1953 paper, On Human Thought, he says:

> Thorndike tried to dispose of the difficulty 55 years ago by denying its existence. He buried thought in 1898, but the ghost insists on walking. Often we decline to say that animals think; but comparative psychology has been unable to avoid concluding that animals have expectancies, insights, hypotheses, conceptual activities, a variable attention and so forth. These are but aspects of thought; and if we cannot deal with the comparatively simple behavior of animals without taking account of thought, how adequate can a thought-less human psychology be [Hebb, 1953b, p. 99].

---

[4]Despite the fact that Hebb himself never attempted a detailed analysis of the temporal interval between stimulus and response, it is interesting that his emphasis on it foreshadowed a renaissance of interest in the use of response latency to explore mental operations (mental chronometry, see Posner, 1978; Chapter 5, this volume), which began in the 1950s and has continued unabated and with great success ever since.

In his 1960 APA presidential address, The American Revolution, Hebb again calls for psychology to balance its analysis of behavior with an analysis of thought. Psychologists eventually got the message. In assessing the state of psychology in 1976, McKeachie reflects on the great progress in cognitive psychology: "I doubt that APA presidential addresses really have the power to redirect our discipline, but whatever its import, Hebb's address was uncannily on target with respect to the course of psychology in the ensuing period [McKeachie, 1976, p. 827]." Of course, it was Hebb's deep commitment to the study of thought that encouraged us to make "the nature of thought" the topic for this collection of essays in his honor.

Critique of S–R and Gestalt Frameworks

To lay the groundwork for consideration of his neuropsychological theory, Hebb first had to point out the weaknesses in the reigning formulations of perception and learning. It is difficult today to conceive of the degree of domination that the Gestalt and S–R frameworks exerted on psychological thinking when *The Organization of Behavior* (1949) was written. Hebb's informed and acute critical examination played an important role in freeing psychological thought from their grasp (see Attneave, 1959, pp. 647–648).

Hebb began by rejecting the S–R connectionist assumption of complete sensory control of behavior:

> Now the tradition in psychology has long been a search for the property of the stimulus which by itself determines the ensuing response, at any given stage of learning. This approach... is no longer satisfactory as theory. Almost without exception psychologists have recognized the existence of the selective central factor that reinforces now one response, now another. The problem is to carry out to its logical conclusion an incomplete line of thought that starts out preoccupied with stimulus or stimulus configuration, eventually runs into the facts of attention and so on, and then simply agrees that attention is an important fact, without recognizing that this is inconsistent with one's earlier assumptions.... Since everyone knows that attention and set exist, we had better get the skeleton out of the closet and see what can be done with it [Hebb, 1949, pp. 4–5].

Hebb also rejected the Gestalt concepts of field theory and equipotentiality and with them the notion that perception and learning depend on the "pattern, or shape of the sensory excitation" rather than on the excitation of any particular neural cells. On the contrary, Hebb assumes that "perception does depend upon exciting specific parts of the receptor surface" and that "the memory trace, the basis of learning, is in some way structural and static." In his revision of perceptual theory, which Neisser (1967) called "the most thoughtful and wide-ranging discussion of visual cognition that we have," Hebb attempts to show, in contrast to Gestalt theory, "that 'simple' perceptions are in fact complex: that they are additive, that they depend on motor activity and that their apparent simplicity is only the end result of a long learning process [Hebb, 1949, p. 17]."[5] Finally, Hebb points out the difficulty Gestalt theory has with learning and the difficultly learning theory has with perception, and he argues that the problems of perception and learning are mutually dependent and must be dealt with in a single framework.

Hebb's strategy here is not merely destructive. To be sure, he is knocking down the reigning theories to make room for his own, but he does so appreciating and often incorporating the contributions each has made:

> It is important as psychology comes of age to avoid, if possible, the extreme positions that have often been adopted in the discussions of the past....The theory to be presented in the following chapters is explicitly designed to deal from the first with the problems of form perception and attention or set— problems whose existence has been most insisted on in recent years by the configurationists—as well as those problems of learning and memory empha- sized by learning theorists. Thus the present argument is based at least as much on Gestalt as on learning theory [Hebb, 1949, p. 59].

A Neuropsychological Theory

For some, like Goddard (Chapter 11, this volume) Hebb's greatest achieve- ment and contribution lies in his neuropsychological theory. Hebb begins by making a fundamental "connectionist" assumption: "When an axon of cell A is near enough to excite cell B and repeatedly or persistently takes part in firing it, some sort of growth process or metabolic change takes place in one or both cells such that A's efficiency, as one of the cells firing B, is increased [Hebb, 1949, p. 62]." Then he proceeds to develop the key concepts of the cell- assembly and the phase sequence. Hebb summarizes their role in his theory as follows:

> Any frequently repeated, particular stimulation will lead to the slow develop- ment of a "cell-assembly," a diffuse structure comprising cells in the cortex and

---

[5]Hebb relies heavily on the very slow development of pattern recognition following removal of congenital cateracts (Senden, 1932) or following the cessation of experimental visual deprivation in the neonate (Riesen, 1947) to support his claim that recognition of simple patterns depends upon a long learning process. Subsequent physiological research (for a review, see Barlow, 1975) demonstrating that early deprivation produces neural degeneration confirmed Hebb's emphasis on the importance of early experience. However, it also suggests (see Thompson, 1969) that recovery from this degeneration rather than learning may be the mechanism responsible for the slow development of pattern recognition (but see Hebb, 1963, for a rebuttal and clarification).

diencephalon..., capable of acting briefly as a closed system, delivering facilitation to other such systems and usually having a specific motor facilitation. A series of such events constitutes a "phase sequence"—the thought process. Each assembly action may be aroused by a preceding assembly, by a sensory event, or—normally—by both. The central facilitation from one of these activities on the next is the prototype of "attention." The theory proposes that in this central facilitation, and its varied relationship to sensory processes, lies the answer to an issue that is made inescapable by Humphrey's (1940) penetrating review of the problem of the direction of thought [Hebb, 1949, p. xix].

The theory is then applied to the problems of visual perception. Hebb assumes that the mammalian visual system has the innate capacity to distinguish figure from ground (which he refers to as primitive unity) but not to distinguish the identity of different patterns. He also assumes an innate system for detection of local features of a pattern, such as edges and corners, and an innate tendency to fixate these features in a more or less random scanning pattern. Although this much innate organization is conceded, by assigning to experience the indispensable role of structuring the cell assemblies that mediate perception, Hebb engaged in "the first serious opposition yet offered to Gestalt nativism [Attneave, 1950, p. 633]." Hebb's theory of perceptual learning and development treats lines and angles as "perceptual elements, not fully innate in perception, but partly so." Figure ground separation and scanning eye movements[6] allow the integration of these elements into higher order assemblies representing configurations. As a mnemonic, Hebb proposes this incomplete analogy: "If line and angle are the bricks from which form perceptions are built, the primitive unity of the figure might be regarded as mortar and eye movement as the hand of the builder [Hebb, 1949, p. 83]." After showing how his theory handles various problems in visual perception, Hebb goes on to analyze other phenomena of behavior: learning, motivation, insight, intelligence, emotional disturbance, and so on, in terms of his general scheme.

When Hebb wrote *The Organization of Behavior,* he knew that some specific proposals might be wrong: "As neurophysiology, this and the preceding chapter go beyond the bounds of useful speculation. They make too many steps of inference without experimental check [Hebb, 1949, p. 79]." And, in fact, while he was writing the book, important and relevant neuropsychological discoveries were being made: Eccles and his colleagues

---

[6]Hebb's emphasis on the role of eye movements in visual perception, and on motor activity generally, seems to be a clear forerunner of efference theories of visual perception (Festinger, Ono, Burnham, & Bamber, 1967). If applied to vocalization it is closely related to the motor theory of speech perception (see MacNeilage, 1970).

(Brock, Coombs, & Eccles, 1952) were discovering neural inhibition,[7] and Moruzzi and Magoun (1949) were uncovering the arousal functions of the reticular formation. Hebb later acknowledged that these results put an end to the specific form of his theory, but "not the universe from which it was drawn":

> It is then on a class of theory I recommend you to put your money, rather than any specific formulation that now exists.... Theories in this class attempt to analyze the central process. They postulate complexity within it, and try to determine how the component subsystems relate to each other and to sensory and motor events. That is, they go further than the postulate of unitary "mediating responses," each involved in a single action.... Psychologically defined, then, the class consists of theories real or potential, present or future, which deal with an interaction of simultaneously present representative or mediating processes in control of behavior, as well as sensory-central interactions [Hebb, 1963, p. 16].

IMPACT AND OUTGROWTHS

Hebb's imaginative and concrete theory stimulated an intensive effort to evaluate it on many fronts. His farsighted ideas foreshadowed several discoveries and anticipated several avenues of exciting research that were not directly aimed at assessing his theory. And finally, his emphasis on mental processes and his critique of reigning frameworks helped redirect the course of psychology from blind alleys into more fruitful ones. Some of these new findings and directions are examined briefly.

Perceptual Learning and Development: Early Experience

In reviewing *The Organization of Behavior,* Attneave (1950) predicted:

> Hebb's ideas can scarcely fail to have an important impact on the thinking and research of psychologists in a number of areas. His views on the importance of perceptual learning...will certainly give rise to much experimental work. The corollary argument that infant and adult learning are markedly different from each other may lead to a reconsideration of conclusions from earlier learning vs. maturation experiments. [p. 635].

---

[7]Hebb had considered proposing inhibitory processes, but felt that the theory was already speculative enough. Moreover, his effort to be grounded firmly in physiological data dictated against further speculation. Milner (1957) later pointed out that inhibition was necessary to prevent positive feedback from eventually activating all cell assemblies once just one was activated, and Hebb (1959; Chapter 2, this volume) later incorporated the concept.

Thirty years after the book was publsihed, J. McVicker Hunt (1979) confirmed Attneave's prediction in his review of the role of early experience in perceptual development (see also McCleary, 1970): "It is usually difficult to locate the specific source of a new stream of investigation, but for this one, as Riesen (1975) has noted, "Hebb's book, *The Organization of Behavior* was the document of that launching [p. 128]." Hunt asserts that Hebb's neuropsychological theory of perceptual development, together with Riesen's discovery (1947) that infant chimpanzees reared in the dark for the first 16 months of life are functionally blind, and Hebb's own work on the effects of early experience on intelligence in the rat, set off three separate streams of investigation into: (1) the relative importance of perceptual versus motor experience (e.g., Forgays & Forgays, 1952; Held & Hein, 1963; Hymovitch, 1952); (2) the effects of variations in sensory experience (e.g., Cynader & Chernenko, 1976; Hubel & Wiesel, 1963; Mitchell, 1978; see Barlow 1975 for a review); and (3) the effects of complexity of rearing conditions on intelligence (Gluck, Harlow & Schlitz, 1973; Harlow, Harlow, Schlitz, & Mohr, 1971; Thompson & Heron, 1954) and on the brain (e.g., see Rosenzweig, 1966). Even if some of Hebb's specific proposals have not been confirmed, it is to his great credit that his imaginative ideas prompted such a vigorous exploration of this enduring theme.

Sensory Deprivation

Hebb's emphasis on sensory experience was not confined to problems of development. In discussing monotony, Hebb (1949) proposed that "the phase sequence continually needs new content to maintain its organization and persistence [p. 227]," therefore, repetitive and monotonous environments should lead to a disruption of the thought process. In the early 1950s, Hebb and his colleagues developed and exploited a technique for studying the effects of sensory reduction or deprivation in the laboratory. Their research was founded in Hebb's theoretical framework and to some extent was designed to test some of its implications, but the immediate impetus for the research was to gain insights into brainwashing. According to Suedfeld (1969), the findings in this new field were exciting and unexpected: "Subjects who had been deprived of patterned sensory input had complicated hallucinations, showed intellectual and perceptual deterioration, became more susceptible to propaganda, and found the situation to be very unpleasant, frequently quitting the experiment in fairly short order [p. 3]." These studies were the first in what was to become a thriving area of investigation. In 1969, John Zubec, a former colleague of Hebb's, edited a volume entitled *Sensory Deprivation: 15 years of Research.* In that book, no less than 20 centers for sensory deprivation research were identified. The volume was dedicated: "To D. O. Hebb and his associates W. H. Bexton, B.

K. Doane, W. Heron, and the late T. H. Scott, who initiated the first experimental studies on sensory deprivation at McGill University."

Attention

Hebb's emphasis on attention (see p. 7) anticipated several decades of intensive research on this topic, beginning with Cherry's (1953) seminal studies of listening with one and two ears and Broadbent's (1958) filter theory. Hebb not only foreshadowed this interest in attention, he also proposed the rudiments of some contemporary attentional concepts. In Hebb's view, for example, the central facilitation of a cell assembly by a preceding assembly or a sensory event is "the prototype of attention." Modern attentional theorists, with the help of signal detection theory (Peterson & Birdsall, 1953), have been able to give Hebb's basic proposal a more precise expression. They might say that context or expectancy acts to lower the criterion of internal dictionary units (see Neisser, 1967, p. 211–212).

Hebb (1949) also addresses the problem of the unity of attention in a manner that is quite relevant to the disagreement between Neisser and Posner in their chapters in this volume:

> It is often supposed that there is an extraordinary unity about attention—that one can attend to one thing, or to another, but not to both at the same time unless the two are a single unit responded to as a whole. These conclusions need qualification... I have emphasized the idea that the motor facilitation of phase or phase sequence may be subliminal; and, to the extent that attention has the unity it is supposed to have, the unity may consist of a control of the motor system by one phase sequence only, when two or more run in parallel. Even then it should be remembered that we very often carry on two familiar activities at the same time. Arguing and driving a car will do as an instance; neither seems possible without "attention." It certainly seems that the unity of attention has been exaggerated, and the phase sequence hypothesis, at least, suggests that it may often by multiple [p. 150-1].

Cognitive Psychology

Finally, and from the point of view of the theme of this book, most important, through his effective attack on radical behaviorism, his unflagging emphasis on internal mental processes, his cogent demonstration of weaknesses in some key assumptions of the Gestalt and S–R frameworks, and his own cell-assembly proposal, Hebb may be said to have plowed the soil from which the renaissance in cognitive psychology would grow and flourish. In his information-processing analysis of cognition and thought, Walter Reitman (1965) acknowledges a great debt of Hebb's work (particularly *The Organization of Behavior,* and Hebb's contribution to the Koch series), and he labels

Hebb's neuropsychological theory as "probably the most seminal theory to appear in the postwar era."

Although the cognitive revolution might have been delayed or even stifled without Hebb's spadework, the "seed" of that revolution lay not in Hebb's cell-assemblies, but rather in "the development of the general purpose digital computer, information theory, and signal detection theory (Antrobus, 1970)."[8] As Reitman (1965) points out:

> Despite Hebb's emphasis upon the need to understand thought, in no sense is his theory a general theory of thinking. Specifically, Hebb never shows how the theory might account for the details of goal directed thinking.... It seems reasonable to ask (for example) how we might account in terms of systems of cell-assemblies for the cognitive processes taking place when a man is deciding to buy a pair of shoes, writing a poem, playing chess, or, or for that matter, adding two and two [p. 7].

Reitman believes that Hebb was lacking an appropriate formal language for an explanation of thought: "Information processing techniques provide us with a way out of these difficulties. They make it possible for us to carry on the *analysis* of central processes (in Hebb's sense) at a level well beyond anything possible at the time Hebb worked out his theory [p. 9]." Chapters, 3, 4, and 5 in this volume, by Simon, Bever and colleagues, and Posner respectively, provide the reader with a first-hand opportunity to evaluate Reitman's confidence in the information-processing framework.

SUBSEQUENT WORKS

Although he is best known for *The Organization of Behavior* (1949), Hebb has authored "A number of papers dealing with perception, intelligence, learning and memory, emotion and motivation in man, chimpanzee, porpoise, dog and rat"[9] many of which are classic, and a highly acclaimed and widely used *Textbook of Psychology*. Some of these papers may be of interest to contemporary scholars. I have therefore selected for brief discussion some of the more important and interesting papers written since 1949.[10]

---

[8]Even if the future of cognitive psychology is not wedded to the information-processing approach (see Neisser, 1976; Chapter 6, this volume), there is no doubt that its origins are.

[9]Seeking a list of Hebb's publications, I asked him for a copy of his vita. Under publications I found only this statement. I got what I was looking for when I asked him for a list of his publications.

[10]I make no pretense of being comprehensive. What follows is something of an idiosyncratic and abbreviated tour through Hebb's post-1949 work.

"Heredity and Environment in Mammalian Behavior" appeared in the first issue of the British Journal of Animal Behavior, in 1953. Hebb began this classic paper on the nature/nurture issue by asserting that if he had to choose sides, his bias would be toward nativism, "as a corrective against the common overemphasis by psychologists and psychiatrists on experience and learning in behavior." Because of his theory's emphasis on experience, Hebb is often incorrectly labeled an "empiricist." Perhaps his "nativistic" bias is a reaction to this inappropriate labeling. In any case, Hebb does not like labels, and does not think one can take sides on this issue. He uses several examples to illustrate how behavior results from a complex interplay between environmental and genetic factors, and claims (1953a): "We cannot dichotomize mammalian behavior into learned and unlearned, and parcel out these acts and propensities to the nativist, those to the empiricist [p. 43]." Hebb (1953a) then presents us with a marvelous metaphor on the nature/nurture issue:

> The question may still be asked, to what extent a given piece of behavior is dependent on one of these influences. Is it fifty-percent environment, fifty-percent heredity, or ninety to ten, or what are the proportions? This is exactly like asking how much of the area of a field is due to its length, how much to its width. The only reasonable answer is that the two proportions are one-hundred-percent environment, one-hundred-percent heredity. They are not additive; any bit of behavior, whatever, is fully dependent on each [p. 44].

Hebb goes on to acknowledge that it *is* meaningful to ask how much of the *variance* in a behavior is due to heredity and how much to environment, but cautions about the pitfalls of misinterpretation.

Hebb's clear thinking on this issue is present in much of his later work. In a 1963 APA address, Hebb defended his theoretical views against critics who:

> still ask the archaic question, whether perceptual organization is wholly dependent on learning during growth, or wholly independent of it.... In the eyes of one critic I had "straddled" the issue, unable to make up my mind; for others I was clearly saying that learning is the whole explanation of perception. Neither is true. Perhaps I may say again, that perceptual organization does not start at zero, but also that adult perception includes experience among its determinants, as it includes the genetic factor and the nutrient factor.

The nature–nurture issue has recently reappeared with a vengence in the often heated and sometimes irrational debate concerning the heritability of IQ. Here as elsewhere, Hebb's cogent and rational analysis (1970, 1971, 1978) has been a welcome relief.

In 1954, together with W. Thompson, Hebb wrote a chapter for the *Handbook of Social Psychology* entitled "The Social Significance of Animal Studies." One of the themes of this chapter was the value of animal studies when direct experiments with humans is not possible:

Failing the possibility of radical rearing experiments with human children, it seems that comparative study offers a solid line of advance in this field. Studies of a number of species will provide some basis for tentative extrapolation of the curves of phylogenetic development through chimpanzee to man, where the ideas thus arrived at can be tested for their value in clarifying clinical and naturalistic observations [Hebb & Thompson, 1954, p. 733].

As mentioned previously, researchers have provided us with fascinating and fundamental facts by performing the kinds of experiments Hebb was advocating here.

In 1955, Hebb incorporated the recently discovered ascending reticular activating system into a general theory of motivation and arousal. The title of the paper, "Drives and the CNS (Conceptual Nervous System)" was a joke on B. F. Skinner. In it Hebb described a continuum of arousal from deep sleep to strong emotion and suggested that optimal levels are in the middle of the continuum. This paper was to become one of the most cited in the psychological literature (see Current Contents, #14, April 2, 1979).

One of Hebb's most important papers was written for Koch's series *Psychology: A Study of a Science.* In this paper, Hebb (1959) discusses the origins, structure, and impact of his neuropsychological theory, as well as the revisions made necessary by subsequent experimentation. In response to the question on the further development of the theory, Hebb presents his views of the course of theoretical research:

If I knew where the next breakthrough would occur, or which of the many are *the* difficulties, I would be able to plan a systematic attack. But this is a misconception of theoretical research—the nub of the matter is so clear in hindsight, unclear ahead of time. We operate by hunches, and one's only strategy is to interest intelligent people of diverse skills, interests, and knowledge, in the problems as one sees them [p. 642].

In the execution of this strategy Hebb was exceedingly successful, as amply demonstrated by the contributions of his own students and others who passed through McGill or were otherwise influenced by his ideas.

Hebb's three major APA addresses make for interesting reading. In one (1963), he discusses the positive evidence for his cell-assembly theory, particularly the pattern of disappearance of stabilized retinal images (see Pritchard, Heron, & Hebb, 1960), and he defends his theory against various criticisms (see p. 17). The other two addresses, "The American Revolution" (1960) and "What Psychology is About" (1974) are like presidential State of the Union messages. Hebb assesses the past performance and present status of contemporary psychology and tries to point the discipline towards a more productive and healthy future.

Every reader will, I believe, enjoy Hebb's "Science and the World of Imagination" (1975). In this paper, Hebb shows that the history of science is full of "fudge factors," that these transgressions are as frequent in the physical sciences as elsewhere, and that they have often been associated with great theoretical advances in our understanding of nature. Hebb claims that what science deals with is an imagined world and that these great advances were advances in imagination. Hebb discusses the implications of this view for the conduct of teaching and research.

Finally, it seems appropriate to draw attention to Hebb's most recent works. Hebb discusses the development of his thinking from a personal perspective in *A History of Psychology in Autobiography VII* (1980). Hebb's new book, *Essay on Mind* (1980), provides his latest ideas on the nature of thought and should be of interest to most readers of this book.

CONCLUSION

In his distinguished career, Hebb has won many honors and awards too numerous to mention here. I can think of no better way of ending this essay than by repeating the citation that was made in 1961 when he was awarded the APA's medal for Distinguished Scientific Contribution:

> For creative, insightful theorizing and ingenious experimentation on psychology's fundamental problems, ranging over the domains of perception, learning, motivation, affectivity, and thought; for bold, challenging, yet flexible and fact-oriented efforts to explain behavior and experience through an informed and resourceful use of physiological concepts. Combining broad scientific knowledge, philosophical clarity, a rich personal research experience involving several species, and synthesizing findings selected judiciously from experimental, naturalistic, clinical and psychometric sources, he has daringly revived and cogently defended neuropsychological conjecture in a form which has generated unusually fruitful research, and which exerts an ever-growing influence upon behavioral scientists [p. 802].

REFERENCES

Antrobus, J. S. Introduction: The renaissance of cognitive psychology. In J. Antrobus (Ed.), *Cognition and affect.* Boston: Little, Brown, & Company, 1970.

Attneave, F. Review of *Organization of Behavior* by D. O. Hebb. *American Journal of Psychology,* 1950, *63,* 633–635.

Attneave, F. Perception and related areas. In S. Koch (Ed.) *Psychology: A Study of a Science* (Vol. 4). New York: McGraw Hill, 1959.

Barlow, H. B. Visual experience and cortical development. *Nature,* 1975, *258,* 199–204.

Broadbent, D. E. *Perception and communication.* New York: Pergamon Press, 1958.

Brock, L. G., Coombs, J. S., & Eccles, J. C. The recording of potentials from motoneurons with an intracellular electrode. *Journal of Neurophysiology,* 1952, *117,* 431–460.

Cherry, E. C. Some experiments on the recognition of speech with one and with two ears. *Journal of the Acoustical Society of America,* 1953, *25* 975–979.

Cynader, M., & Chernenko, G. Abolition of direction selectivity in the visual cortex of the cat. *Science,* 1976, *193,* 504–5.

Festinger, L., Burnham, C., Ono, H., and Bamber, D. Efference and the conscious experience of visual perception. *Journal of Experimental Psychology,* 1967, *74,* 1–36.

Forgays, D. G., & Forgays, J. The nature of the effect of free-environmental experience in the rat. *Journal of Comparative and Physiological Psychology,* 1952, *45,* 322–328.

Gluck, J. P., Harlow, H. F., & Schlitz, K. A. Differential effect of early enrichment and deprivation on learning in the rhesus monkey (macaca mulata). *Journal of Comparative and Physiological Psychology,* 1973, *84,* 598–604.

Harlow, H. F., Harlow, M. K., Schlitz, K. A., & Mohr, D. J. The effect of early adverse and enriched environments on the learning ability of rhesus monkeys. In L. E. Jarrad (Ed.), *Cognitive processes of nonhuman primates.* New York: Academic Press, 1971.

Hebb, D. O. Man's frontal lobes: A critical review. *Archives of Neurology and Psychiatry (Chicago)* 1945, *54,* 10–24.

Hebb, D. O. *The organization of behavior.* New York: Wiley, 1949.

Hebb, D. O. Heredity and environment in mammalian behavior. *British Journal of Animal Behavior,* 1953, *1,* 43–47. (a)

Hebb, D. O. On human thought. *Canadian Journal of Psychology,* 1953, 7, 99–110. (b)

Hebb, D. O. Drives and the CNS (conceptual nervous system). *Psychological Review,* 1955, *62,* 243–254.

Hebb, D. O. A neuropsychological theory. In S. Koch (Ed.), *Psychology: A study of a science* (Vol. 1). New York: McGraw–Hill, 1959.

Hebb, D. O. The American revolution. *American Psychologist,* 1960, *15,* 735–745.

Citation for D. O. Hebb, on receipt of award for Distinguished Scientific Contribution. *American Psychologist,* 1961, *16,* 802.

Hebb, D. O. The semi-autonomous process: Its nature and nurture. *American Psychologist,* 1963, *18,* 16–27.

Hebb, D. O. A return to Jensen and his social science critics. *American Psychologist,* 1970, *25,* 568.

Hebb, D. O. Whose confusion? *American Psychologist,* 1971, *26,* 736.

Hebb, D. O. What psychology is about. *American Psychologist,* 1974, *29,* 71–79.

Hebb, D. O. Science and the world of imagination. *Canadian Psychological Review,* 1975, *16,* 4–11.

Hebb, D. O. Open letter to a friend who thinks the IQ is a social evil. *American Psychologist,* 1978, *33,* 1143–1144.

Hebb, D. O. *Essay on mind.* Hillsdale, N.J.: Lawrence Erlbaum Associates, 1980.

Hebb, D. O. D. O. Hebb. In G. Lindzey (Ed.), *A history of psychology in autobiography* (Vol. VII). San Francisco: W. H. Freman & Company, 1980.

Hebb, D. O., & Thompson, W. R. The social significance of animal studies. In D. Lindzey (Ed.), *Handbook of social psychology* (Vol. 1). Cambridge, Mass.: Addison-Wesley, 1954.

Held, R., & Hein, A. Movement produced stimulation in the development of visually guided behavior. *Journal of Comparative and Physiological Psychology,* 1963, *56,* 607–613.

Hubel, D. H., & Wiesel, T. N. Receptive fields of cells in striate cortex of very young visually inexperienced kittens. *Journal of Neurophysiology,* 1963, *6,* 994–1002.

Hunt, J. McVicker. Psychological development: Early experience. *Annual Review of Psychology,* 1979, 30, 103–143.

Hymovitch, B. The effect of experimental variations on problem solving in the rat. *Journal of Comparative and Physiological Psychology,* 1952, *45,* 313–321.

Lashley, K. S. The problem of serial order in behavior. In L. A. Jeffress (Ed.), *Cerebral mechanisms in behavior: The Hixon symposium.* New York: Wiley, 1951.

MacNeilage, P. Motor control of serial ordering of speech. *Psychological Review,* 1970, *77,* 182–196.

McCleary, R. A. *Genetic and experiential factors in perception.* Glenview, Ill.: Scott, Foresman & Co., 1970.

McKeachie, W. Psychology in America's bicentennial year. *American Psychologist,* 1976, *31,* p. 819.

Milner, P. M. The cell assembly: Mark II. *Psychological Review,* 1957, *64,* 242–252.

Mitchell, D. E. The effect of early experience on the development of certain perceptual abilities in animal and man. In H. Pick & R. Walk (Eds.), *Perception and experience.* Plenum Press, 1978.

Moruzzi, G., & Magoun, H. W. Brain stem reticular formation and activation of the EEG. *Electroencephalography and Clinical Neurophysiology,* 1949, *1,* 455–473.

Neisser, U. *Cognitive psychology.* New York: Appleton-Century-Crofts, 1967.

Neisser, U. *Cognition and reality.* San Francisco: W. H. Freeman, 1976.

Peterson, W. W., & Birdsall, T. G. *The theory of signal detectability.* (Technical Report No. 3). University of Michigan: Electronic Defense Group, 1953.

Posner, M. I. *Chronometric explorations of mind.* Hillsdale, New Jersey: Lawrence Erlbaum Associates, 1978.

Pritchard, R. M., Heron, W., & Hebb, D. O. Visual perception approached by the method of stabilized images. *Canadian Journal of Psychology,* 1960, *14,* 67–77.

Reitman, W. R. *Cognition and thought: An information processing approach.* New York: John Wiley & Sons, 1965.

Riesen, A. H. The development of visual perception in man and chimpanzee. *Science,* 1947, *106,* 107–108.

Riesen, A. H. *The developmental neuropsychology of sensory deprivation.* New York: Academic Press, 1975.

Rosenzweig, M. Environmental complexity, cerebral change and behavior. *American Psychologist,* 1966, *21,* 321–332.

Senden, M. V. *Raum- und gestaltauffassung bei operierten blindgeborenen vor und nach der operation.* Leipzig: Barth, 1932.

Skinner, B. F. *The behavior of organisms: An experimental analysis.* New York: Appleton-Century, 1938.

Suedfeld, P. Introduction and historical background. In J. P. Zubec (Ed.), *Sensory deprivation: 15 years of research.* New York: Meredith, 1969.

Thompson, R. F. Neurophysiology and thought: The neural substrates of thinking. In J. Voss (Ed.), *Approaches to thought.* Columbus, Ohio: Merrill, 1969.

Thompson, W. R., & Heron, W. The effects of restricting early experience on the problem-solving capacity of dogs. *Canadian Journal of Psychology,* 1954, *8,* 17–31.

Zangwill, O. L. Review of *Organization of Behavior* by D. O. Hebb. *Quarterly Journal of Experimental Psychology,* 1950, 2, 142–143.

Zubec, P. *Sensory deprivation: 15 years of research.* New York: Meredith, 1969.

2 The Structure of Thought

D. O. Hebb
Dalhousie University

This chapter is concerned with the operation of thought as it takes place in the ordinary conditions of life. That is, the effects of brain injury are excluded as well as neurotic and psychotic disorder, and it does not attempt to deal with Hilgard's (1977) very important discovery of separate streams of consciousness in certain cases of hypnosis—very important, but one that would take us too far afield[1].

WORKING ASSUMPTIONS

It is best to begin by making explicit some working assumptions, as follows. The study of thought must be a theoretical one, not introspective and descriptive. Thought is solely an activity of the brain; neurological information is fundamental but not sufficient and cannot be sufficient; and cell assemblies are the basis of thought.

I have discovered to my surprise that the meaning of the term *introspection* is not understood by many of the present generation of psychologists, who quite properly insist that experience and private evidence have an important contribution to make to our understanding of the mind but who confuse the use of private evidence with introspection. "Introspection" literally means looking inward, and the introspective study of mind and thought was the attempt by such workers as Wundt, Külpe, and Titchener to observe mental activity directly and describe it. Modern objective psychology has given up

---

[1]See Chapter 8 in D. O. Hebb, *Essay on Mind* (1980), on which the present lecture was based.

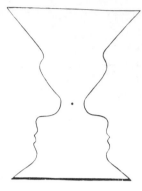

FIG. 2.1. The ambiguous or reversible figure. With gaze fixed on the center dot, one can perceive either goblet or profiles, so eye movement is not necessary to the change from one percept to the other. After Rubin, from Hebb (1972). Reprinted by permission.

that attempt, but we can still make use of private evidence as a valid basis of inference concerning what does go on in mental activity. Let me illustrate.

Private evidence consists of the awareness of one's own body, in the form of somatosensory perception; awareness of the rest of the physical world; and imagery or representative activity, in which one seems to perceive events of the physical world but knows from other accompanying evidence that this is illusory. In none of the three cases does one observe one's mental activity. When you bark your shin, what you are aware of is not a process going on in your head but the state of your shinbone. From that awareness you can discover the duration of the theoretically known process of pain perception and something about the way it affects, and is affected by, other perceptual processes, but this is not direct observation of your own mental activity. By looking at Rubin's ambiguous figure, you discover that the same visual stimulation can give rise to different perceptions. With certain preliminary preparation (e.g., looking at a series of vaselike figures), you discover that prior experience affects what is perceived, but the discovery depends on inference and the comparison of perceptions of external objects made at different times or in different circumstances. You do not perceive the perceptions but the external objects. In the case of imagery, the role of inference is particularly clear. What you are aware of is some visual, auditory, or tactual object or event, but at the same time there is conflicting evidence to tell you that the apparent perception is not real—that is, it will not be confirmed if you explore it further. In the case of vision, one usually may distinguish image from percept by a certain faintness or lack of vivid detail, but still this is a characteristic of the object one seems to be perceiving, not of the imaginal process itself.

So far are we in fact from such a direct acquaintance with our perceptual activity that we may even be unable to discriminate between vision, hearing, and touch, apart from the circumstances in which the sensory stimulation occurs (e.g., if what one is perceiving is at a distance it cannot be tactual; or if it is at a distance and behind the head, it must be auditory). This at least is suggested by the formerly held theory of "facial vision." It is a familiar experience in complete darkness to know that one is approaching some large solid object, though how one knows it may be very puzzling. The theory of facial vision proposed that the skin of the face must have a sensitivity, somewhat like that of the eye, which makes possible the awareness of nearby objects. Actually, the perception is auditory (Supa, Cotzin, & Dallenbach, 1944). It is a case of echolocation; the ear is stimulated both by the sound of one's breathing or the rustle of one's clothing and by the echo, the sound wave that is bounced back from the nearby surface a milisecond or so later. The fact that the theory could be seriously considered is enough to show that auditory sensation, at least, is not automatically distinguishable as such.

All this means is that our mental processes are not directly known. One cannot prove that such knowledge does not exist, for that would be proving the null hypothesis, but all our present knowledge points to that conclusion. Modern psychology is basically an objective science; even in its use of private evidence, which others can only know from verbal report, what the observer can actually report is not mental self-observation but observation of the physical world, real or illusory. The observer tends to confuse inference with observation, as Titchener's group did (Humphrey, 1951), but that is a mistake. The study of the mind is a theoretical enterprise, not descriptive.

It is important also to see that this conclusion applies equally to physiologically based study. It might seem, if thought is an activity of the brain, that it could be recorded and studied physiologically, but this neglects the complexity of the brain. Ten thousand electrodes, even if they could be inserted in the right places, would not be sufficient. Not only are there an estimated 10 or 12 billion neurons in the human brain, but the number of ways in which they may group themselves in functional systems, units of thought, is enormously greater. Scott (1977) quotes Legendy's conclusion that the number of cell assemblies (each of 10,000 neurons) in the individual brain is of the order of a billion, and the number of different ways in which such a number of assemblies might be established, in different brains, is almost infinite. Even if human beings were willing to have a great number of electrodes inserted through holes in their skulls, for single-cell recording, it would not be possible to work out gradualy where to put them by studying a series of subjects, for each brain must be different in this respect. Familiar as it may seem to be, human thought is both as real and as impossible to observe directly as the quarks that the physicist is concerned with these days, and a lot more complicated.

So we must theorize, testing the implication of theoretical ideas against the observable evidence of behavior (including, of course, the behavior of reporting private evidence). Obviously, it is implied also that theory must be ultimately concordant with histological and physiological fact.

THE CONSTITUTION OF THOUGHT: IDEAS

The two main problems of classical theory concerned the constituent parts (the elements or items of which thought is made up) and the direction of thought (how to account for its temporal sequence and apparent order). For the first of these the obvious candidate was the image—images evidently do occur in thought—but this notion had difficulties when it came to generalization and abstraction. This in turn led to the theory that thought is mainly verbal. I come to the second problem shortly; here I must try to show first that thought must be primarily nonverbal, even when it generalizes and abstracts, which it does all the time.

The trouble with the image as vehicle of thought was mainly that no one had any good alternative to thinking of the image as the reinstatement of a specific perception, though it was recognized that this was not satisfactory. William James made fun of the notion but offered no alternative. Obviously, an image of a particular animal as it is seen in one position at one time cannot represent that animal in all its different postures and activities, let alone represent animals in general. What then do such general ideas consist of? And how is a trait of an animal represented, apart from the animal itself? An image of a fox by itself cannot sometimes represent foxes, sometimes animals at large, sometimes foxiness or cunning. When you think of a person as "foxy," you might have an image of a fox, but even so, the image would not be of something that is seen in people. Various attempts were made to provide for some modification of the image, to make it less rigid, but this was never really successful.

However, it *could* be supposed that the word "animal" is associated in your mind with each of the different creatures you know of, and the word "foxy" as a purely verbal event can of course be associated with people about as readily as with foxes. That sort of solution for the problem of abstraction and generalization had its own difficulties—if there is not some common property that is *perceived* in both people and foxes, how did the verbal association with people occur in the first place? Nevertheless, this did have the advantage of being an intelligible theory of thought: Thought is verbal, and the way you perceive and think about your world is determined by the way you have learned to talk about it. If I am right, the real support for such a theory was the lack of any other explanation for generalization and abstraction. That support may now be removed.

In this century there has been a revolutionary change in our understanding of the brain, which has opened new possibilities for psychological explanation. The new ideas come from Berger, Adrian, Lorente de Nó (following up and making us aware of some forgotten work of the great Ramón y Cajal), Moruzzi & Magoun, Eccles, Hubel, & Wiesel, and—I may add—two psychologists, Olds & Milner. These men have provided solid factual data that make possible new theoretical ideas. For my purpose here, this concerns cell assemblies of lower and higher order, abstraction and generalization increasing as one goes from first-order to third- or fourth-order assemblies (Hebb, 1968). Generalization for example: In essence, suppose that the child's perception of an adult is the excitation of, say, 100 million neurons, a different set each time, but suppose also that there may be a thousand neurons common to all those different excitations. If those thousand become organized in an assembly, because of being active every time the child sees a human being, the activity of that assembly will be the idea of a *person,* generalized. Abstraction is involved also, for the assembly is representative only of characteristics that people have in common—head, hands, voice, and so forth. The idea of a particular person, or a particular voice, would require the added activity of other assemblies ("schema with correction").

If the classical difficulty of generalization and abstraction can be met in that way, the theory that thought is primarily verbal (with imagery to liven it up) is no longer inescapable. The explanation of course is theoretical, but it is no longer true that there is no alternative to the verbal theory. Moreover, some aspects of verbal thought itself may become more intelligible in terms of the theory. Hebb, Lambert, and Tucker (1971) have shown how a nonverbal mechanism of imagery may deal with a problem raised by Bever, Fodor, & Weksel (1965), who "had to assume that the underlying form from which the passive [voice] derives is . . . an abstract structure never realized in speech [p. 473]." What we proposed is that memory of an event in which A hits B may be recalled either with A in the center of attention followed by impact on B, in which case verbal report would naturally take the active form, *A hit B*; or with B in the center of attention, in which case the sequence of ideas is image of B, impact, A, tending to excite the verbal formulation *B was hit by A*. In terms of a thought process that integrates verbal and nonverbal imagery, an otherwise puzzling problem looks simpler.

Again, Slobin (1966) proposes that a child must develop criteria of what he calls "nounness," an apparently esoteric conception. We were able to show how such a thing might be made physiologically intelligible as a product of experience. In brief, the suggestion is that a higher-order cell assembly would be formed when the neurons organize that are common to all the sets that are excited when the child sees something concrete and hears its name. Later, the child generalizes this to include words that act in the same way in adult speech—i.e., abstract nouns. The proposal is that thereafter exposure to a noun excites both lower-order assembly activity, specific to that word, and also higher-order activity representative of the class of the word: namely, nounness. Similarly with verb, adjective, and adverb. This is best illustrated in the context of Chomsky's famous sentence: COLORLESS GREEN IDEAS SLEEP FURIOUSLY in which no word is reasonable in its context but which as a whole is undeniably an organized English sentence. The reasonable "feel" of that semantically preposterous affirmation comes from the higher-order assemblies representative of *adjectiveness–adjectiveness–nounness–verb-*

ness–adverbness: all in order at this level, despite the conflict at the level of lower-order assemblies.

Now back to the main argument. If we need not have recourse to verbal symbols to account for generalization and abstraction in human thought, we can look afresh at the question of verbal thought. And as soon as we do, it becomes apparent that the main structure of thought cannot be verbal, though it may of course have verbal components, and in the case of adult human thought normally does. Consider: Generalization can be demonstrated in chimpanzee thought an in the 18-month-old human infant, both of whom are capable of more complex thought than their command of verbal behavior, if any. Again, Levy, Trevarthen, & Sperry (1972) show that it is the right hemisphere, which mostly lacks verbal control, that can see the broader picture and functions holistically, rather than in the more detailed analytic style of the left hemisphere. Clearly that molar style is essential to abstract thought, and it cannot be primarily verbal.

The essential argument, however, is the difficulty all of us meet in putting thought into words. Think how far it is from knowing something about electricity to communicating the knowledge to someone else, or from knowing how the political system works to putting your knowledge into words intelligibly. Think how much easier it is to respond appropriately in social situations and know that one's behavior is appropriate than to explain why it is appropriate. In general: If thought is verbal, in content and organization, how can it ever be hard to find the words, ready organized, to communicate your thoughts to others?

So primary thought, the main stream, must be nonverbal; verbal thought certainly exists, it is a powerful tool, but it is only a tool or adjunct to a primarily nonverbal mechanism. Not the boss, the straw boss.

ORGANIZATION AND DIRECTEDNESS
IN THOUGHT

The second classical problem, concerning the "direction" of thought, was how to account for the capacity of thought to stick to the same topic until a conclusion is reached. Thought was treated as a single series of ideas—images and verbalizations—one after another in single file, each link in the chain determined by whatever association of the preceding link happened to be strongest at the moment. There is no way in which such a sequence could ever maintain direction or ever solve a problem. A recent comic strip shows where the difficulty lies ("Beetle Baily" by Mort Walker, April 19, 1977). An instructor, apparently, says "Now the theory of atomic fission is" at which point one of the class interrupts: "Speaking of women—." The instructor objects—the student explains: "You said fission, which makes one think of fishin for tuna, piano tunas make music, music makes me want to dance, and who do you dance with? Women!" There in a nutshell is the problem of the direction of thought. The problem is radically changed if thought is not a series of ideas one at a time, if a considerable number of ideas or ideational components (assemblies and subassemblies) are active together, including a maintained background activity of assemblies that constitute the *Aufgabe,* the task or the guiding idea of the goal.

That surmounts the classical difficulty, but this recourse to physiological considerations raises a new problem. Having a big brain may not be a help in all respects, if there are many more neurons than is necessary for any particular task. (That this is a real consideration is shown by the lack of effect of some quite large brain lesions, and the extensive loss of neurons in old men who still seem to have all their marbles.) Neurons not called on by external excitation nevertheless will be active spontaneously. That activity must be "noise," disruptive of the organized activity of other neurons. One aspect of this is the familiar student's problem of "concentration," when the extra activity is organized and takes the form of daydreams. How is that extra activity to be avoided or made nondisruptive?

It is implausible to suppose that a minority of neurons—the organized ones constituting the main train of thought—can actively inhibit a much larger majority, and I have proposed that the organization can be maintained only by incorporating within itself that "extra" activity (Hebb, 1976). We know, of course, that the ease of concentration varies with the topic, being self-maintaining with some topics, at best intermittent with others because of the persistent intrusion of irrelevant content. The first kind is what we call "interesting." The interesting topic is, I propose, one that immediately commands a wide organization of cerebral activity because it excites cell assemblies with manifold associative connections. This is the physiological formulation. Psychologically (from the point of view of the thinker, that is) such a task is one that at once gives rise to further ideas, and these to still further ones; it is one that can be seen from this angle and that, each such sequence interconnected with the others as the whole process develops and breaks new ground. If the physiological proposal is right, if this coherence depends on such a rich network of connections between assemblies, it becomes more intelligible why the level of thought at maturity is a function of exposure in childhood to the complexity of the home. It makes more intelligible Goldfarb's (1943) extraordinary observations of the deleterious effects of 3 early years in an orphanage, compared to the same 3 years in a foster home. In a well-run orphanage things are orderly, with minimal variety, and lack the multitudinous contingencies and coincidences of the ordinary untidy home.

What then is the function of the very large number of inhibitory neurons in the human brain? In the same paper (Hebb, 1976), it was proposed that instead of suppressing "extra" neuronal activity, inhibition serves to streamline thought by a prompt cutoff of activity in the cell assembly once it has served its function of exciting the next one (or a motor pathway). Continued firing thereafter would be a form of noise. In 1949 I thought that the closed pathways of the cerebral cortex must have the function of making possible a holding of activity in reverberatory circuits, because it was thought then that a neuron fired once would be subnormal and would need to be strongly stimulated to fire a second time. Not long after the theory was published, however, it was found that a neuron fired once tends to fire repeatedly. If assemblies active in sequence also had to keep on firing, this could be disruptive indeed. It would be as if a key on a piano could not be struck once only, or as if the note could not be damped but had to keep on sounding loudly while subsequent notes were sounding, preventing the player from producing a clear quick run of single notes. The exceptionally high frequency of inhibitory neurons in the human brain (Rakic, 1975) may thus have the essential function of streamlining thought—a point that I will return to.

PERCEPT AND CONCEPT

Turn now to the nature of concepts. If one assumes, as I think we must, that conceptual activities all originate in perception, though characteristically in new combinations and new sequences (which is creativity, since the resulting pattern does not correspond to any one part experience), one may also assume that these processes retain some of the properties of perception. From that assumption some interesting conclusions follow.

First, a concept cannot be a static unchanging process, and it must vary to some extent with the context in which it appears. The simplest case of a concept—regarded as an activity originating in perception but occurring in the absence of the adequate environmental stimulus—is the image or idea of some object or event, relatively unmodified: that is, an ordinary visual or auditory or tactual memory. As soon as one examines it, one finds that a visual image of a car, for example, is an active series of part -images— dynamic, as perception itself is, not static (Hebb, 1968). I have also argued that the perceptual process involves higher-order abstractions as well as lower-order processes specific to the object perceived, and this also must must apply to the concept.

This bears on a remarkable statement made in a letter by Wolfgang Mozart, who in describing the process of developing (creating) one of his musical pieces said that when it was completed in his mind—in the course of a walk after dinner or during a sleepless night—he could hear the new piece as a whole, all at once, as one can see a picture at once. The authenticity of the letter has been doubted, perhaps because the statement sounds so unlikely. A musical piece is necessarily a sequence and can only be heard as a sequence—

even in imagination, how could Mozart hear the whole thing without starting at the first and going on to the end? But we can see now how such an illusory impression would be possible. In the visual realm, when one has an image of a street scene or of a familiar printed word, it seems as though the whole lies before one, complete and clear in detail. We know in fact that this is illusion; the imagery in detail is a series of part-images, just as seeing in detail is (Hebb, 1968), but that ability to "look at"—call up an image of—any of the parts of the scene inevitably makes one feel that the whole is there being looked at like a picture. In the same way, because Mozart could hear at will any part of the whole and had at the same time higher-order abstract ideas representative of larger segments of the piece and of the piece as a whole, it could well have seemed to him that it was all there, active in his mind all at once. If the authenticity of his letter is still in doubt on the ground of the improbability of making such a statement, the doubter should consider a parallel report of whose authenticity there is no doubt whatever. Henri Poincaré remarked in his famous lecture on creativity in 1913, that although he had a poor memory for the details he could still recreate a long and difficult mathematical argument because he "perceived at a glance" the course of the argument, and this served to remind him of the detail in the proper order. This observation is particularly interesting because it denies that the process was merely a rapid run-through of the component parts: The "seeing-as-a-whole" came first, detail second. Something else was involved at a higher level. A mathematical demonstration is as sequential as a piece of music and cannot literally be recalled as a single event. Nevertheless, it might well seem so, when the argument is seen in thought as spatially ordered (as Mozart's music may have been seen) and any part can be reinstated in imagery as if an external representation were being looked at.

It is interesting to see how wide the ramifications are of supposing that concepts share the fluidity and dynamic Gestalt properties of the percept. N. R. Hanson (1958) in *Patterns of Discovery* has related the phenomena of the ambiguous figure to the scientist's world view, ostensibly in terms of perceiving the world but really with respect to knowledge, which is conceptual. He posed a riddle for philosophy: How can two scientists looking at the same event see different things? And Kuhn (1962, p. 220) also is "acutely aware" of the difficulties caused by the fact that Aristotle and Galileo looking at a swinging stone could have seen different things (because of their different ideas about the nature of motion). But these difficulties are merely verbal; they arise from implicitly giving the word "see" its figurative meaning instead of its ordinary one signifying the reception of visual stimulation. In the fundamental sense of the word, both observers see the same thing, but perceive it differently. Visual perception is, or includes, the activity of cell assemblies (experimentally demonstrated: Pritchard, Heron, & Hebb, 1960), and is thus a part of thought rather than sensation. In effect, the two see the same thing but think about it differently. No problem for philosophy.

And Hanson (like others, including myself, who have discussed the ambiguous figure) has overlooked the fact that an observer of Rubin's famous diagram of the vase and profiles perceives three things, not two: (1) the vase; (2) the profiles facing each other; and (3) the diagram itself, as a set of lines drawn on paper. Thus, Tycho Brahe and Johannes Kepler looking at the sunrise, in Hanson's discussion: In that situation it was possible to perceive: (1) the sun rising in its revolution about the earth, as Tycho did; or (2) the earth revolving downward to give the illusion of sunrise, as Kepler saw it. But in either case both men would see and perceive the change of light, the color reflected from the clouds, and the sun's gradual appearance above the horizon, whatever else they might also "see."

The point is obvious, but there is still somthing of interest here, that relates for example to the logical problem for the mathematician of proving that $2 + 2 = 4$. This has been a more complicated matter than it may seem. Bertrand Russell (1961, p. 786) for example says that the proof is long and arduous and that the resulting knowledge is "merely verbal knowledge." In fact it is not verbal in origin, and the difficulty of proof results only from treating the problem entirely as a verbal and symbolic one.

Consider Fig. 2.2, and the Gestalt phenomena of grouping. At one moment the four items appear as a single group; at another, as two and two; again as two groups, one item left and three right, or vice versa; or as four single items. At the same time one also perceives that the source of this variety, the set of four stimulus objects, remains all the while unchanged. It is *the same set* that is perceived as two and two, and as four. Thus, *the referent of the idea of two and two is also the referent of the idea of four,* and this is evidently true of any other four objects or events, not only those of Fig. 2.2. A very high order of

O O O O FIG. 2.2.   To show Gestalt phenomena of grouping.

abstraction but common in thought is the idea of *something* (Hebb, Lambert, & Tucker, 1971). The Gestalt grouping is still possible when one thinks of four somethings, a phrase that may properly be translated as any four things—a fully generalized proposition. The conclusion drawn from the figure is therefore not restricted to any particular set of four. The figure offers an example of a nonverbal visual logic (which might be auditory or tactual also since the Gestal phenomenon of grouping is found in those fields, too) showing directly that two plus two equals four.

CREATIVITY

But there are bigger fish in this pond, or at least ones that are closer to current psychological interest. The parallel between percept and concept is enlightening also for the fundamental problem of creativity. I am talking here

FIG. 2.3. Illustrating a proposal concerning the creative idea. *A, C, E,* and so on represent randomly firing cell-assembly groups that constitute the occurrence of ideas about the problem (they are, of course, not spatially separated as in the figure). The solution is represented by *K–L–M,* firing in that order. From D. O. Hebb (1974). Copyright 1974 by the American Psychological Association. Reprinted by permission.

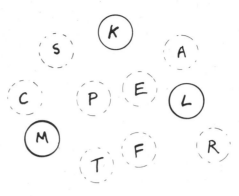

about scientific creativity because there is more detailed evidence available in the history of scientific thought, but I do not suggest that creativity in science is of a special kind—quite the contrary.

In an earlier preliminary attack on the problem of scientific problem solving (Hebb, 1974), the letters of Fig. 2.3 were used to represent the ideas, regarded as activity in cell assemblies or assembly groups, that occur in the presolution period. The letters *K, L,* and *M,* encircled with solid lines, represent elements needed for the ultimate solution; the rest, with broken lines, other ideas with which the thinker approaches the problem. For the thinker, all these represent data or ideas possibly relevant to the solution, but which of them are really relevant he does not know. They are active and subside, appear in his thought and disappear, more or less at random and in varied combinations, until the crucial sequence *K–L–M* occurs by itself. The sequence is crucial because it is able to initiate a new line of thought: A new way of looking at the data that reveals order or a new idea of how to deal with the situation.

This is a crude and mechanical formulation but we will see that it can be developed further, and it already has some value. It shows for example how to understand that element of chance in technical discovery that is so evident in the historical record. It shows how a pre-existent bias can prevent discovery; if for example *K* is strongly associated with *E,* and *E* is incompatible with *L* (either because of inhibition or because the two share some of the same assemblies, differently organized), the sequence *K–L–M* cannot occur and the thinker does not solve the problem even though the necessary components of the solution are available to him. And the scheme shows how, when one is stuck in problem solving, it may help to set the problem aside for a time; for one's first attempts at solution may have produced a temporary connection of *K* with *E* that will weaken if both are left inactive for a time.

All this depends on assuming that a concept like a percept is a sequential activity of subordinate elements. The parallel with perception can be taken further, in the figure–ground relation. Figure 2.3 clearly implies that segregation of relevant from irrelevant items in thought is crucial for the creative process. Once the ideas *K, L,* and *M* are active separately from the others, the probability of arriving at the solution (i.e., the correct sequence) is high. The proof that rickets is caused by a lack of sunshine may have been long and laborious, but the problem was solved in principle when the question was put in terms of the relation of sunshine to a child's skin and the high frequency of the disease in smoke-obscured Northern cities. The old saying is familiar, that stating a problem in the right way is halfway to a solution. This itself is a half-truth, but the truth it does contain lies in the fact that the right formulation separates out the relevant from the irrelevant: Is rickets due to persistent lack of sunlight, where there is smog? Can there be two different atomic weights with the same set of chemical properties? Is the heart truly a pump—can the blood in the arterioles somehow reach the veins by vessels too small to be seen? *Does* Nature abhor a vacuum, or does the suction pump work instead because of the weight of the air outside?

Now this need of sorting out the relevant items in thought has its perceptual parallel in the figure–ground phenomenon, especially with the hidden figure—and especially a difficult one like that of Fig. 2.4. Some of you may already know this one and have discovered the figure it contains, a Christlike representation of a man. Some of you instead, though seeing the whole for the first time, may at once discover the figure, for there is an element of chance here that adds to the similarity to scientific problem solving. For others the figure is well hidden—and then, when you do see it, you will hardly be able again to look at it without seeing the figure of the man. Having once detected

FIG. 2.4.   Hidden figure. From Paul B. Porter (1954). Copyright 1954 by the Board of Trustees of the University of Illinois. Reprinted by permission.

it, it is perfectly obvious. The same is true of scientific ideas like those of torque, of inertia, or of allergy, which took genius to develop but became simplicity itself once discovered.

Treating the hidden figure as a paradigm of discovery allows us to improve on the crudity of the discussion based on Fig. 2.3. The new idea in that case was supposed to consist of three items of thought, *K–L–M,* in that order and in the absence of others. In the real world, with a problem of any complexity, the likelihood that such a sequence could result from random activity, in a very much larger number of possibly relevant facts and ideas, would be small indeed. A less simplistic treatment can now be suggested.

It is clear that perception of the male head and shoulders in Fig. 2.4, when it does occur, does so independently—or even in spite of—any attempt at systematic examination of details of the presentation. Seeing what is figure and what ground, among these details, *follows* the discovery of the figure. The parallel with scientific discovery implies that the discovery occurs first, and only then can the thinker know which are the relevant ideas and the relevant facts. So much is perhaps obvious, but we can go further. In Fig. 2.4 one recognizes a man but not a man that one has seen before; the recognition is of a member of a *class* of objects.[2] A necessary condition for a perception that involves such generalization is the possession of a perceptual program, a pre-existent cortical organization that can be excited by exposure to any member of the class. (That means the excitation of higher-order cell assemblies, but the argument can be pursued without reference to that aspect of theory.) What is implied by the parallel with scientific discovery is that the scientist who comes up with a new idea must already have a template of abstract thought into which his data suddenly fit. The chance element is still present with this proposal and still great, but in a different way.

If it seems that this is a lot to conclude from a possibly false similarity of percept and concept, from a parallel between the child's game of "find the hidden figure" and serious research, there are some supporting considerations. I draw attention to the ubiquitous role of analogy shown by the figures of speech in scientific language. I argued earlier (Hebb, 1949) that it was not merely a verbal convenience to speak of a "rise" in blood-sugar "level," or of a "cycle" of sunspots. These figures of speech point instead to a use of existing patterns of thought to accommodate and organize new data and new ideas. "Sound waves" for example have no concrete similarity to waves seen in the ocean, but at a higher level of abstraction they both share a pattern of opposed states that alternate rhythmically. The water moves up and down, the air is alternately compressed and rarefied; and in both cases energy is transmitted, diminishing with distance. Again, Rutherford's ideas about the

---

[2]If you do not see the figure I have described and have given up trying to discover it, I reluctantly direct you to page 35 at the end of this chapter.

atom utilized the familiar schema of sun and planets, while today's physicists are talking about quarks of which some have "charm," and some lack it—a succinct way of saying that two of them, like two people, may be identical in definable characteristics but also have an important difference that is detectable only in its effects. Such aspects of scientific thought seem to mean that long-established and sometimes very primitive ideas are used to impose order on new ideas. Primitive, at times even of childish origin? Is a weather system a whirlpool of air, over half a contintent instead of in the kitchen sink? Is the double helix a coil of wire? With the necessary and successive corrections, these schemata tend to become complex indeed, but their origin may still go back to childhood experience.

UNEXPECTED IMPLICATIONS

What is suggested here is that developments of adult thought, not only in science but generally, are elaborations of ideas that originate in childhood, and this unexpectedly takes us back to an old problem, long forgotten. What is the nature of the special learning of childhood that determines mental age, the MA of the intelligence testers? It is learning as well as maturation, for it depends on an adequately stimulating environment, but it ceases in adolescence, somewhere between, say, 12 and 18 years of age. Thereafter of course learning goes on, but not of the same kind, for no exposure after the age of 15 or so can raise an MA that was depressed by lack of a good environment earlier. What is the nature of the learning that can only happen during childhood?

The preceding discussion suggests an answer. Theoretically, learning can be either the development of new cell assemblies or the recombination of ones already in existence. Childhood then may be the only period in which new cell assemblies are formed, all learning thereafter being the recombinative kind. This proposal does not of course imply a sudden shift from one to the other at 15 years of age. From 1 or 2 years of age onward both forms of learning must go on, the combinative kind steadily increasing in amount, the formation of new assemblies reaching a peak perhaps at 6 or 7 and then petering out gradually in adolescence. From then on *all* learning is in terms of what has already been learned, and limited of course in kind and extent by any limitation of the earlier development in childhood—to a great extent, very early childhood.

It is fun to speculate, and it may even be useful when it shows you how to look at such old problems in a new way. Let me add a final example.

There has been a fundamental problem about the relation between intelligence and the size of the brain. It seems, on the face of it, that size must be important, but it cannot be the whole story in view of the fact that the elephant and the great whales have brains three to five times as big as the human brain; even the porpoise has a somewhat bigger one. Around the first of the century attempts were made to deal with the problem by reference to the brain-weight/body-weight ratio, apparently on the assumption that the elephant, for example, needs a very big brain to manage his big body and has not much left over as a basis for intelligence. Man is more intelligent because he has a relatively big brain and a relatively small body. But the assumption is false; there are big animals with very small brains that control body movement very well. Nowadays the evolutionist talks instead about indices of encephalization (see Jerison, 1973), but this is still based on a relation of brain size to body size and so lacks any rationale in explaining the basis of the intellectual superiority of modern man. Human brain substance seems markedly superior in itself. Some other variable must operate, and this conclusion is supported by the fact that there is only a low relation of brain size to level of intellectual function *within* the human species. Eminent men have had brains as small as 1100 gm and as large as 2000 gm (the average for the species is about 1300 gm) but "sundry nitwits"—I quote an anatomist—have had very big brains too, as well as small ones. Given a minimal size of, say, 1100 gm, the other variable can be decisive. What can it be? For years, when lecturing on this question, I told students that no answer was available. The only guess I could make was that there must be some metabolic difference between the human brain and that of other animals and, to a less extent, between individual human brains. But I could not see how this would operate, and the whole thing was a mystery to me.

And then during a discussion of the idea that the function of cortical inhibition may be to shut off a cell assembly promptly after it has fired—the suggestion made earlier in this chapter—Peter Milner drew my attention to Rakic's (1975) report of the frequency of the presumptively inhibitory local-circuit neurons in the cortex at different phylogenetic levels: for the rabbit, 31%; for the cat, 35%; for the monkey, 45%; and for man, 75%, an astonishing difference. If those short-axon cells are as it seems inhibitory, and if the inhibition has the function that I have proposed, of streamlining the thought process and increasing its efficiency, then those values can plausibly explain the high efficiency of the human brain compared to that of other species. Conversely, we can now suggest to the comparative neurologist what the evolutionary advantage is of that surprisingly high proportion of short-axon cells in the human cerebral cortex; they made possible a more effective thought, clearer and quicker, and what could have been of greater value for the nascent species in its competititon with others?

REFERENCES

Abercrombie, M. L. J. *The anatomy of judgment.* London: Hutchinson Publishing Group, Ltd., 1960.

Bever, T., Fodor, J. A., & Weksel, W. On the acquisition of syntax: A critique of "contextual generalization." *Psychological Review*, 1965, *72*, 467–482.

Goldfarb, W. Effects of early institutional care on adolescent personality. *Journal of Experimental Education*, 1943, *12*, 106–129.

Hanson, N. R. *Patterns of discovery*. Cambridge: Cambridge University Press, 1958.

Hebb, D. O. *Organization of behavior*. New York: Wiley, 1949.

Hebb, D. O. Concerning imagery. *Psychological Review*, 1968, *75*, 466–477.

Hebb, D. O. *A textbook of psychology* (3rd ed.). Philadelphia: Saunders, 1972.

Hebb, D. O. What psychology is about. *American Psychologist*, 1974, *29*, 71–79.

Hebb, D. O. Physiological learning theory. *Journal of Abnormal Child Psychology*, 1976, *4*, 309–314.

Hebb, D. O. *Essay on mind*. New York: Lawrence Erlbaum Associates, 1980.

Hebb, D. O., Lambert, W. E., & Tucker, G. R. Language, thought and experience. *Modern Language Journal*, 1971, *55*, 212–222.

Hilgard, E. R. *Divided consciousness*. New York: Wiley, 1977.

Humphrey, G. *Thinking*. London: Methuen, 1951.

Jerison, H. J. *Evolution of the brain and intelligence*. New York: Academic Press, 1973.

Kuhn, T. S. *The structure of scientific revolutions*. Chicago: University of Chicago Press, 1962.

Levy, J., Trevarthen, C., & Sperry, R. W. Perception of bilateral chimeric figures following hemispheric deconnection. *Brain*, 1972, *98*, 61–78.

Porter, P. B. Another puzzle picture. *American Journal of Psychology*, 1954, *67*, 550.

Pritchard, R. M., Heron, W., & Hebb, D. O. Visual perception approached by the method of stabilized images. *Canadian Journal of Psychology*, 1960, *14*, 67–77.

Rakic, P. Local circuit neurons. *Neurosciences Research Program Bulletin*, 1975, *13*, No. 3.

Russell, B. *History of western philosophy*. London: Allen & Unwin, 1961.

Scott, A. C. *Neurophysics*. New York: Wiley, 1977.

Slobin, D. I. Comments on "Developmental psycholinguistics." In F. Smith & G. A. Miller (Eds.), *The genesis of language*. Cambridge, Mass.: MIT Press, 1966.

Supa, M., Cotzin, M., & Dallenbach, K. M. "Facial vision": The perception of obstacles by the blind. *American Journal of Psychology*, 1944, *57*, 133–183.

FIG. 2.5.   Revealing the hidden figure. From Abercrombie (1960). Copyright 1960 by Hutchinson Publishing Group, Ltd. Reprinted by permission.

II INFORMATION-PROCESSING ANALYSIS

3 Information-Processing Explanations of Understanding

Herbert A. Simon
Carnegie-Mellon University

The explanation of human mental processes that Donald O. Hebb provided some 30 years ago in his *Organization of Behavior* (1949) is now a permanent part of the conceptual equipment of psychology. The cell assembly is as familiar a construct as the reflex. In rereading the book, one is immediately struck again with the insight and imagination of its author in building a coherent picture of mind from a mass of complex and confusing evidence. What may be less evident—unless one has a long memory—are the reasons why *Organization of Behavior* produced such a violent shock wave when it impacted on the hard shell of a behaviorism reluctant to look inside the human head, much less populate it with structures as rich as cell assemblies. The courage of the author in rejecting the dominant S–R psychology and reintroducing central mental processes is quite as remarkable as his psychological insight.

That shock wave continues to reverberate through psychology. We are no longer satisfied with external descriptions of regularities that say nothing about the mechanisms producing them. We want to formulate and test, however indirectly, what is going on inside. I don't know how sympathetic Donald Hebb is with the particular form of explanation that today is known as *information-processing psychology*. Whatever his sympathy or lack of it, his courage in exploring the mechanisms of mind must bear a large share of the responsibility for setting others on this path. Without the example of that courage, few would be foolhardy enough to investigate phenomena as intricate and cloudy as the phenomena of human understanding.

"Understanding" is one of those global terms referring to processes of the human mind whose importance we acknowledge even as its meaning remains vague and ambiguous. No one—certainly no practicing teacher—doubts for a moment that there is a fundamental difference between learning through understanding and learning by rote and that the former is infinitely to be preferred to the latter. There is even a modest body of empirical evidence (Katona, 1940) indicating that material learned through understanding is retained longer and transferred more readily to new tasks than material learned by rote. If the distinction merits the significance we attach to it, then we need to provide it with some operational foundations and to explore the mechanisms that enable understanding to arise.

SOME MEANINGS OF "UNDERSTANDING"

In a recent survey of artificial intelligence approaches to understanding (Simon, 1977), I undertook to provide some definitions of the term, building on an earlier proposal by Moore and Newell (1974). Just as intelligence is defined by specifying tasks the intelligent person is able to perform ("Intelligence is what intelligence tests measure"), so understanding is defined by specifying tasks the understanding person can perform. Let me enumerate what I think are some of the relevant tasks.

Understanding, like intelligence, has many facets: We can speak of someone understanding knowledge or of someone understanding a task. In the first case, following Moore and Newell (1974), we can say that "S understands knowledge K if S uses K whenever appropriate." Notice that this definition distinguishes clearly between *having* knowledge and *understanding* it. I may know (i.e., be able to repeat on request) the definition, "the sine of an angle is the side opposite over the hypotenuse," without being able to answer the question, "What is the sine of 45 degrees?". It is precisely this kind of difference we are trying to get at when we distinguish between rote learning and learning through understanding.

Similarly, we would not say that someone understands the game of chess simply because that individual can recite the rules for a legal move. We would want to test further to make sure the individual can actually apply the rules in a chess situation. We may say that S understands task T if S has the knowledge and procedures needed to perform T.

Some important ambiguities remain even in these definitions. One may know how ("understand how") to play chess without knowing how to play it well. In fact, we commonly make a rather strong distinction between understanding a problem and being able to solve it. There is a celebrated mathematical hypothesis, Goldbach's conjecture, that any even number can be expressed as a sum of exactly two prime numbers. It is not at all difficult to understand Goldbach's conjecture—that is, to know what it would mean for it to be true or false. However, no one has yet been able, after a century of effort, to prove whether the conjecture is true, or false, or undecidable.

Understanding how to perform a task may or may not entail understanding the principles underlying task performance. Most automobile drivers have only the vaguest idea of how a clutch operates or how carburetor and spark plugs control the injection and ignition of fuel. We presently examine an example of alternative solution algorithms for solving a problem that correspond to different understandings of the problem structure. There are many other nuances to the term "understanding" that I cannot go into here.[1] My main goal is to illustrate, with concrete examples, how processes that mediate understanding, in one or the other application of that term, are represented in information-processing models of human thinking. In the next section, I sketch out the modeling strategy in general terms. In the two succeeding sections I describe in greater detail two examples of information-processing systems that simulate human understanding.

MODELING UNDERSTANDING PROCESSES

The basic strategy for modeling understanding processes is identical with the general strategy for computer simulation of human thinking. A task is selected, successful performance of which is regarded as evidence of some particular form of understanding. On the basis of any knowledge we may have of how people perform this task, together with our general knowledge of human cognitive processes, we construct a computer program capable of performing the task we have selected, and of doing so without using any computer capabilities—rapid arithmetic operations or unlimited short-term memory—that we know people do not possess. After testing the program's performance on the understanding task, we carry out various comparisons with data (e.g., latencies, thinking-aloud data, error statistics) obtained from human performance of the same task. If we regard the computer program as a theory, which it is, this is simply an application of the general procedure for testing theories that is used throughout science. Let us look at a few examples.

One of the earliest understanding programs was described in Robert Lindsay's 1961 doctoral dissertation (Lindsay, 1963), which undertook to understand Basic English in the context of making inferences about kinship relations. Given such sentences as "John is Mary's father" and "Alice is John's sister," Lindsay's system could infer and report that "Alice is Mary's aunt" and "Mary is Alice's niece." This act of understanding required two basic abilities: the ability to carry out syntactical analyses of simple English prose, and the ability to carry out inferences based on lexical definitions like "a parent's sister is an aunt." The demonstrated success of Lindsay's system in performing the language-processing and inference task allows us to hypothe-

---

[1] For a more elaborate taxonomy of forms of understanding, see Simon (1977).

size that it is precisely the possession of these abilities that enables people to exhibit understanding in these kinds of tasks. Lindsay's system was, of course, only a first step toward the construction of more flexible, general, and powerful language-understanding schemes with inference-making capabilities, but it illustrates how computer models can illuminate the nature of the human processes.[2]

Other aspects of understanding are illustrated by Winograd's well-known SHRDLU program (Winograd, 1972). Understanding "cat" involves more than having a lexical definition for the term. A "real" understanding of what the word means requires the ability to recognize a cat when one appears on the scene. Any system that understands words having real-world referents must have intentional definitions of these words in the form of tests that can be applied to real-world objects.

SHRDLU has this capability in principle, although the "real world" on which it operates is in fact a simulated Block World that exists in a computer memory. The Block World contains blocks of various shapes and colors resting on a table or on each other. SHRDLU is able both to answer questions about the Block World (e.g., "Is there a blue cone standing on a yellow cube?") and to obey instructions that involve moving blocks (e.g., "Place the small cube on the large cylinder."). Executing such commands requires not only an ability to understand what is meant by them, but also a problem-solving ability for finding a sequence of actions that will actually carry them out. The problem-solving component of SHRDLU uses forms of means–ends reasoning very similar to those embodied in the General Problem Solver (Newell & Simon, 1972).[3] By storing the reasons for its sequences of actions, SHRDLU acquires another kind of understanding: the ability to explain why it did certain things. It can carry on a conversation like this: "Why did you move the green pyramid?"; "In order to clear the large cylinder?"; "Why did you want to clear the large cylinder?"; "In order to place the small cube on it."; "And why did you want to do that?"; "Because you told me to."

A major product of the first two decades' research on systems that understand in various task environments, including the systems described briefly above, was to identify a small set of mechanisms that showed up again and again as essential components of understanding systems. The first of

---

[2]Anderson & Bower (1973) contains an extensive survey of langauge-understanding systems that have been constructed in the intervening years. See also Siklóssy & Simon (1972).

[3]In brief, means–ends reasoning involves comparing the present state of the system with the desired goal state, detecting one or more differences between them, recovering from long-term memory one or more operators that are relevant to reducing differences of the kinds that were detected, and applying one of the operators. The process is then repeated until all differences between present state and goals have been eliminated. For a fuller discussion of this and other terms from information-processing psychology, see Newell and Simon (1972).

these are mechanisms for syntactical parsing of natural language. The second are mechanisms for mapping input information into canonical representations that can be stored in semantic memory. (Lindsay's system, for example, stored its information in family trees.) The third are mechanisms for inferring implied meanings by exploiting the relations among several input sentences, including mechanisms for doing means–ends reasoning. The fourth are matching mechanisms for assessing schemas of semantic information stored in long-term memory and relating these to new information provided explicitly in input strings. The fifth are mechanisms that can recognize instances of concepts and classify objects in terms of those concepts. The sixth are mechanisms for generating objects that satisfy specified relations. The seventh are mechanisms for finding reasons for the system's own actions.

This is certainly not a complete inventory of the range of mechanisms that will be required to simulate human understanding in all of the task environments where it manifests itself. What is shows, however, is that of the substantial number of "understanding" programs that have been constructed, each one is usually capable of operating in only a very restricted range of task environments, and all rest on a common base of quite general processes.

I have referred to these programs as simulations of *human* understanding. Many of them were written, of course, not with the specific goal of simulating human processes, but with the aim of exploring and extending the capabilities of computers for intelligent action. In spite of that, I believe that most of the mechanisms they use are essential also to human intelligence. In the two examples I discuss in the following sections, we have a certain amount of empirical evidence that this is so.

THE *UNDERSTAND* PROGRAM

In an earlier section of this chapter, Goldbach's conjecture was used to illustrate the distinction between understanding a problem and understanding how to solve it. This is simply one instance of the vast number of situations we encounter where we have to understand a set of instructions expressed in natural language before we can carry them out. More homely and practical examples are the instructions on a can of soup or medicine bottle, or instructions for filling out an income tax form.

In these situations, and others like them, we are engaged in a two-stage process: first to extract the meanings of the written instructions, and then to use our problem-solving abilities to follow those instructions. There are two classes of such situations (really a continuum, but I consider the extreme possibilities). On the one hand, the instructions may be entirely self-contained, so that, once we understand them, we possess all the knowledge that we need in order to solve them. In that case, we may conceive of the second stage as being carried out by some kind of general problem-solving process that incorporates one or more general procedure for attempting to solve problems but no specific knowledge or information about any particular problem domain. We call problems that, once understood, can be attempted by a general problem solver, "puzzlelike" problems. Most of the problem-solving tasks that have been studied in the psychological laboratory fall in this category: e.g., the Tower of Hanoi problem, the Missionaries and Cannibals problem, water-jug problems, and so on.

The second class of problems are those that, even after they are understood, require domain-specific knowledge as well as general problem-solving capabilities for their solution. For example, solving a textbook problem in physics stated in natural language may require the ability to understand not only general English-language text, but also the specific meanings of physical terms like "acceleration" and "lever," and knowledge of some physical laws—the law of mechanical advantage for levers or the law of falling bodies—that govern the behavior of physical systems. We call problems that require specific knowledge for their solution, "semantically rich" problems.

The UNDERSTAND program (Hayes & Simon, 1974) was designed to simulate the processes for understanding puzzlelike problems. UNDER- STAND takes the written instructions in natural langauge as its input and produces as output the information that would be needed, in turn, as input to the General Problem Solver (GPS) so that the latter program could go to work on the problem (without guarantees, of course, that it would be successful in solving it).

The input for GPS that UNDERSTAND produces consist of: (1) a representation for problem states,[4] which permits a description of the objects appearing in the problem instructions and their relations; and (2) routines for legal move operators that can transform one problem state into another. We claim that the program understands because it uses its knowledge appropriately to construct the representation and the routines.

What knowledge does UNDERSTAND call on in its performance? Its only external source is the set of written problem instructions. Its internal sources, embodied in the program, include: (1) a natural language parser; (2) capabilities for transforming the parsed text into an internal list structure representation of objects and relations; (3) stored programs capable of modifying list structures in a variety of ways and of making tests on list structures; (4) capabilities for mapping the legal move descriptions in the instructions on appropriate moves and tests selected from among these stored programs; and (5) capabilities for executing the stored programs and tests

---

[4]Problem states are situations reachable by applying "legal move" operators from the initial problem situation.

interpretively so that they operate correctly on the particular representations constructed by the processes that transform the parsed text.

I must digress to explain some of the computer science terminology I have used in this description and to motivate its use in the context of simulation of human thought processes. In particular, what do "list structures" have to do with human memory? A list is simply an ordered set of elements—which could be used, for example, to represent a simple chain of associations. A list structure is an assemblage of lists—which could be used to represent an assemblage of associations (more precisely, of *directed* associations, in the Wuerzburg sense of the term). A more complete explanation of the use of list structures to represent an associational memory may be found in Newell and Simon (1972, Chapter 2), or in Anderson and Bower (1973).

To account for storage of new information in such an associational memory, for the modification of existing information, or for the accessing of information, only a few basic processes need be postulated, and—most important—these processes depend only on the structure of memory, and not on its content. They include, for example, processes for adding an item to a list, for deleting an item from a list, for copying an item from one list to another, for comparing two items for identity, and the like. Once represented as list structures, all problems look alike to such a system—that is to say, they all can be attacked with processes that are indifferent to real-world content, and responsive only to the organization of the abstracted list structures. The "stored programs" referred to are simple combinations of these basic processes.

Consider the familiar puzzle of moving three missionaries and three cannibals across a river, with the conditions that they must be rowed across in a boat holding at most two persons and that missionaries must never be left alone with a larger number of cannibals. The list-structure description of this problem might consist of a list of missionaries and cannibals on the left side of the river, a list of those on the right side of the river, and a list of those in the boat. A "move" operator would transfer members of these lists from one location (list) to another, as the boat is loaded, moved across the river, and unloaded. Another simple operator would compare the relative number of missionaries and cannibals on each list. Of course, the system would need no knowledge of the meanings of "missonary" and "cannibal"—they could as well be labeled "hobbits" and "orcs." Nor would "boat" and "river" have any but abstract properties, unrelated to real-world knowledge about boats and rivers.

UNDERSTAND parses the natural-language text of the problem instructions and discovers in the parsed text the classes of objects that are being talked about ("missionaries," "cannibals") and the properties and relations of those objects (location, number). By examining the formal properties of the legal moves described in the instructions (the number and types of arguments), it assembles from the basic operators stored in its memory a legal move operator (in this case, an operator for transferring objects from one list to another, and checking that the legal move conditions are satisfied). This is essentially all the information that GPS needs in order to conduct a heuristic search for a problem solution.

The UNDERSTAND program is demonstrably capable of understanding the instructions for simple, puzzlelike problems. J. R. Hayes and I (Hayes & Simon, 1974; Hayes & Simon, 1977; Simon & Hayes, 1976) have carried out several empirical studies to compare the program's behavior with that of human subjects faced with the same task. Human thinking-aloud protocols show generally good correspondence with the processes postulated by the program. Moreover, the program predicts correctly the alterations that can be induced in human subjects' problem representations by manipulating the text of the problem instructions. I think it fair to say that, on the basis of the available evidence, UNDERSTAND provides a good first-order theory of human understanding processes in abstract problem environments.

Some progress has been made, also in simulating the understanding process for semantically rich domains, but much remains to be done. The central difficulty, of course, is that in understanding such problems, people make use of the knowledge of the domain they already possess, and therefore that knowledge must be represented in the memory of the problem-solving system. This means that we must make a reasonably complete inventory of such knowledge for a particular domain before we can build an understanding system for that domain.

Such knowledge bases have now been constructed, for example, for some restricted domains of chemistry (Buchanan & Lederberg, 1971) and for broad areas of medical diagnosis (Pople, Meyers, & Miller, 1975; Shortliffe, 1976), but, in these cases, for the purpose of constructing artificial intelligence systems, and without concern for detailed simulation of human processes. However, several knowledge bases have also been constructed for limited domains of physics that simulate in various ways the organization of human knowledge in these same domains. I mention just one of them.

Novak (1976) has constructed an ISAAC system that can understand and solve physics word problems in elementary statics, relating to levers and the equilibrium of weights. The system's domain-specific knowledge is stored in *schemas* that describe common components of such systems: schemas for pivots, for levers, for surfaces with and without friction, for weights, and so on. Concrete objects (ladders, walls, men standing on ladders) are abstracted to the corresponding appropriate schemas. A ladder is a lever, a wall is a surface, and so on. When a problem is presented to ISAAC, it is analyzed in terms of the elementary schemas represented in it and their relations. A new complex schema is built up in memory to represent the whole physical situation of the problem. This schema is used in turn to specify the equations that govern the behavior of the system, and, finally, the equations are solved.

Similar systems have been built for simple problems in kinematics (Simon & Simon, 1978), dynamics (de Kleer, 1977), and chemical engineering thermodynamics (Bhaskar & Simon, 1977). They have been compared with human behavior to a limited extent only but show considerable initial promise of casting light on the human processes.

UNDERSTANDING PROBLEM SOLUTIONS

Space does not permit a survey of all the meanings of "understanding"—the range of tasks to which knowledge can be applied. Consider, for example, the HEARSAY speech recognition system (Reddy & Newell, 1974). Its task is to produce a translation of a sound stream into written language, a task that would not appear to require understanding of the meaning of the sound stream at all. Attempts to build speech-understanding systems have taught us, however, that it is very difficult to decode a sound stream without bringing to bear on it all the syntactic and semantic information we can marshal. No one has been able to show how simple phonemic encoding and word recognition can be made to work without the use of rich syntactic and semantic information. As a consequence, although understanding meanings is not one of the direct goals of HEARSAY, the program makes extensive use of semantics and indeed requires virtually all the kinds of mechanisms I have described as constituting an understanding system.

Chess-playing programs illustrate a rather different point. Here, depth of understanding might be measured by quality of play. Yet existing programs achieve a given quality of play by a whole continuum of methods ranging from large-scale brute-force search of all legal moves to some depth, to highly selective search making use of feature recognition and other knowledge-interpreting devices. Looking at these programs, we might decide that strength of play does not capture what we usually mean by "understanding" and that the programs that play more selectively somehow understand more deeply the situations in which they find themselves than do the programs that rely on brute-force search.

Every experienced teacher makes a similar distinction between a student's depth of understanding and a student's ability to perform on particular tests. The teacher knows that some students learn by rote whereas others learn through understanding and that this is an important difference even if it does not show up in the grades on the Friday quiz. How can we characterize the distinction, and what is its significance?

Returning from humans to computers for a moment, there is a temptation to say that everything a computer knows it knows by rote, for "it can only do what it is programmed to do." The vast differences among chess programs noted previously should warn us, however, against equating "doing what the program says" with "doing by rote." In any event, the question deserves a deeper examination.

In order to have a simpler environment than chess in which to explore the issue, let us consider the Tower of Hanoi puzzle (Simon, 1975). This puzzle consists of three vertical pegs and a number of doughnutlike disks of different sizes, which are initially stacked in a pyramid on one of the pegs, say A. The task is to move all the disks to another peg, say C, under the constraints that (a) only one disk may be moved at a time, and (b) a disk may never be placed on top of another smaller than itself. The minimum number of moves for a solution of the n–disk problem is 2^n-1.

Three examples illustrate the wide variety of relatively simple programs that solve the Tower of Hanoi problem. Moreover, these different programs exhibit quite different kinds of understanding of the problems. I think these programs are simple enough that I can describe their fundamental characteristics in English, without getting into programming formalisms.

The first possibility is simply a *rote* solution. The correct sequence of moves is stored in a list in memory. A simple interpreter retrieves the moves from memory in the order of storage and executes each in turn. When the list is exhausted, it halts, with the problem solved.

To execute the rote strategy, only a single place-keeping symbol need be retained in short-term memory, and no perceptual tests need be made in order to determine what move to make next. The reasons for regarding this as a rote strategy are obvious: No analysis is involved, but simply recall of a list of items in order; the solution only works for a specified number of disks; and it only works for a specified initial problem situation and a particular goal situation. Hence, the program has no capability for transfering what it knows about the problem to variants involving a different number of disks, or even trivially different starting and goal points.

In sharp contrast to the rote program is a program incorporating the usual *recursive solution* for the Tower of Hanoi problem. This solution rests on the observation that in order to move a pyramid of n disks from Peg S to Peg G, one need only: (1) move a pyramid of $(n-1)$ disks from S to Peg $O;$ (2) move the largest remaining disk from S to $G;$ and (3) move the pyramid of $(n-1)$ disks from O to G. To execute this solution, however, the program must be able to store in short-term memory, in a sequence corresponding to their order in the goal hierarchy, all the goals that at the given time have not yet been completely executed. The maximum number of goals that have to be held simultaneously in short-term memory is $(2n-1)$ for an n-disk problem. Hence, it is unlikely that a human subject would be able to carry out this strategy unmodified form with more than three or four disks.

From the standpoint of understanding, however, the important difference between the rote and recursive solutions of the problem is that the latter, but not the former, possesses and makes use of implicit knowledge of important aspects of the problem structure. This additional knowledge is knowledge that the problem is recursive—that the n-disk problem can be dissected into problems of exactly the same form, but with fewer disks. Notice that "possession" of knowledge here means that it is built into the program, hence available for solving the problem, not that it is available in explicit declarative form. A subject having and using such a program may, or may not, be able to state the recursive rule.

The recursive strategy is knowledgeable about the Tower of Hanoi problem and can solve problems of any number of disks, and with any starting point and number of goal pegs. It must start from the beginning, however, and if it loses its place (loses the stack of subgoals), it cannot recover. It is very introverted, paying no attention to the current arrangement of disks on pegs but deciding what to do next solely on the basis of which goal lies uppermost in its goal stack in STM. It can easily be fooled by an outside intervention that changes the disk arrangement between two of its moves and is then not able to continue.

There is a very different strategy, the *perceptual strategy,* that makes considerable use of its knowledge of the current problem situation in order to decide on its next move. The perceptual strategy first notices the largest disk that has not yet reached the goal peg. It determines whether this disk can be moved legally to the goal. If not, it notices the largest disk that is blocking the move and determines the peg to which this latter disk must be moved to get it out of the way. Taking the move of the blocking disk as its new subgoal, the strategy now repeats the same cycle: checking the legality of the move, noticing the largest blocking disk if it is not legal, and setting up the goal of moving that disk. Eventually, the strategy finds a move that can be made and makes it. Now it starts at the beginning again and repeats.

The perceptual strategy solves not only the problem of moving an n-disk pyramid from one peg to another, but it does this starting from any arbitrary (legal) arrangement of the disks. Moreover, it need retain in short-term memory a maximum of only two symbols, no matter how large n is, instead of the entire goals stack required by the recursive strategy.

This difference in performance capabilities derives from differences among the means the various strategies have available for conceptualizing the problem. In the recursive method, the successive moves are governed by the goal structure in short-term memory; in the perceptual method, they are governed by the current state of the stimulus. The rote strategy knows only of individual legal moves. The recursive strategy employs the concept of a macromove: moving a subpyramid of disks. The perceptual strategy lacks this latter concept, but it has the notion of "the largest disk blocking the move of disk X," is able to determine perceptually which disk this is, and can use this knowledge to progress toward its goal.

Even this simple puzzle environment reveals additional dimensions to the meaning of understanding. The understanding that different subjects, who have learned to use different strategies to solve the Tower of Hanoi problem, have acquired is quite different in each case. Each has touched a different part of the elephant.

UNDERSTANDING AND AWARENESS

Let us return again from computer programs to human behavior. In order to test a student's understanding of the Tower of Hanoi problem:

1. We could test the speed with which the student learned a solution strategy, how well the student retained it over time, and to what range of similar tasks the student could transfer it. Research by Katona (1940) has shown that "meaningful" solutions of problems are learned faster, retained better, and transferred more effectively than rote solutions.

2. We could infer the nature of the strategy the student used to solve the problem and evaluate it with respect to its parsimony and generality, just as we have been evaluating the computer programs.

3. We could measure the student's ability to evoke the strategy when it was appropriate for solving a problem. (This is the criterion that comes closest to fitting our initial definition of understanding.)

4. We could test the student's ability to paraphrase or describe the strategy in alternative expressions.

5. We could test the student's ability to explain or prove how or why the strategy works.

The final two tests in this list raise entirely new issues beyond those discussed up to this point—issues of what might be called "awareness." But why are we interested in a student's ability to paraphrase, explain, or prove? And how can we give an information-processing explanation of being aware in these latter senses? We take up the second question first.

Because the three strategies have not been described in formal detail but have already been paraphrased in the text, we can take those paraphrases as examples. Note that they are expressed in natural language; they omit much of the detail of the formal strategies; and they are in a form that a program having the general characteristics of UNDERSTAND might use as input for generating the programs themselves. Stated otherwise, a paraphrase of a program corresponds closely to an informal description of the top levels of that program. Hence, it might serve as input to an understanding program. A system that could paraphrase programs and create programs from para-phrases would have ways of understanding its knowledge that go beyond those previously described. It is not hard to think of contexts in which people appear to use this kind of understanding (e.g., in learning to perform tasks from brief English-language descriptions).

Explaining a program or proving its efficacy (the fifth of the tests listed earlier) is similar to paraphrasing but goes a step further in paying attention to the performability of each step and to the effectiveness of the procedure in attaining its goal. Knowledge in the form of paraphrase, explanation, or proof of strategies is knowledge about knowledge, which is how I define awareness. To the extent that a system can examine its own programs, analyze them, and modify them, it has additional forms of knowledge that have their own appropriate uses. It appears plausible that these uses are especially closely related to the system's capacity for learning, and for acquiring new forms of understanding.

CONCLUSION

There appears to be no end of "understanding" problems. Research in artificial intelligence and information-processing psychology has identified and attacked at least a half-dozen such problems during the past decade. Understanding was initially viewed in this research as the ability to extract meanings from natural language inputs and to make explicit by inference information contained implicitly in those inputs. At a later stage, emphasis shifted to capabilities for combining information derived from multiple sources (two or more input sources, or input information with information already available in semantic memory). Just appearing on the horizon, and likely candidates for the next decade's research, are questions about the forms of understanding called "awareness."

In surveying a considerable range of tasks calling for understanding, we have found a much smaller variety of basic mechanisms for performing these tasks. This is encouraging and comforting if we have, as most of us do, a taste for parsimony in explanation. However, it should not make us complacent in thinking that we have already discovered the main mechanisms required for all forms and types of understanding of which people are capable. The understanding of the process of understanding continues to be an important, even central, research target in cognitive psychology today.

ACKNOWLEDGMENT

This research was supported by Research Grant MH-07722 from the National Institute of Mental Health.

REFERENCES

Anderson, J. R., & Bower, G. H. *Human associative memory*, Washington, D.C.: V. H. Winston, 1973.

Bhaskar, R., & Simon, H. A. Problem solving in semantically rich domains: An example from engineering thermodynamics. *Cognitive Science*, 1977, *1*, 193–215.

Buchanan, B. G., & Lederberg, J. The heuristic DENDRAL program for explaining empirical data. *Proceedings of the International Federation of Information Processing Societies*. Ljubljiana, 1971, 179–188.

Hayes, J. R., & Simon, H. A. Understanding written problem instructions. In L. W. Gregg (Ed.), *Cognition and knowledge*, Potomac, Md.: Lawrence Erlbaum Associates, 1974.

Hayes, J. R., & Simon, H. A. Psychological differences among problem isomorphs. In G. Potts (Ed.), *Indiana Cognitive Symposium*, Potomac, Md.: Lawrence Erlbaum Associates, 1977.

Hebb, D. O. *Organization of behavior*, New York: Wiley, 1949.

Katona, G. *Organizing and memorizing*. New York: Columbia University Press, 1940.

de Kleer, J. Multiple representations of knowledge in a mechanical problem-solver. *Proceedings, Fifth International Joint Conference On Artificial Intelligence*. Pittsburgh: Department of Computer Science, Carnegie–Mellon University, 1977, 299–304.

Lindsay, R. K. Inferential memory as the basis of machines which understand natural language. In E. A. Feigenbaum & J. Feldman (Eds.), *Computers and thought*. New York: McGraw-Hill, 1963.

Moore, J., & Newell, A. *How can MERLIN understand?* In L. W. Gregg (Ed.), *Cognition and knowledge*. Potomac, Md.: Lawrence Erlbaum Associates, 1974.

Newell, A., & Simon, H. A. *Human problem solving*, Englewood Cliffs, N.J.: Prentice-Hall, 1972.

Novak, G. S. *Computer understanding of physics problems stated in natural language*. (Tech. Rep. NL-30) Austin Tex.: Department of Computer Sciences, The University of Texas, March 1976.

Pople, H., Meyers, J., & Miller, R. DIALOG, a model of diagnostic logic for internal medicine, *Proceedings of the Fourth International Joint Conference on Artificial Intelligence*, Tiblisi, USSR: 1975, 848–855.

Reddy, R., & Newell, A. Knowledge and its representation in a speech understanding system. In L. W. Gregg (Ed.), *Knowledge and cognition*. Potomac, Md.: Lawrence Erlbaum Associates: 1974.

Shortliffe, E. H. *Computer-based medical consultation: MYCIN*. New York: American Elsevier, 1976.

Siklóssy, L., & Simon, H. A. Some semantic methods for language processing. In Simon, H. A. & L. Siklóssy (Eds.), *Representation and meaning*, Englewood Cliffs, N.J.: Prentice-Hall, 1972.

Simon, H. A. The functional equivalence of problem solving skills. *Cognitive Psychology*, 1975, *7*, 268–288.

Simon, H. A. Artificial intelligence systems that understand. *Proceedings of the Fifth International Joint Conference on Artificial Intelligence*. Pittsburgh: Department of Computer Science, Carnegie–Mellon University, 1977, 1059–73.

Simon, H. A., & Hayes, J. R. The understanding process: Problem isomorphs. *Cognitive Psychology*, 1976, *8*, 165–190.

Simon, H. A., & Simon, D. P. Individual differences in solving physics problems. In R. S. Siegler (Ed.), *Children's thinking: What develops*. Hillsdale, N.J.: Lawrence Erlbaum Associates, 1978.

Winograd, T. *Understanding natural language*, New York: Academic Press, 1972.

4

The Comparative Study of Serially Integrated Behavior in Humans and Animals

T. G. Bever
R. O. Straub
H. S. Terrace
D. J. Townsend
Columbia University

INTRODUCTION

An enduring problem for psychology is whether it should be kept from reductionist dissolution in a sea of neurological details. Those psychologists who view such reduction as a scientific necessity focus on the learning of single responses. They indefinitely postpone study of the "chaining" of such isolated responses into "higher order" structures. Single stimulus-response connections are interpretable in terms of isolated behavioral units for which there is hope of finding sensory-motor analogues.

Yet, most behavior involves highly organized *sequences* of "responses," a fact that forces the question of how an organism represents the transition from one response to the next. The obvious recourse of the reductionist is to argue that a given response *itself* serves as the stimulus for the next response. This *leger de pensée* creates a coherent description but one that is empirically inadequate for a variety of well-known reasons. Response sequences can occur too fast for each one to be separately stimulated; response sequences themselves can be organized into subsequences, and an entire sequence can have a goal or meaning quite independent of the goal or meaning of each response unit in the sequence.

Such facts force us to refer to "mediating central processes" that bind and organize a response sequence. But even here one often hopes to keep the "mediator" close to the sensory-motor ground; "In a single rapid series of skilled movements, highly practiced, it is possible that behavior may be momentarily without sensory guidance—*but only momentarily*." (Hebb,

1958, p. 63, emphasis ours.) In the case of most sequential behaviors, however, the only available evidence about their organization is what appears at the sensory-motor level itself. Language is a singular exception to this and has often been idealized as the "sequential behavior *par excellence,*" which illuminates our understanding of all other sequential behaviors. At the outset, one must admit that a response–response chaining model is inadequate to describe language behavior: "No one... has succeeded in explaining a speaker's sentence construction, during the course of ordinary speech, as a series of (conditioned responses) linked together by feedback alone." (Hebb, 1958, p. 60).

Language is many things—*too* many to serve as a clean case study of serially ordered behavior. "Evidence concerning speech is complex, and may not be decisive" (Hebb, 1958, p. 60). What can we do to make it more decisive? In this paper we present two related investigations of serial behavior. These investigations show how we have tried to break the problem down into natural constituents. First, we show that certain serial constraints on sentence structures may be due to the interaction of speech comprehension mechanisms with experimentally distinguishable cognitive search strategies. Then we show that it is possible to vary and test models of how animals represent and execute serial behaviors. Our results demonstrate that similar theoretical mechanisms can underlie serial behavior in humans and animals.

This coincidence suggests that our effort to simplify the study of serial behavior by using simple paradigms and studying animals has boomeranged: In humans, we found that serial search strategies are under immediate subconscious control and can be instantly shifted. We found evidence that animals deploy complex mechanisms similar to those that humans use to organize and perform sequences. That is, rather than reducing the complexity of a serial behavior by studying it in animals, we may have discovered that they have unsuspected processing capabilities. Our studies suggest that, once a sequential behavior is acquired, it is organized in terms of internal processing mechanisms. Those mechanisms presuppose a serial representation of the behavior and utilize operations that are not directly modeled on the overt behaviors. Because of this lack of isomorphism, the mechanisms cannot be simple "maps", "plans," or internal, sequentially triggered "(cell) assemblies." Rather, they are internal processes that operate to yield the observed serial behaviors. This is part of the answer to a classical property of complex integrated behavior: Originally isolated responses "consolidate" into a coherent structure (cf. Hebb, 1963). In our view, the first step is to recognize that the organism develops an abstract organizing structure, which is not necessarily isomorphic to the behavior, but which underlies it. This chapter concentrates on the internal nature of such structures and their application to behavior in different species.

THE SOURCES OF LINGUISTIC STRUCTURES

Language is the most elaborate serially organized behavior known to us. Linguists search for universal contraints that are true of the grammars of all languages. These universals comprise the body of a hypothetical Universal Grammar, a store of what every child is prepared to learn at birth. A major part of our research over the past few years has been devoted to showing that specific universal properties of languages are not contained in Universal Grammar, but rather are true of all languages because of constraints on the way language is *learned* and *used*.

Consider some obvious cases. No language has complete ambiguity of the underlying grammatical relations in every sentence. No language has a word consisting of 20 consonants in a row. No language relies on half a quarter-tone as a distinctive acoustic feature. Every language has at least one verb for existence (to be). Every language distinguishes the first person from others. Every language has a way of expressing requests.

Each of the previously mentioned universals of languages is not necessarily a property of Universal Grammar, because each would have to be true in any case for language to be usable by humans. Consequently, it would be a mistake to require that such universals of language be an intrinsic part of Universal Grammar. Of course, the achievements of recent linguistic investigations have been to isolate language universals of far greater interest than the previous six obvious ones. The following are directly related to serial properties of language.

The Most-General-First Principle

There are several principles governing how to apply a rule to a structure that offers more than one point at which the rule could apply. The basic constraint is that the rule applies to the "most general" instance or domain of application available. In syntax, one version of this principle is known as the "A-over-A principle." This principle governs how a syntactic rule is applied to a hierarchy in which a constituent subject to the rule appears more than once. The principle requires that the rule always apply to the highest available instance of that constituent. For example, if a rule applies to a "noun phrase" in a sentence in which one of the noun phrases dominates another, then the rule applies to the dominating noun phrase.

A parallel constraint has been suggested that governs the application of a phonological rule to a sequence containing a subsequence that could also be affected by the rule. The phonological principle is to check first for the longest domain that the rule can apply to, and only apply it to a shorter domain if a longer domain is not available.

These principles are technical contraints that operate internally within grammar. As such, they appear to be prima facie examples of "pure" linguistic universals, true of grammars because of the nature of Universal Grammar. This may be so; however, it is intriguing that the principles ensure that the most general application of a rule will occur whenever it can. This is an intuitively appealing generalization, independent of its application to language. Furthermore, there is some evidence from the literature on serial pattern learning in humans that this principle is true in nonlinguistic domains. However, it could be the case that human subjects import their mastery of language into nonlinguistic domains and that such experiments do not serve as nonlanguage tests of the principle. It becomes clear, however, in the following section that such questions *can* be addressed with nonspeaking animals, thereby making it possible to see if such principles apply to subjects that do not know a human language.

Save the Hardest for the Last

This principle applies to rules (both in syntax and phonology) that reorder constituents of differing complexity. The generalization is that placing the more complex constituents after the simpler constituents is stylistically preferred and sometimes obligatory (see J. R. Ross, 1968). We can interpret this in light of constraints on short-term memory. The order "hard-task/easy-task" requires that the hard task be held in immediate memory while waiting for the subsequent processing. The opposite order requires that only the easy task be held, making for less overall computational complexity.

The Penthouse Principle

This is an observation across languages about the distribution of rules that apply to main and subordinate clauses. The basic insight (due to J. R. Ross, 1968) is that optional reordering rules in syntax apply more freely to main clauses than to subordinate clauses. For example, (1a) is an optional version of (1b), but (2a) is not an optional version of (2a):

1a. Quickly John left.
1b. John left quickly.
2a. *After quickly John left, Mary was upset.
2b. After John left quickly, Mary was upset.

Why should this be true? There is no obvious or intuitive explanation for this difference between main and subordinate clauses. Perhaps here we see an unambiguous instance of a true property of Universal Grammar. Recently, we have been exploring the way that information in main and subordinate clauses is stored during immediate processing. We have found that main clause information is accessed in parallel, whereas subordinate clause information is accessed serially. This offers an explanation of why more word rearrangement is allowed in main clauses—they are processed in parallel anyway, so rearranging the order of the words in itself can have no deleterious affect on processing. Subordinate clause processing, on the other hand, would be impaired by reordering the words, out of the standard behavioral order because subordinate clauses are accessed initially in serial form (see Townsend & Bever, 1978).

This explanation is consistent with the facts, but there is a potential circularity. The difference in accessing style could itself be a processing accommodation to the linguistic universal, rather than its cause. That is, it could be argued that main clauses are accessed in parallel *because* their serial form is subject to greater reordering; subordinate clauses are accessed serially because they more reliably present a canonical phrase order. One way to resolve this question is to show that the different kinds of accessing style can occur in homogeneous materials that are not linguistic. We did this, and found subjects can allocate a serial search to one part of a string and a parallel search to another part of the same string, depending on how important it is to encode each part correctly. This strengthens our claim that the Penthouse Principle could be a linguistic consequent of different scanning strategies for main and subordinate clauses.

The scanning explanation of the Penthouse Principle presupposes that subjects can rapidly shift the way in which they access sequential material— scanning a main clause in "parallel," but scanning a subordinate clause "serially." We studied this in two steps. First, we demonstrated that subordinate clauses are accessed serially, whereas main clauses are accessed in parallel. Then we showed that humans have the ability to shift rapidly from a serial recognition access technique to a nonserial access in a nonlinguistic domain.

Propositional Processing Theory

Our findings about the serial and parallel processing of clauses are set within a particular framework of a model of speech comprehension. In the study of speech comprehension, considerable research has also been devoted to the reception and comprehension of sentences and clauses (see Clark & Clark, 1977, Chapter 2; Fodor, Bever, & Garrett, 1974, Chapter 6; Johnson-Laird, 1974). The main focus has been on how listeners isolate propositions in clauses and the relations between them.

The end of the first surface structure clause in a complex sentence defines a major break in the structural description of the sentence. The surface structure clause can function as a unit during comprehension in at least three ways (Fodor, Bever, & Garrett, 1974):

1. The listener determines the location of major surface structure breaks during listening. This segmentation process is shown by experiments demonstrating that detection of a nonspeech noise is poorer when it occurs within a clause than when it occurs between clauses (Garrett, 1965; Garrett, Bever, & Fodor, 1966; Holmes, 1970; Holmes, & Forster, 1970; see also Bever, & Hurtig, 1975; Bever, Hurtig, & Handel, 1977; Bever, Lackner, & Kirk, 1969; Chapin, Smith, & Abrahamson, 1972; Dalyrymple-Alford, 1976; Forster, 1970; Reber & Anderson, 1970; Wingfield & Klein, 1971).

2. The listener applies perceptual mapping rules to assign the words of a clause to their semantic roles. Strategies for this mapping operation may include the use of semantic constraints, which suggest the more plausible logical subject (Bever, 1970; Slobin, 1966; but see Forster & Olbrei, 1973; Glucksberg, Trabasso, & Wald, 1973, for instances where semantics is irrelevant), direct mapping of words onto underlying structure on the basis of the order of elements in underlying structure (Baird & Koslick, 1974; Tanenhaus, 1977; Wanner & Maratsos, 1971), and mapping on the basis of syntactic properties of individual words occurring within the clause (Fodor & Garrett, 1967; Hakes & Cairns, 1970; Holmes & Forster, 1972).

3. As the listener determines a set of underlying logical relations within a clause and an interpretation for the clause, the exact word sequence of the clause fades. This process of "erasure" of words from immediate memory is shown by experiments that demonstrate abrupt shifts in verbatim recall and word recognition performance at clause boundaries (Caplan, 1972; Jarvella, 1971; Jarvella & Herman, 1972; Perfetti & Goldman, 1976). The process of deciding about an underlying structure for a clause, and removal of the exact wording from immediate memory has typically been assumed to have occured by the clause boundary (Bever, Garrett, & Hurtig, 1973).

Relations Between Clauses

Recent research has emphasized the effect of "functional completeness" on the processes of segmentation and semantic recoding. For example, in the following sentences, there is a progressive deterioration of the extent to which the explicit information in the italicized clause determines what the semantic representation is:

3a. *I felt sorry for the old bum* so I gave him a dollar.
3b. *After the crook stole the woman's bag* he ran for safety.
3c. *Meeting the pretty young girl* was the highlight of Peter's trip.
3d. *The old painted wooden pipe* was on display at the local museum.

This has been shown by Tanenhaus and Carroll (1975) to be reflected in the extent to which recoding of the sequence has occurred. For example, if a probe word is presented following the different kinds of clauses, the latency to report the next word is greater when the stimulus word is the last word of a clause that is functionally more complete. This is taken as reflecting the fact that those clauses are more strongly sequential and semantically recoded.

This line of argument has been extended to relations between clauses themselves. For example, Carroll, Tanenhaus, & Bever (1977) report stronger segmentation after main clauses than after subordinate clauses. This could be so because the main clause can always be semantically recoded, whereas a subordinate clause may have to be held in memory while one listens to the main clause, in order to recode the subordinate clause in a manner consistent with the meaning of the main clause. This variable has been explored systematically by Townsend & Bever (1978). They followed sentence fragments such as,

4a. Bob did put down some tiles in the...
4b. Bob did put some tiles down in the...
4c. While Bob did put down some tiles in the...
4d. While Bob did put some tiles down in the...

with either a synonomy judgment task (is "covering a floor" consistent with the meaning of this fragment?) or a word probe task (was "down" in the fragment?). Table 4.1, summarizes the results of this study. They found that listeners accessed the meaning of main clauses more quickly than the meaning of subordinate clauses, whereas there is evidence of a serial scanning strategy in the word probe task in subordinate clauses and not in main clauses.

TABLE 4.1
Response Times (Sec) to Initial Main and Subordinate Clauses[a]

	Subordinate		Main	
Meaning				
Probe	1.3		1.2	
F (1,16)		4.85,	p < .05	
	Early	Late	Early	Late
Word				
Probe	1.1	1.2	1.1	1.1
F (1,16)	6.35 p < .05		< .1 ns.	

[a]From Townsend and Bever (1978, tables 2 & 4). Copyright 1978 by Academic Press, Inc. Reprinted by permission.

Townsend and Bever (1978) also found that both of these effects were reliably influenced by the kind of subordinating conjunction that introduced the subordinate clause. Certain conjunctions showed more effects of "closure," e.g., "if." Other conjuctions showed weak effects of closure, e.g. "though." They suggest that this is related to the extent to which the information in the subordinate clause is semantically independent of the information in the main clause in the comprehension of the entire sentence. According to this view, the information in an "if" clause can be analyzed entirely independently as a whole, but the information in a "though" clause must be held in abeyance because the appropriate part of it has to be related to the main clause information in order to understand the relevance of the use of "though."

These studies extend the originally structurally determined theory of clausal processing into a more functional interpretation. We can view the listener's task as attempting to organize propositional relations corresponding to the sequence.

The original purpose of this investigation was to show that the Penthouse Principle could be explained by a difference in immediate access technique between main and subordinate clauses. To a first degree of approximation, our results confirm that there is a difference. However, they also reveal that the clause difference in immediate access technique is a function of the type of subordinating clause conjunction—clauses with conjunctions introducing relatively functionally independent material (e.g., "if") more often are responded to as if they were main clauses than other conjunctions (e.g., "although"). It follows that the Penthouse Principle effects may also be weaker in clauses with functionally independent subordinating conjunctions. Again, to a first degree of approximation, this is a correct observation: Consider the relative acceptability of the following clauses (with the noncanonical placement of the adverb). They appear to be ordered according;

5a. That loudly John left...,
5b. ? Why loudly John left...,
5c. ?? If loudly John leaves...,
5d. *after loudly John left...,

to acceptability, with the only difference being the extent to which the clause is dependent propositionally on what follows. However, it is possible that the Penthouse Principle is codified for all subordinate clauses without exceptions for specific conjunctions because of the simplicity of formulating it as applicable to *all* subordinate clauses of certain structured types.

Our primary concern here is to isolate for study some properties of sentence processing that can occur in all serially organized behavior. Regardless of the individual differences between conjunctions, we can argue that the initial representation of main and subordinate clauses differ, with related consequences for immediate access of meaning and lexical material in each type of clause.

Different Kinds of Serial Access Strategies

What does this show about human processing capacity? If it is not limited to language, it demonstrates that humans can rapidly organize adjacent sequential material with different *kinds* of representations, and can access those representations in distinct ways. Many demonstrations of serial "chunking" in humans show that distinct parts of a sequence can be represented separately; but it is characteristic of such phenomena that the distinct chunks are represented and accessed in the *same way*. Our results show that in language comprehension, listeners make simultaneous use of different kinds of representational systems for different verbal "chunks." To study this in an area outside of language, we adapted standard studies of nonlinguistic serial processing. We found that humans can also rapidly shift the kind of representation and access pattern with nonlinguistic materials.

LIST SEARCH IN HUMANS

In the well-known Sternberg (1966, 1969) paradigm, a subject is presented with a set of digits, letters, or words. After seeing the set, the subject is shown a probe item from the same class as the items in the set. The subject is instructed to indicate as quickly as possible whether or not the probe was contained in the set. Sternberg's results show that reaction time (RT) increases with the size of the memory set, and the slope of this RT function is similar for positive and negative trials. In addition, Sternberg reports that RT does not vary with the serial position of the target item within the memory set. The fact that RT increases with set size rules out a parallel scan, in which the subject simultaneously compares all memory set items with the probe. The lack of serial position effects the similar slopes for positive and negative trials, and the equality of RTs to positive and negative trials all rule out a self-terminating scan, in which the subject compares the memory set items with the probe one at a time and responds as soon as a match occurs. Instead, Sternberg interprets his data to indicate that subjects conduct a serial exhaustive scan in which items are compared one at a time with the probe, but a response is not made until all items have been compared with the probe.

Within the limits of Sternberg's procedures, his findings have been replicated numerous times and are now fairly well accepted as an established, though perhaps curious, fact about retrieval from active memory. The current research considers whether Sternberg's serial position results are a general sequence of scanning in active memory, or whether different types of serial position effects are obtained under different conditions. In our experiments, we manipulated the conditions of scanning within a memory set and hence provide the strongest test that different serial position effects are obtained under different conditions. To the extent that different serial position effects are indicative of different scanning strategies, our experiments demonstrate that different scanning strategies can be applied to different portions of a list.

Although the exhaustive models have received broad support, several investigators have found reason to doubt the generality of the exhaustive model (see Sternberg, 1975, for a review). One source of doubt is the frequent presence of serial position effects in memory scanning experiments. Recency effects have been found in several experiments (Baddely & Ecob, 1973; Burrows & Okada, 1971; Clifton & Birnbaum, 1970; Corballis, 1967; Corballis, Kirby, & Miller, 1972; Corballis & Miller, 1973; Juola & Atkinson, 1971; Kennedy & Hamilton, 1969; Morin, DeRosa, & Stultz, 1967), although some of these effects could be explained in terms of a sensory store, which retains the final items of the memory set. Even more problematical for the exhaustive serial model are those studies that found that RTs increase with the serial position of the target (Burrows & Okada, 1971; Corballis, Kirby, & Miller, 1972; Kennedy & Hamilton, 1969; Klatzy & Atkinson, 1970; Klatzky, Juola, & Atkinson, 1971; Sternberg, 1967). These increasing serial position curves suggest a self-terminating scan and certainly cannot be explained in terms of a sensory store. In addition, two of these studies (Corballis et al., 1972; Klatzky & Atkinson, 1970) obtained greater slopes for negative trials than for positive trials, which also suggests the self-terminating scan.

A second source of doubt about the generality of the exhaustive model is evidence that shows scanning can be limited to a part of the memory set. Several studies (Clifton & Gutschera, 1971; Darley, Klatzky, & Atkinson, 1972; Naus, 1974; Naus, Glucksberg, & Ornstein, 1972; Williams, 1971) indicate that one portion of the memory set can be omitted from a subject's exhaustive scan. Other studies suggest that subjects use a self-terminating scan within sets of letters partitioned by a pause (Wilkes & Kennedy, 1970a) or within different constituents of a sentence (Kennedy & Wilkes, 1969; Shedletsky, 1974; Townsend & Bever, 1978; Wilkes & Kennedy, 1969; Wilkes & Kennedy, 1970b).

The hypothesis that different scanning strategies can be used on different portions of a memory set was examined by providing subjects with incentives for responding accurately to only one portion of the set. Although previous experiments (Banks, cited in Atkinson, Hermann, & Wescourt, 1974; Swanson & Briggs, 1969) have found that subjects do not use substantially different scanning strategies when given incentives for accuracy versus speed on different memory sets, these studies have not shown the effect of incentives on scanning strategy within a memory set.

EXPERIMENTS

We used 10-item auditory lists of 5 adjacent randomly organized letters and 5 randomly organized digits (e.g., 6a, 6b following). The sequences were recorded at the rate of 3 items/sec.

6a. 5 9 4 7 2 X B N R F–TONE–PAUSE–PROBE (e.g. "N")
6b. X B N R F 5 9 4 7 2–TONE–PAUSE–PROBE (e.g. "N")

A brief tone marked the end of each segment followed by a one-half-second pause and then a probe letter or digit. The subjects' task on each trial was to signal as fast as possible whether the probe occurred in the 10-item list. This technique is typical of the experiments we reviewed earlier, with one important difference. Before each trial, subjects were told whether a correct letter or digit probe would be rewarded; this technique marked one subsequence of each trial as potentially "paid," and the other as "unpaid." Our intention was to make one-half of each sequence more important for the subject as the subject heard it (although the subject could not be sure that the probe would be drawn from the paid subsequence, so the subject also had to attend to the unpaid subsequence (see Townsend, Bresnick, & Bever, 1979, for discussions of these experiments).

We have run a number of paradigms of this sort, all of which generate similar data. Table 4.2 presents a typical set of data, in this case drawn from the last block of trials from eight subjects who had considerable pretraining. Subjects recognized the probes correctly in both paid and unpaid subsequences, with better performance in response to the paid subsequences. A superficial examination of the data suggests that the paid subsequences were searched serially and the unpaid ones randomly; the first four paid positions were responded to with a steady increase in latency, whereas there is no orderly serial effect for the unpaid sequences. Before considering the difference in response latency pattern as indicating different search processes, we must show that there is no systematic trade-off between latency and response accuracy. If there were, it could indicate that subjects shifted their

TABLE 4.2
Reaction Times (Sec) to Recognized Items From Paid and Unpaid 5-Item Lists

	Probe Serial Position					Mean Identification	Mean Correct Rejections
	1	2	3	4	5		
Paid	1.24	1.33	1.40	1.59	1.27	1.36	1.68
Unpaid	1.58	1.61	1.50	1.67	1.63	1.59	1.70

accuracy–speed priority between paid and unpaid subsequences but not their item access processes. Several features of the data argue against the trade-off hypothesis. First, the error rate for the paid subsequences is uniformly low ($<$ 5%), whereas the error rate for the unpaid sequences does not increase with serial position—that is subjects do not "compensate" in the unpaid condition for the flat latency curve by allowing the error rate to increase. Second, the false–positive frequencies for the paid and unpaid condition are virtually identical; the subsequences differ only in the correct recognition scores they elicit—that is, subjects are not simply indiscriminate in their responses to unpaid subsequences, nor has their response criterion seriously shifted—rather, they specifically fail to recognize more target items. Finally, the correlation between speed and errors was *positive* both for paid (r = .31) and unpaid (r = .43) subsequences, that is, the latency pattern tended to correlate positively with the error pattern, a correlation specifically *not* characteristic of a speed–accuracy trade-off.

We can analyze the different latency patterns with some degree of confidence that they are neither caused nor undermined by systematic variations in accuracy. Can we make more precise the observation that the latency response pattern to paid subsequences appears to be consistent with a self-terminating serial search? The fact that there is an orderly inverse in the first few latencies and that correct-rejections are the largest correct response category can be expressed by the following search principle:

7. Search the list for the probe from left-right; if a match appears, respond, "yes"; if the end is reached without a match, respond "no."

The relatively fast recognition time of the item in the fifth position could be accommodated by assuming an echoic "buffer" that stores the last item and the following rule that applies together with (7):

8. Search the buffer immediately for the probe.

These principles are an adequate description, but they do not provide precise predictions, nor do they utilize a general formal technique for representing processes that can be directly related to the unpaid condition, nor to related paradigms with other conditions or kinds of subjects.

So-called information-processing models offer such a formal language (see Simon & Newell, 1977). Characteristically, these models utilize a small set of operations (match–mismatch; read a symbol; change a symbol; move to next symbol on a "tape"; respond) combined in a restricted manner. The latency data from the paid subsequences are generated by such a model in Fig. 4.1. If we set each pointer moving operation as taking 120 msec and assume a base response time of 1220 msec, we can predict the first four response times to a

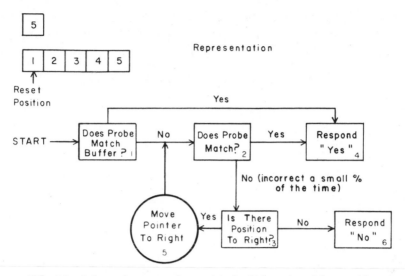

FIG. 4.1. Information-processing model of paid items in serial recognition task. (In the representation, the single box indicates the contents of the buffer, and the sequence of five boxes indicates the representation of the sequences.)

reasonable approximation (see Table 4.3). We also predict that the time for a correct rejection is the equivalent of running through to the fifth serial position (1700 msec) before saying "no," also a reasonably accurate prediction. Finally, the relatively fast latency to identify positively the item in the fifth position is explained by the assumption that the last-heard item is represented in an immediate store, the "buffer." The buffer is checked initially, along with the first position. If we assume a small miss rate, we can also predict that the fifth item will take slightly longer to recognize than the first: This follows from the fact that in a small number of cases the fifth item will be missed in the buffer and then correctly recognized in the fifth position. The empirically derived overall rate of misses is about 6%: This predicts the slightly longer response time for the fifth item shown in Table 4.3.

TABLE 4.3
Reaction Times (Sec) Predicted to Recognized Items (From Experiments in Table 4.2).[a]

	Probe Serial Position					Mean Identifi- cation	Mean Correct Rejections
	1	2	3	4	5		
Paid	1.22	1.34	1.46	1.58	1.24	(1.37)	(1.70)
Unpaid	(1.58)	(1.58)	(1.58)	(1.58)	(1.58)	1.58	1.82

[a]Latencies in parentheses represent nonindependent predictions.

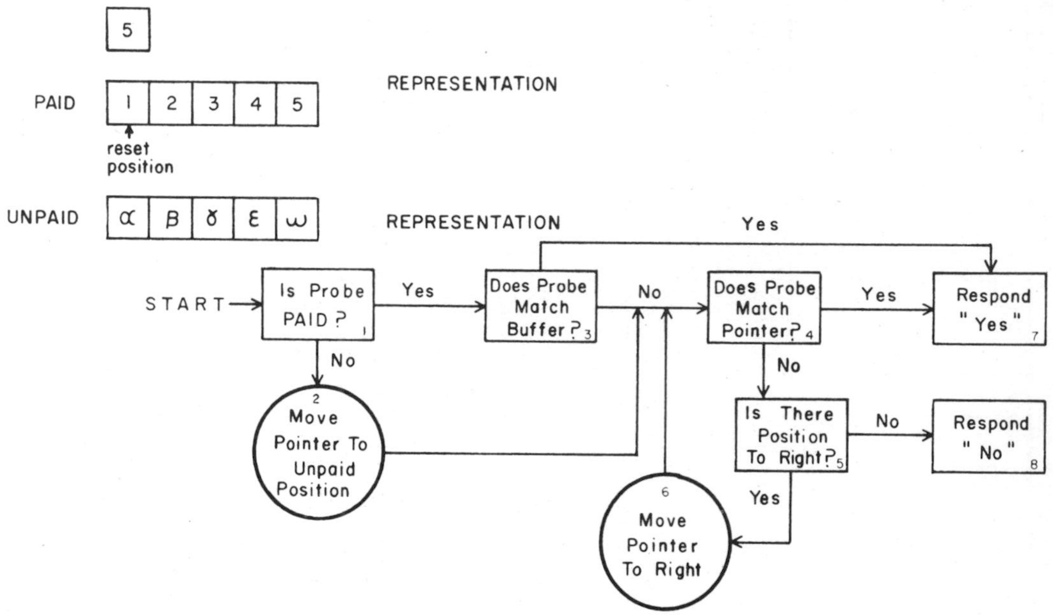

FIG. 4.2. Information-processing model of paid and unpaid items in serial recognition task. (In the representation, the single box indicates the contents of the buffer, and the sequence of five boxes indicates the representation of the sequences.)

This model can be adapted to generate responses to the unpaid condition as well, as shown in Fig. 4.2. Basically, this model assumes that the subject is set to examine the paid list—if the probe is from the unpaid subsequence, then the first operation is to move the pointer to the representation of the unpaid subsequence. Thereafter, the search proceeds serially. However, the unpaid list is assumed to have been represented in a random order so the average recognition time of the pointer is the mean of the time to scan one-half of the list in addition to the initial shift from scanning the unpaid to scanning the paid list. (See Appendix for sample derivations in this model.)

This model uses one latency variable (the time to move the pointer once) and a constant (the time to respond) to predict eight distinct behaviorally observed latencies. The empirical adequacy of this model is hard to demonstrate conclusively. First, it is the case that no observed value is more than one standard error from its predicted value. A further test of such a model is to assess the extent to which it predicts the variance in the observed data. In this case (with the value suggested earlier) more than 96% of the observed variance in the data is accounted for, using fairly simple and intuitive assumptions. (Table 4.4 presents the eight independent predicted latencies paired with the corresponding observed latencies).

TABLE 4.4
Predicted and Observed Probe Latencies (Presented in Increasing Predicted Time)

Predicted	1.22	1.24	1.34	1.46	1.58	1.58	1.70	1.82
Observed	1.24	1.27	1.33	1.40	1.59	1.59	1.68	1.78

We should emphasize that this model is valuable primarily because of the extent to which it allows us to make precise certain aspects of our theory of how the internal search process is organized. There are other, more complex models that could handle the same data with somewhat greater completeness. (For example, there is considerable variation in the individual latencies to the unpaid subsequence position (though, none of them individually departs from the predicted mean latency by more than one standard error). Furthermore, the miss rate is much higher in the unpaid condition, and there is much wider variation in position. Both of these phenomena *could* be accommodated by the assumption that the items in the unpaid condition are lost during the entry phase *into* a memory representation.)

Our subjects were humans, which makes it plausible to infer complex internal processes because such processes could be explicitly carried out by the same subjects. It is useful to consider what we could conclude from such a model if we did not have access to introspective subjective reports from members of the same species performing similar tasks. In its own right the model suggests the following:

9a. Subjects encode a representation of the sequence.

9b. Subjects apply an orderly internal procedure to access the representation.

9c. The representation (and/or) the search procedure differs internally as an interpretable function of external variables. (That is, the external differences are intuitively related to the form of the internal ones.)

Each of these observations centers around the existence of a neutral "representation." Several empirical features indicate that such a representation is "internal," rather than an expressive behavioral habit. First, the hypothesized search speed of 1/8sec per item is faster than the stimulus list and faster than almost any list could be spoken—especially spoken and analyzed as well. Second, the presence of dual representation of the last item, in the buffer and at the beginning of the full sequence, presupposes the distinctness of the latter in processing. Finally, the serial difference in the representation of the unpaid stimulus sequence and the sequence itself suggests further that there is a difference between the actual sequence and its representation.

The observations in (9) may seem abstract and stilted in light of the fact that many human behaviors explicitly demonstrate such representations and processes. But this exercise is useful to give perspective on analogous experiments with nonhuman subjects which we discuss in this next section.

SERIAL LEARNING IN ANIMALS

Serially ordered behavior is the norm rather than the exception in nature. Animals ordinarily execute complex plans, even in such basic tasks as nestbuilding, flying south for the winter, or courting a mate. Such behaviors are composed of many intermediate steps, which are not rewarded by any direct environmental change. In light of such a homely truth, it is striking that virtually all laboratory work with animals has concentrated on the learning and forgetting of separately reinforced responses: Even in the rare instances in which an animal is trained on a sequence, each response in the sequence is separately rewarded. We have developed a paradigm in which the animal is reinforced only after an entire sequence of responses has been executed (see Straub, 1979; Straub, Seidenberg, Bever, & Terrace, 1979). Pigeons are trained to peck a complete sequence of colors in a particular order, e.g., "*A B C D*," presented in randomly varying physical arrangements.

The subjects were trained in an operant conditioning chamber containing four response keys. (During a trial, each key was a different color, e.g., "white, green, red, or blue," hereafter referred to by letters "*A B C D*"). In order to earn a reward the pigeon had to peck the colors in the sequence, regardless of the position of these colors within the array of four keys. For example, on one trial the left–right arrangement of the simultaneously lit colors might be B A D C. On the next trial the pigeon might be presented with *C B D A*. In each case access to food was provided if and only if the pigeon had pecked the keys in the order "*A B C D*." If the subject made an error, the array was turned off and a new array was presented on the next trial. With the exception of the response to the last color (which was followed by reinforcement), no feedback was provided following correct responses.

Straub et al. started their training by exposing the pigeons only to the last color, "*D*." We did this following the learning-theoretic hypothesis that a backward spread of reinforcement accounts for serial learning. After training on the last color, the birds were shifted to the last two colors, (preparatory to being shifted to the last three, and ultimately to all four). After many fruitless sessions with the last two colors, we shifted the paradigm (with the same birds) so that it built up from the beginning; first they responded to *A*, then *A B*, then *A B C*, and finally to *A B C D*.

During the training phase of the experiment, three subjects were exposed to 15 of the 24 possible physical configurations that could be generated from 4 colors in a left–right array. At the end of the training, the range of trials completed correctly was 59–64%. This performance, though well above chance, could have resulted if the subjects memorized the 15 different arrays and somehow associated a different pattern of responding with each array. Under that interpretation each pigeon would have had to learn 15 different spatially defined orders. If, however, each subject was responding to the sequence *A B C D*, regardless of the position of the colors, they should be able to respond to new arrays at levels above chance.

During subsequent test sessions, four of the original 15 arrays were replaced by four physically novel generalization arrays. Although there was some initial decrement of performance on the new arrays, performance in each case was considerably above chance levels. We therefore concluded that the subjects did indeed learn the behavior "peck *A* first, then *B*, then *C*, and then *D*."

Straub et al. present this experiment in detail. However, certain features of their procedures, results, and their interpretation are worthy of comment here. There are two main issues—possible artifacts that could have allowed the subjects to mimic serial behavior without learning it; qualitative analyses that provide positive evidence for the claim that the birds acquired a "representation" of the sequence, rather than a pair-by-pair chain of responses.

Possible Artifacts. Two aspects of the procedure of Straub et al. might have allowed subjects to construct a nonserial set of independent responses. First, they allowed subjects to generate an arbitrary number of "repeat" pecks on each correct key without counting them as errors—for example, a possible "correct" sequence was "*A B B C D.*" This allowed subjects, conceivably, to "pace" themselves and to create potential ways of discriminating the next response without attending specifically to the preceding response. For example, subjects might have differentiated each color according to the time from the beginning of the trial (e.g., "peck *A* at time 0; peck *C* at 1 sec; ..."). The "repeat" pecks could have been used to "fill" intervals (cf. Heise, Keller, Kharari, & Laughlin, 1969) and allowed the subjects to peck a sequence on the basis of independent time-discrimination. Straub et al. analyzed this by examining the temporal distribution of correct and incorrect pecks with and without repeats and found no independent effects as a function of time. They performed a similar analysis to check on the possibility that subjects were differentiating the responses by "counting" the previous number of pecks (e.g., "after 0 pecks, peck *A*; after n pecks, peck *B*; after n + m pecks, peck *C*..."). This analysis also failed to show any systematic effects. Finally, as a more general check on the possible effects of allowing "repeats," they analyzed the number of correct responses to the next key that did and did not follow a repeat on the previous key—again there was no effect on correct performance to the key. In brief, we do not know how important the possibility of "repeat" pecks is to the birds' capacity—but they do not appear to be the source of obvious artifacts in the birds' serial behavior.

The second way that birds could have mastered the task without learning the color sequence would be if they had mastered the 15 independent training configurations as independent problems. For example, the subjects might have followed a general rule of not going back and pecking a previously pecked key (which brings the probability of a correct sequence up to ca. .04. If they also mastered the rule "at trial start, peck *A*," the probability would rise to ca. .18. Although this is considerably less than their performance on both the training and generalization arrays, it could provide a solid base for the birds to work from—for example, if they learned in addition the physical instructions necessary to peck white after green that differ for each array (e.g., "on the array *B A D C*, peck key 4 after key 1; on *B C A D*, peck key 2 after 1..."), their performance would rise to 50%. Of course, such separate "physical routing" learning for each array, would be quite a prodigous achievement in its own right and one that includes serial order learning differing for each array. However, the fact that it is in terms of "physical ordering" would be consistent with a peripheralist interpretation of what the subjects learn (see the following discussion).

Several features of the data suggest that the role of separate array learning is minimal. There are no consistent correlations across birds of the relative difficulty of each array. No pattern of difficulty is obvious that accounts for the relative difficulty of the arrays. Finally, the immediate above-chance performance on the novel generalization physical arrays indicates that the subjects were sensitive to the color sequence itself.

TABLE 4.5
Response Times (Sec) and Frequencies (in Brackets)
from Three Pigeons, Initially Given Backward Training

	Response			
	A	B	C	D
Position or last key pecked				
Start	1.5 (86%)	2.3 (12%)	3.0 (2%)	.8 (< 1%)
A	.5 (34%)	1.0 (54%)	1.6 (12%)	2.0 (1%)
B	.9 (1%)	.4 (41%)	.9 (53%)	1.4 (4%)
C	.1 (< 1%)	.7 (1%)	.3 (63%)	.9 (36%)

[a]From Straub et al. (1979, table 1—about 8000 pecks). Copyright 1979 by University of Indiana. Reprinted by permission.

Representation Versus Chain.   We have emphasized the fact that our paradigm is one of "simultaneous chaining," in which the birds are presented with all colors simultaneously and do not receive any step-by-step feedback after each correct response. This makes it possible to assume that what they learn is the entire sequence in some form of "representation" (physical or central, see the following). This would be in contrast to a sequential chaining of separate S–R links. Several features of the data are consistent with the view that the pigeons have acquired a representation of the sequence.

Table 4.5 presents the data from the last three sessions of the three birds, a data pool of almost 10,000 pecks. This table demonstrates several important features of the birds' response patterns. First, the probability of an error decreases the further "downstream" it is from the correct response. The overall probability of a one-step error is larger than that for a two-step error, which is larger than that for a three-step error. Furthermore, the response latency to an error also increases the further downstream the error is.

These facts are most consistent with the view that forward errors are generated when the bird "runs through" the sequence internally and skips over a key without pecking it—this adds increased latency but decreasing likelihood of errors as they occur further downstream. Of particular import is the presence of backward errors—a representation model allows for them as a function of losing one's place in the representation—a forward S–R chaining model cannot account for them, because there are no backward associations. A second argument concerns the speed of responding—we found a class of extremely fast correct sequences, roughly .1 sec per response—faster than studies on pigeon discrimination learning response suggest are possible as separate responses.

The best demonstration that the birds' achievement was not an artifact or fluke is to replicate it with other birds, with slightly varying techniques.

TABLE 4.6
Training Procedures for Serial Learning Experiments[a]

	(Straub et al.) Backwards	(Straub, Group 1) Forwards	(Straub, Group 2) Pair
Pretraining	D, CD	A,B,C,D,(separate)	AB,BC,CD
Training	A	A	A
Phases	AB	AB	AB
	ABC	ABC	ABC
	ABCD	ABCD	ABCD

[a]From Straub et al. (1979).

Straub (1979) succeeded in training two groups of birds on a simultaneously presented four-color sequence. The new groups responded in a chamber that had six keys, rather than four, making possible many more physically unique color arrays. The training method also differed from our original experiment. Rather than receiving initial "backward" training on D, one group of four pigeons received "forward" training only, progressing from A, A B, A B C, A B C D; another group of three birds received initial adjacent "pair" training before the forward training, A B, B C, C D. Table 4.6 presents the three paradigms schematically.

Straub's subjects ultimately achieved a 70% success rate on the four-color sequences. Table 4.7 and 4.8 present the data from three sessions of each group of birds when they were responding at the 50% level (this level is chosen to be similar to the success rate of subjects in our original experiment). Despite the differences in training procedures, the response patterns are similar to those of the original experiment. In each case, forward and backward errors decrease and latencies increase as a function of distance from the correct response. Straub demonstrated further that the birds learned the

TABLE 4.7
Response Times (Sec) and Frequencies (in Brackets)
from Three Pigeons, Initially Given Forward Training[a]

	Response			
	A	B	C	D
Position or last key pecked				
Start	1.1 (83%)	2.2 (16%)	2.0 (< 1%)	0
A	0.2 (41%)	0.9 (53%)	1.6 (5%)	2.0 (2%)
B	1.0 (2%)	0.3 (61%)	1.0 (32%)	1.9 (5%)
C	0	1.5 (3%)	0.3 (56%)	1.3 (41%)

[a]From Straub (1979, Group 1; 50% level of accuracy;—about 2000 pecks).

TABLE 4.8
Response Times (Sec) and Frequencies (in Brackets) from Four Pigeons,
Given Initial Training on Sequence Pairs[a]

	Response			
	A	B	C	D
Position or last key pecked				
Start	1.1 (86%)	2.0 (11%)	1.8 (2%)	3.1 (< 1%)
A	0.2 (35%)	0.8 (53%)	1.2 (7%)	1.3 (4%)
B	1.1 (2%)	0.2 (69%)	0.9 (24%)	1.5 (6%)
C	0	0.8 (5%)	0.3 (47%)	0.9 (48%)

[a]From Straub (1979, Group 2; 50% level of accuracy—about 3000 pecks).

color sequence in two ways: He administered a generalization test with physically novel arrays and found virtually no performance decrement; he tested the birds on ordered pairs drawn from the full sequence $A\ B\ C\ D$, e.g., $A\ C,\ A\ D,\ B\ C,\ B\ D,\ C\ D$. He found an impressive, almost immediate transfer to these subsequences, demonstrating that the birds had acquired some representation of the separate ordinal relations among the colors.

We can tentatively conclude that the birds' mastering of the color sequence is not a matter of chance, although it remains to be seen how long such a chain can become without intermediate reinforcement. The establishment of a new paradigm in which serial behavior can be studied in animals is important for comparative psychology. We will be able to use it to study whether certain universals of language are also true of animal serial behavior. For example, the principles of "most-general-first" and "save-the-hardest-for-the-last" can be studied with expansions of the paradigm used in Straub et al. In this way, we can develop a true comparative study of the structural laws governing all serial behaviors. Part of this study involves a close examination of how animals might represent these complex performances—we turn to this in the next section.

What Is Learned?

Certain methodological difficulties force us to be cautious in claiming that we have conclusive proof that subjects mastered the color sequence, as opposed to memorizing the separate physical arrays. We *can* ask, however, what we will know about the mastery of sequences once the methodological limitations are overcome. There are two independent questions: At what physiological "level" is the chain represented? Is the representation ordered or unordered? The answers to the physiological question range from the "peripheral" to the "central"—at one extreme one could claim that the "representation" is encoded as a series of *sensorimotor–color–peck* pairs. The alternative claim is that there is a central arrangement of *encoded-color–encoded-peck* pairs. It is important to remember that, however the physical question is answered, it does not determine whether the representation is itself of an integrated sequence or of a sequence of otherwise isolated responses. A complete solution to the problem of serial behavior may include an answer to the physiological question. But we will be in a better position to ask it intelligently if we have determined *what* is learned—how is the chain per se represented?

With respect to this question there are two extremes—on the one hand we could follow the implication of Lashley's considerations and claim that the chain is represented as an integrated response program. The alternative is the claim that the sequence is represented by uniquely encoded S–R complexes that can only be ordered in behavior in a single way. (See Wickelgren, (1969), for a presentation of such a model of sequencing in language.) The essentials of such a model rest on the attachment of mediating response–stimulus units, which bind the adjacent members of a sequence. For example, one could interpret the subsequence *A B* as composed of the following, unordered, set of learned behaviors:

1. At the start, peck *A*.
2. If *A* was just pecked, peck *B*.

Stated in this way, (1) and (2) are formally equivalent to a *sequence* representation. If we require that the representation account automatically for the order, the rules could be:

1. At the start, peck *A*; when pecking *A*, produce response "a."
2. If in bodily state "a," peck *B*....

In this way, the very manner of pecking *A* is itself the discriminative stimulus for pecking *B*; accordingly, "*A*" and "*B*" do not have to be represented as ordered—rather they are expressible only in the appropriate order, even though they are represented as unordered. At first, such a model appears to be compatible with an associative learning theory. For example, a bird might isolate the previously arbitrary distribution of body weight as the discriminative stimulus associated with each color-peck response:

1. At the start peck *A*; (when pecking *A*, shift weight to left claw).
2. If weight is on left claw, peck *B*.

There is a class of (peripheral) models in which no appeal to sequence-processing is necessary: those in which the discriminating mediator, "a," is produced following *A automatically* as a function of pecking *A*, rather than being actively isolated by the bird. For example:

1. At start, peck *A* (pecking involves approaching and withdrawing from a color).
2. If withdrawing from *A*, peck *B*....

This class of models could be acquired without any explicit ordering of responses or processing of subsequences during acquisition.

Such a model can be extended to describe the four-color sequence, in such a way that the sequence itself is not explicitly represented. There is a corresponding nonperipheral model:

1. The starting configuration is the stimulus for pecking *A*....
2. Having pecked *A* is the stimulus for pecking *B*....

Both models appear to allow unordered statements to represent the ordered behavior. Now we come to two questions:

1. How does the organism isolate "a" as a possible discriminative stimulus—except by "noting" the sequence?
2. When isolated, how does the peripheral model differ from a nonperipheral sequence-representation model, except metaphysically?

The first question is crucial: Why should and how can an organism differentiate a response "a" that is uniquely associated with pecking *A* unless it is in response to the need to use it as a sequence mediator? To put it another way, how does the organism associate "a" as the mediator between *A* and *B* unless it *already* is processing what is being mediated, namely the subsequence "*A B*"? If the organism must first process the sequence in order to extract the mediators, then the mediator is hardly a formal replacement for sequential capacity: Rather, it is at best, a mnemonic device for the organism's representation of an already processed sequence.

It would seem that there is no associative model that easily accounts for the phenomena. However, the failure of a simple-minded associative theory is not a convincing argument that the birds learn a representation of the sequence. That is a negative argument. In the next section we show that the birds' behavior is efficiently represented by a computational model of how the response sequence is both represented and executed. This model also accounts in an intuitive way for the slight differences in the results from the three experiments. The model assumes the existence of a sequence representation; accordingly, the model's descriptive success can count as an empirical confirmation of the view that the birds acquire such a representation.

A Computational Model

The study of how representations are used is typical of research on human cognition and problem solving. For example, in the previous section, we presented an information-processing model of strategies that human subjects use to search lists. Recently, such models have been applied to certain instances of animal behavior (e.g., Blough, 1977).

These models have varied interpretations concerning their "psychological reality." Indeed it can be argued that they merely simulate human performance rather than model human knowledge (cf. Tanenhaus, Carroll, & Bever, 1976). Such objections may have even more force when such models are applied to animal behavior, because we have no introspective evidence to aid our choice of a model. However, information-processing models have proven useful in organizing large amounts of data and in providing a precise basis for new experimental predictions. The orderliness of our data indicated that it might be correspondingly useful to apply such a model. As we outlined in the following section, we found a general model that deals with our result quite efficiently. This model presupposes both a representation of the sequence and a computational mechanism for the expression of that representation. We show that slight differences in three serial learning experiments with pigeons result in three similar models, each of which differs from the others in a way that is intuitively related to unique aspects of its experimental paradigm. This correspondence lends support to the appropriateness of such models for the description of animal behavior. Furthermore, the success of such models with our data may provide a start toward a new way of uniting the study of human and animal behavior, using such models as a common form of representation.

It was the error pattern of our data in Table 4.5 that first prompted us to apply computational modeling techniques. We noted previously that the probability of a forward or backward slip error decreased with the number of skipped colors. This suggests a probabilistic error function that iterates across the sequence. Suppose we postulate a model with two modes of operating—moving a pointer from the beginning to the end of a tape of the sequence and pecking the color that the pointer indicates. If the model corresponded with the errors, as in AVIAN in Fig. 4.3, it would always peck its way correctly through the sequence. If we now introduce error functions for the "peck" and "move" opeations, we can account better for the mean frequency of repeats and skips, as in Fig. 4.4.. The overall performance in these sessions is about 56%; if the errors occur equally frequently at each point, this requires that each individual transition be correct $\sqrt{.56\%}$ = .86. The frequency of repeat pecks (41%) is simply set empirically to match the overall mean of repeats. It is straightforward that, if after pecking, the device returns in a loop to peck again 41%, then 41% of the responses will be repeat pecks. Similarly, 14% of nonrepeat responses will skip at least 1 color, since the pointer moves to the right 14% of the time without pecking; $(14\%)^2$ of the nonrepeat pecks skips

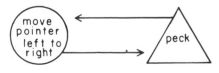

FIG. 4.3.   Basic model of ordered responding in pigeons.

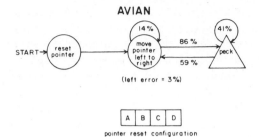

FIG. 4.4. AVIAN. Preliminary
model of serial pecking in pigeons
with initial backward training.

over at least two color positions, and so on. Finally, an assumption that the
pointer erroneously moves *backward* in 3% of the cases that it moves at all
generates the prediction that backward errors occur 3% of nonrepeat
responses, and two-step backward errors occur $(3\%)^2$ of nonrepeat responses.
The second column in Table 4.9 presents the predicted frequency of the
different response categories as against the observed frequency presented in
the first column.

TABLE 4.9
Predicted and Observed Latencies and Frequencies for AVIAN

	AVIAN			
Correct	*Observed Frequency* %	*Predicted* 86% 41%	*Observed Latency*	*Predicted* m = .56 p = .38
A	86	86	1.5	1.5
B	54	51	1.0	.9
C	53	49	.9	.96
D	36	49	.9	.9
Repeats				
A	34	41	.5	.4
B	41	41	0.0	.4
C	63	41	.3	.4
Forward Skips				
Start—				
B	12	12	2.3	2.0
C	1.9	1.7	3.0	2.6
D	.1	.2	1.6	1.5
A–C	11.7	6.9	2.1	2.1
D	1.1	1.1	1.4	1.5
B–D	4.3	8.0		
Backward Skips				
B–A	1.7	1.5	—	—
C–B	1.1	1.5	—	—
C–A	0.0	.1	—	—
Correlation		.956		.859
Variance		91%		74%

The efficacy of an information-processing model such as AVIAN can be tested by examining how much of the variance in the actual data it accounts for (see Table 4.9). AVIAN accounts for 91% of the variance in the observed probabilities—this is supportive but not fully convincing. One way to gain additional support for AVIAN is to set temporal parameters that correspond to the "move" and "peck" operations: We set the move-pointer time at .56 sec and the peck time at .38 sec. The columns in Table 4.9 present the observed and predicted latency values for AVIAN (we do not compute predicted latency values for those response categories with less than 4% of the data because of the small number of responses in those categories). This analysis accounts for 73.8% of the variance in the latencies—again suggestive, but certainly not overwhelming confirmation of AVIAN.

Further consideration of the latencies stimulated us to develop a more sophisticated model, AVIAN *B*, presented in Fig. 4.5. It contains, like AVIAN, a move-pointer operation (on the left) and a pecking operation (on the right). This model allows us to take into account several systematic facts about the latencies. First, the repeat peck latencies decrease to colors later in the sequence. Second, the amount by which latency increases in forward skips decreases to colors later in the sequence. Finally, the latency to correct responses decreases to colors later in the sequence. AVIAN B captures this property by having a second pointer on the same tape, the "checker," that moves back from the end of the sequence to the color to be pecked. Only when the checker and pointer coincide can an actual peck be executed; the checker

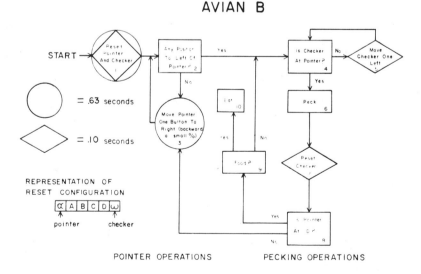

FIG. 4.5.   AVIAN B. Information-processing model model of serial pecking in pigeons with initial backward training.

TABLE 4.10
Predicted and Observed Latencies in the Three Experiments

	Backwards		Forward		Pair	
	Obs.	Pred.	Obs.	Pred.	Obs.	Pred.
Correct						
A	1.51	1.66	1.10	1.36	1.07	1.40
B	.96	1.03	.87	.93	.75	.85
C	.94	.93	.99	1.03	.91	.87
D	.91	.83	1.27	1.13	.93	.93
Repeats						
A	.51	.50	.19	.20	.22	.24
B	.38	.40	.29	.30	.19	.22
C	.33	.30	.34	.40	.24	.24
Forwards Errors						
St → B	2.32	2.19	2.21	2.09	1.84	2.01
St → C[a]	2.98	1.72	1.96	2.82	1.68	2.66
St → D[a]	.81	3.25		3.55	3.10	3.35
A → C	1.60	1.56	1.56	1.66	1.24	1.50
A → D[a]	2.07	2.09	1.89	2.39	1.29	2.19
B → D	1.40	1.46	1.87	1.76	1.47	1.56
Backwards Errors						
B → A[a]	.95	1.13	.99	.83	1.15	.87
C → B[a]	.73	1.03	1.53	.93	.84	.85

[a]Response categories that accounted for less than 2% of the data overall.

then resets to its end position. Because the early colors require more leftward moves of the checker, their latencies are predicted to be correspondingly longer. We assessed the adequacy of AVIAN B by postulating the move-pointer operation as requiring .63 sec and the move-checker operation as requiring 0.1 sec. The observed and predicted latencies are presented in the first two columns of Table 4.10, (as stated, only the 10 data points with more than 4% of the possible responses are tested for latency predictions— although the reader can satisfy himself that AVIAN B accounts quite well for all the latencies): The predictions account for 99% of the variance, which is well within accepted limits for confirmation of such a model. Furthermore, the model is a strong one in the sense that only two variables are needed to account for the 10 independent data points. (See Appendix for sample derivations).

AVIAN B can also account for the frequency pattern if we assume the same sort of error functions as in AVIAN. If the device erroneously answers "no" 14% of the time to the question "Is there a position to the left of the pointer?," then it will generate the same forward skip-error functions as AVIAN; 41% erroneous "yes" to the question "Is the pointer at D?" produces the same proportion of repeats; and an erroneous 3% leftward movement of the pointer when it should be to the right produces the same pattern of backward skips. These functions could be repeated in AVIAN B and would account for the variance in frequencies in the same way as AVIAN. Accordingly, AVIAN B accounts for 98% of the variance in 10 latencies and 91% of the variance in 16 percentages with a total of five variables, applied to a single model.

The efficacy of this model and its ability to account simultaneously for the error pattern and the latency pattern are convincing features. However, unlike the case with humans, we have no independent evidence that the subjects (pigeons) ever "think" in terms of such devices as postulated by the model. These devices are themselves descriptively powerful, which raises the question of the ontological claims we make about their arrangement in the particular model. Is it a model of the birds' "knowledge"? Is it (only) a simulation of the birds' behavior?

We can attempt to resolve such questions in the usual way: by appealing to further data and showing that the model accounts for them in a revealing manner. If the models are "only" a simulation, then they cannot be expected to generalize to new paradigms. We found that a slight change in AVIAN B produces a new model that can account for the latency pattern of the birds in the "forward" training experiments, as shown in AVIAN F (Fig. 4.6). AVIAN F accounts for 97% of the variance in the latencies (see the second pair of columns in Table 4.10). This model is nearly identical to that for the original birds; most important, it uses the exact same two physical values (.63 sec for a pointer opertion, .1 sec for a checker). In fact, it has only one difference—*the "checker" moves from left to right rather than right to left.* This difference is necessary to account for the fact that the latency for repeat pecks goes *up* for

AVIAN F

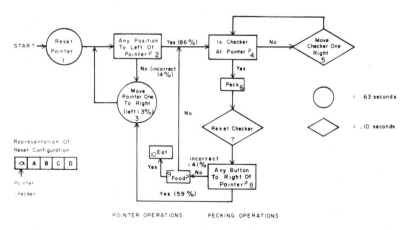

FIG. 4.6.   AVIAN F. Information-processing model of serial pecking in pigeons with initial forward training.

AVIAN P

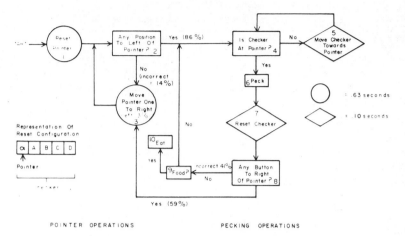

FIG. 4.7. AVIAN P. Information-processing model of serial pecking in pigeons with initial pair training.

the later colors, as does the added time for an error of each size (recall that the opposite patterns held for the backward pretraining experiment). We do not discuss further the prediction of relative frequencies because the frequency patterns are similar in the three experiments, and all the models make the same frequency predictions.

It is a confirmation of our original model, AVIAN B, that it can account for the new data with the same constraints. Even more striking is that the one difference in the new model has an understandable basis in the different pretraining techniques. In the original experiment, birds were first trained extensively on the end of the sequence and then shifted to the beginning—it is those birds whose model assumes that the checker starts at the end of the sequence on each peck: The later birds were trained equally on all colors in isolation and then shifted to the beginning of the sequence. That is, the first presented pair in this experiment was *A B* rather than *C D*. This is reflected in the model by having the checker always reset back to the beginning.

A further modification in the checker-reset position yields a model that accounts for the latency data in a third, pair-pretraining experiment. AVIAN P (Fig. 4.7) is identical to the previous two, using the same configuration and the same physical variables *except that the checker resets randomly to each position.* This parallels the behavioral fact that there is no serially ordered increasing or decreasing trend in repeat and incremental error latencies, and the fact that overall, *all* the latencies are faster than in the other paradigms (see the last two columns in Table 4.10). Like AVIAN F, AVIAN P is also related to the pretraining procedure given the birds. They were exposed to isolated pairs *A B, B C, C D,* which can be understood as diffusing their

TABLE 4.11
Variance Accounted for by AVIAN Model for
All Response Catergories in Each Experiment

	Model		
Experiment	AVIAN B	AVIAN F	AVIAN P
Backwards Training	98%	88%	94%
Forward Training	79%	97%	65%
Pair Training	69%	97%	97%

attention evenly throughout the sequence. This diffusion is reflected in the fact that the checker in AVIAN P resets to each position equally frequently and randomly.

We have presented what we think are the best models for each of these separate experiments. Before interpreting the meaning of the differences in the models, it is necessary to make sure that they are empirically distinguishable—that is, that no single model designed for one experiment can predict the data from another experiment equally well. Table 4.11 presents the extent to which each model accounts for the variance in the latencies for each experiment. (For the purposes of this discussion, the same response frequencies are predicted by each model, so we can concentrate on the latencies.) AVIAN B, constructed for the backward experiments, does not strongly predict the other experiments and AVIAN P predicts the data from the pair experiment better than the other experiments. AVIAN F, however, originally designed to account for the forward experiment, accounts as well overall for the data from the pair experiment as does AVIAN P. This is mathematically due to the fact that the main qualitative difference predicted by the models is in the times for repeat pecks—but these latencies are extremely short compared with the other data points—thus any difference in the adequacy of predicting these points are obscured by the roughly equal ability of the models to predict the longer latency data points. We could have avoided this difficulty by calculating correlations between predicted and observed values, based on frequency-weighted latencies. We did not do this, however; we treated all reliable latencies equally to arrive at the best *qualitative* model.

It should be noted that the repeat pecks are a major component of the data in each experiment—comprising about one-half of all the pecks actually made. Accordingly, ceteris paribus, the relative ability of a model to predict these responses is decisive: By this criterion the model chosen for each experiment is the best. AVIAN B is clearly the most adequate for the repeats in the backward experiment, and close analysis shows that the AVIAN F is best for the forward experiment repeats; AVIAN P remains the best for the repeats in the pair experiment. Furthermore, we have a separate way of conclusively demonstrating the superiority of each AVIAN model in accounting for its corresponding experiment. The models make exact quantitative predictions for each response category. For example, "repeat *A*" is predicted to take .50 and .20 by AVIANs B and F, respectively. We can note that this *relative* ordering is confirmed by the actual data on the observed repeat "*A*" pecks, .51 and .19. For the 10 response categories with at least 1% of the data in each experiment, the pair-by-pair directional predictions between AVIAN B and F are confirmed in all 10 cases; this is also true for AVIAN B and P; and for AVIAN F and P, the relative predictions are confirmed in nine cases (the reversal of .03 sec for correct *A* was also the smallest observed difference in the two experiments). (See Table 4.10.) In brief, the ambiguity left by the correlation test is resolved by careful nonparametric analysis: Each model is best for its corresponding experiment, and vice-versa.

To Sum Up. We have analyzed the performance of pigeons on three four-color serial experiments. *The exact same two quantitative variables* (.63 sec for a pointer operation; .1 sec for a checker operation) provide a convincing prediction of the latency data obtained in each experiment. The slight differences in the form of the predictive model for each experiment have a natural interpretation, based on the different pretraining procedures:

Backward Experiment: Subjects were pretrained on the final color alone. The final color is the checker reset position in the model for this experiment.

Forward Experiment: Subjects were pretrained on each color in isolation and then given initial color training alone. The initial color is the checker reset position in the model for this experiment.

Pair Experiment: Subjects were pretrained on paired subsequences, rein-forcing each color as the member of a two-color chain. The checker resets randomly to any position, in the model for this experiment.

That is, according to the models, subjects "scan" the color sequence with the checker before each response, starting in each different condition at the position(s) on which they were pretrained. The intuitive nature of this interpretation is itself support for the models. Furthermore, the consistency of the quantitative variables across the experiments provides a strong basis for accepting the models: The models use two variables to predict 30 independent latency data points from three separate experiments.

Despite their success and intuitive consistency, the details of the models must be cautiously interpreted. For example, as the models are constructed, the time to execute a peck response is not separately represented—rather it is embedded within the other times. This could be interpreted as claiming that each "peck" is a behavior that is inextricably linked to the decision process governing where to do it—certainly a possibility, but not one that we are likely to prove or disprove easily. Furthermore, the specific mechanics of the checker operations are constructed to generate the following generalization:

1. In experiment 1, focus on the end of the sequence.
2. In experiment 2, focus on the beginning of the sequence.
3. In experiment 3, attend equally to all positions.

These generalizations could be captured by formal devices other than those we have used.

Given these cautionary notes, we can still conclude from the models of how pigeons deal with serial order problems:

10a. Subjects encode a representation of the sequence.
10b. Subjects apply an orderly internal procedure to access the representation.
10c. The search procedure differs internally as a direct function of external variables.

The reader is invited to compare our conclusions in (10 a–c) to those made from the human studies, cited in (9 a–c), p. 66.

It is interesting to note that, the simplest model, AVIAN, could be interpreted as a model of two *physical* processes, "pecking" and "moving along in the sequence." In this sense, the model is consistent with a "peripheralist" interpretation of the representation of the sequence. An error is generated when the bird "skips over" a color, by "air-pecking" it: that is, by executing a response toward the color that is not sufficiently complete to close the recording circuit. This would account for the fact that downstream errors take additional time the further downstream they are. We pointed out previously that the nature of the physiological representation is important but orthogonal to the structural organization of the representation. The weakness of the original AVIAN does not involve its reducibility to physical terms but its inadequacy to predict the data. As we found models that are more adequate to the data empirically, we found them harder to interpret in sensorimotor terms. In particular, the checker and the various internal scanning mechanisms in the later three models are not easy to understand this way. Even if one interpreted the different patterns in the distinct experiments as due to a difference in focus (involving no checker at all), one would have to accept the concept of "focus" as a psychological entity in animals. Although such a notion is not unreasonable, given the manifest behavior of many wild and domestic animals, it certainly is not "peripheral."

We do not mean to suggest that no physiological representation can underlie the acquisition of mechanisms such as those we have isolated. Rather, there is no simple sensorimotor basis for these organized behaviors.

In our view, the integration of a sequence of originally isolated responses involves the emergence of an internal organization.

CONCLUSION—BACK AGAIN

We opened this chapter by raising the question of the explanation of serial behavior. We recalled that the existence of integrated subsequences of behavior, such as language, raises immediate conceptual problems for a response-by-response model of behavior. We reported on two attempts to reduce serial constraints in language to simpler terms: examining non-linguistic list search strategies that can explain certain properties of language and developing a paradigm for the study of serial behavior in nonlinguistic organisms.

In each case we have found that learning a serial behavior appears to force the subject to a complex organization. Our evidence suggests that humans and animals alike utilize sequence representations. Their behavior is efficiently modeled by scanning procedures that are similar and similarily dependent on environmental contingencies. This statement, of course, would not be startling to an S–R chaining theorist, who is committed to the belief that all behavior in humans and animals can be reduced to environmentally transparent processes. What should be startling to everyone, however, is that we have not succeeded in finding paradigms in which human behavior can be reduced to the simplicity of animal behavior. Rather, humans use intricate structures in serial behavior outside of language and animals spontaneously generate similar kinds of structural organizations for their serial behavior.

APPENDIX:
AN INTERPRETATION OF
INFORMATION-PROCESSING MODELS

The text in this chapter presents several information-processing models of behavior. It is important to understand how these models operate, because they make exact quantitative predictions that are crucial to the main argument of the paper. We present the following derivations of different kinds of responses produced by the models. The numbers indicate that operation is referred to in the corresponding model.

SEQUENCE MODEL
(as shown in Fig. 4.2)

This model basically executes a left–right serial search on the sequence representation (ordered in paid subsequences; randomized in unpaid sequences). As constructed, the model generates predictions for all correct responses. It could be adapted to predict the incorrect responses as well, but this involves considerable complexity, and, consequently we have not included them.

Operation	Mode of Exit	Latency	Position of Pointer
1. Time to recognize "N" in example (6), (5 9 4 7 2 X B N R F), as Paid Sequence Item.			
Start	—	—	1
1	yes	—	1
4	no	—	1
5	yes	—	1
6	—	120	2
4	no	—	2
5	yes	—	2
6	—	120	3
4	yes	—	3
7	respond yes	1220	3
		1460(predicted latency)	
2. Time to recognize "F" as a Paid Sequence Item in the same sequence.			
a. Via Buffer			
Start	—	—	1
1	yes	—	1
3	yes	—	1
7	respond yes	1220	1
		1220(predicted latency)	
b. Via Pointer			
Start	—	—	1
3	no	—	1
4	no	—	1
5	yes	—	1
6	—	120	2
4	no	—	2
5	yes	—	2
6	—	120	3
4	no	—	3
5	yes	—	3
6	—	120	4
4	no	—	4
5	yes	—	4
6	—	120	5
4	yes	—	5
7	respond yes	1220	5
		1720(predicted latency)	

Mean latency predicted for sequence—final items = P_c = probability of an incorrect "no" on operation 3 or 4.

$(1 - P_c) (1220) + P_c (1720) = 1240.$

Operation	Mode of Exit	Latency	Position of Pointer
3. Time to recognize any Item as an Unpaid Sequence Item.			
Start			
1	no	—	
2	—	120	
—	—	—	
—	—	—	
—	—	—	

The number of cycles through 4, 5, 6, is the average number of pointer moves through the entire 5-item sequence ÷ 2 = 240 msec.

		240
7	respond yes	1220
		1580

4. Time to miss any paid item.
   Same as (2b).
5. Time to miss any unpaid item.
   Same as (2b) with an additional 120 msec for operation (2).

AVIAN MODELS

As presented, these models can predict the latency of every response category (although they are tested only on responses with at least 1% frequency). The models could also be adapted to predict the relative frequencies of responses. However, there is an extremely high correlation across the experiments of the relative frequencies of responses; the models make the same frequency predictions for each experiment. The latencies are less well-correlated across the experiments; the models make different predictions, due to the different reset configuration of the checker, and the corresponding differences in operation 5.

Each model had the following basic processes (numbers indicate specific operations in Figs. 4.4–4.6.):

1. Resetting pointer to position before the sequence representation.
2–3. Stepping the pointer through the sequence.
4–5. Stepping the checker toward the pointer until it coincides with the pointer.
6. Pecking at the coincident pointer/checker position.
7. Resetting the checker to its canonical position.
8. Checking if the sequence is finsihed (cycling to 3 if it is not).
9. Checking for food (cycling to 6 if there is not any).
10. Eating.

REPEAT RESPONSES AND ERRORS

Repeat responses and errors are generated in the following ways:

Repeats.   An incorrect "yes" to question 8 (i.e., "Is the sequence over?") generates a cycle back to 4–5–6, producing a peck without moving the pointer.

Forward Errors.   An incorrect "no" to question 2 (i.e., "Is the sequence at the beginning?") generates an extra pointer move (operation 3) before going to the pecking operations 4–6, thus creating a skip.

Backward Errors.   A small "jitter" function in the rightward pointer moving operation (operation 3) allows for erroneous backward movement of the pointer and a consequent backward peck.

AVIAN B

		Correct A		
	Exit Response	Latency Increment	Pointer Position	Checker Position
Start		—	—	—
1[a]		.63	α	w
2	no	—	α	w
3		.63	A	w
1	yes	—	A	w
4	no	—	A	w
5		.1	A	D
4	no	—	A	D
5		.1	A	C
4	no	—	A	C
5		.1	A	B
4	no	—	A	B
5		.1	A	A
4	yes	—	A	A
6	peck	—	A	A
		1.66 predicted latency		

[a]Note that the Start operations of resetting the pointer and checker are assumed to be parallel, thus adding only the longer latency of the pointer operations to the overall time.

		Correct B		
Operation	Exit Response	Latency Increment	Pointer Position	Checker Position
6 (Peck A)	—	—	A	A
7	—	.1	A	w
8	no	—	A	w
3	—	.63	B	w
2	yes	—	B	w
4	no	—	B	w
5	—	.1	B	D
4	no	—	B	D
5	—	.1	B	C
4	no	—	B	C
5	—	.1	B	B
4	yes	—	B	B
6	Peck B			
		1.03 predicted latency		

		Repeat A		
Operation	Exit Response	Latency Increment	Pointer Position	Checker Position
6 (Peck A)	—	—	A	A
7	—	.1	A	w
8	yes[a]	—	A	w
9	no	—	A	w
4	no	—	A	w
5	—	.1	A	D
4	no	—	A	D
5	—	.1	A	C
4	no	—	A	C
5	—	.1	A	B
4	no	—	A	B
5	—	.1	A	A
4	yes	—	A	A
6	Peck			
		.5 predicted latency		

[a]Incorrect operation.

Forward Error from A → C

Operation	Exit Response	Latency Increment	Pointer Position	Checker Position
6 (Peck A)	—	—	A	A
7	—	.1	A	w
8	no	—	A	w
3	—	.63	B	w
2	no[a]	—	B	w
3	—	.63	C	w
1	yes	—	C	w
4	no	—	C	w
5	—	.1	C	D
4	no	—	C	D
5	—	.1	C	C
4	yes	—	C	C
6	Peck	—	C	C
		1.56 predicted latency		

Backward Error C → B

Operation	Exit Response	Latency Increment	Pointer Position	Checker Position
6 (Peck C)	—	—	C	C
7	—	.1	C	w
8	no	—	C	w
3[a]	—	.63	B[a]	w
4	no	—	B	w
5	—	.1	B	D
4	no	—	B	D
5	—	.1	B	C
4	no	—	B	C
5	—	.1	B	B
4	yes	—	B	B
6	Peck			
		1.03 predicted latency		

[a]Incorrect operation.

AVIAN F

		Correct A		
Operation	Exit Response	Latency Increment	Pointer Position	Checker Position
Start	—	—	—	—
1	—	.63	α	α
2	no	—	—	α
3	—	.63	—	α
2	yes	—	—	α
4	no	—	—	α
5	—	.1	A	A
4	yes	—	A	A
6	peck	—	A	A
		1.36 predicted latency		

		Correct B		
6 (Peck A)	—	—	A	A
7	—	.1	A	α
8	no	—	A	α
3	—	.63	B	α
2	yes	—	B	α
4	no	—	B	α
5	—	.1	B	A
4	no	—	B	A
5	—	.1	B	B
4	yes	—	B	B
6	peck	—		
		.93 predicted latency		

Note: Other categories of AVIAN F responses are generated analogous to Avian B, except that the checker reset position is always α.

AVIAN P

(Essentially the same as AVIAN B, and AVIAN F, except that the checker
resets randomly to each position.)

		Correct A		
Operation	Exit Response	Latency Increment	Pointer Position	Checker Position
Start	—	—	—	$(\bar{\Sigma}=B)^a$
1	—	.63	—	$\alpha-D$
2	no	—	—	$\alpha-D$
3	—	.63	A	$\alpha-D$
2	yes	—	—	$\alpha-D$
4^a	—	—	A	$\alpha-D$
5^a	—	$.14^a$	—	$\alpha-D$
.	.	.	.	.
.	.	.	.	.
.	.	.	.	.
.	.	.	.	.
6	peck			
		$\overline{\hspace{2cm}}$ 1.4 predicted latency		

^{a}If the checker reset varies evenly over the five representation positions, the average number of checker moves to A is:

From proportion weighted moves
$$\alpha-1 \times .2 = .2$$
$$A-0 \times .2 = 0$$
$$B-1 \times .2 = .2$$
$$C-2 \times .2 = .4$$
$$\underline{D-3 \times .2 = .6} \quad 1.4 \text{ moves} = .14 \text{ sec}$$

The checker moves in operations 4–5 for all the buttons are:

From	To A		To B		To C		To D	
α	1	.2	2	.4	3	.6	4	.8
A	0	0	1	.2	2	.4	3	.6
B	1	.2	0	0	1	.2	2	.4
C	2	.4	1	.2	0	0	1	.2
D	3	.6	2	.4	1	.2	0	0
moves	1.4		1.2		1.4		2.0	
$\bar{\Sigma}$ latency increment	.14		.12		.14		.20	

Repeat and error responses are generated in the same way as AVIAN B and AVIAN F, except that the latency increments produced by operations 4–5 follow the above calculations corresponding to the actual pecked button.

ACKNOWLEDGMENTS

This research was supported by NSF and NIE grants to T. G. Bever and D. J. Townsend, and by a grant from NIH to H. S. Terrace. The authors are particularly indebted to N. Gould and R. Shanor for assistance in preparation of the manuscript, and to C. Daiute for advice on the manuscript.

REFERENCES

Atkinson, R. C., Hermann, D. J., & Wescourt, K. T. Search processes in recognition memory. In R. L. Solso (Ed.), *Theories in Cognitive Psychology: The Loyola Symposium.* Potomac, Md.: Lawrence Erlbaum Associates, 1974.

Baddeley, A. D., & Ecob, J. R. Reaction time and short term memory: Implications of repetition effects for the high-speed exhaustive scan hypothesis. *Quarterly Journal of Experimental Psychology,* 1973, *25,* 229–240.

Baird, R., & Koslick, J. D. Recall of grammatical relations within clause-containing sentences. *Journal of Psycholinguistic Research,* 1974, *3,* 165–171.

Bever, T. G. The cognitive basis for linguistic structures. In J. R. Hayes, (Ed.), *Cognition and the development of language.* New York: Wiley, 1970.

Bever, T. G., Garrett, M., & Hurtig, R. The interaction of perceptual processes and ambiguous sentences. *Memory and Cognition,* 1973, *1,* 277–386.

Bever, T. G., & Hurtig, R. Detectability of a non-linguistic stimulus is poorest at the end of a clause, *Journal of Psycholinguistic Research,* 1975, *4,* 1–7.

Bever, T. G., Hurtig, R., & Handel, A. Response biases do not account for the effect of clause structure on the perception of non-linguistic stimuli. Unpublished manuscript, 1977.

Bever, T. G., Lackner, J. R., & Kirk, R. The underlying structures of sentences are the primary units of immediate speech processing. *Perception and Psychophysics,* 1969, *5,* 225–231.

Blough, D. S. Visual search in the pigeon: Hunt and peck method, *Science,* 1977, *196,* 1013–1014.

Burrows, D., & Okada, R. Serial position effects in high-speed memory search. *Perception & Psychophysics,* 1971, *10,* 305–308.

Caplan, D. Clause boundaries and recognition latencies for words in sentences. *Perception & Psychophysics,* 1972, *12,* 73–76.

Carroll, J. M., Tanenhaus, M. K., & Bever, T. G. *The perception of relations: The interaction of structural, functional and contextual factors in the segmentation of sentences.* Yorktown Heights, N. Y.: I.B.M. Research Report RC (# 28234), 1977.

Chapin, P., Smith, T., & Abrahamson, A. Two factors in perceptual segmentation of speech. *Journal of Verbal Learning and Verbal Behavior,* 1972, *11,* 164–173.

Clark, H., & Clark, E. *Psychology and language.* New York: Harcourt, Brace Jovanovich, 1977.

Clifton, C., & Birnbaum, S. Effects of serial position and delay of probe in a memory scan task. *Journal of Experimental Psychology,* 1970, *86,* 69–76.

Clifton, C., & Gutschera, K. D. Hierarchical search of two-digit numbers in a recognition memory task. *Journal of Verbal Learning and Verbal Behavior,* 1971, *10,* 528–541.

Corballis, M. C. Serial order in recognition and recall. *Journal of Experimental Psychology,* 1967, *74,* 99–105.

Corballis, M. C., Kirby, J., & Miller, A. Access to elements of a memorized list. *Journal of Experimental Psychology,* 1972, *94,* 185–190.

Corballis, M. C., & Miller, A. Scanning and decision processes in recognition memory. *Journal of Experimental Psychology,* 1973, *98,* 379–386.

Dalrymple–Alford, E. C. Response bias and judgements of the location of clicks in sentences. *Perception & Psychophysics*, 1976, *19*, 303–308.

Darley, C. F., Klatzky, R. L., & Atkinson, R. C. Effects of memory load on reaction time. *Journal of Experimental Psychology*, 1972, *96*, 233–234.

Fodor, J. A., Bever, T. G., & Garrett, M. *The psychology of language: An introduction to psycholinguistics and generative grammar.* New York: McGraw Hill, 1974.

Fodor, J. A., & Garrett, M. Some syntactic determinants of sentential complexity. *Perception & Psychophysics*, 1967, *2*, 289–296.

Forster, K. I. Visual perception of rapidly presented word sequences of varying complexity. *Perception & Psychophysics*, 1970, *8*, 215–221.

Forster, K. I., & Olbrei, I. Semantic heuristics and syntactic analysis. *Cognition*, 1973, *2*, 319–347.

Garrett, M. F. *Syntactic structures and judgments of auditory events.* Unpublished doctoral dissertation, University of Illinois, 1965.

Garrett, M. F., Bever, T. G., & Fodor, J. A. The active use of grammar in speech perception. *Perception & Psychophysics*, 1966, *1*, 30–32.

Glucksberg, S., Trabasso, T. & Wald, J. Linguistic structures and mental operations. *Cognitive Psychology*, 1973, *5*, 338–370.

Hakes, P., & Cairns, H. Sentence comprehension and relative pronouns. *Perception & Psychophysics*, 1970, *8*, 5–8.

Hebb, D. O. The semi-autonomous process: Its nature and nurture. *American Psychologist*, 1963, *18*, 16–27.

Hebb, D. O. *A textbook of psychology.* Philadelphia: W. B. Saunders, 1958.

Heise, G. A., Keller, C., Kharari, K., & Laughlin, N. Discrete-trial alternation in the rat. *Journal of Experimental Analysis of Behavior*, 1969, *12*, 609–622.

Holmes, V. *Some effects of syntactic structure on sentence recognition.* Unpublished doctoral dissertation, University of Melbourne, 1970.

Holmes, V., & Forster, K. Detection of extraneous signals during sentence recognition. *Perception & Psychophysics*, 1970, *7*, 297–301.

Holmes, V., & Forster, K. I. Perceptual complexity and underlying sentence structure. *Journal of Verbal Learning and Verbal Behavior*, 1972, *11*, 148–156.

Jarvella, R. Syntactic processing of connected speech. *Journal of Verbal Learning and Verbal Behavior*, 1971, *10*, 409–416.

Jarvella, R., & Herman, S. Clause structure of sentences and speech processing. *Perception & Psychophysics*, 1972, *11*, 381–384.

Johnson–Laird, P. N. Experimental psycholinguistics. *Annual Review of Psychology*, 1974, *25*, 135–160.

Juola, J. F., & Atkinson, R. C. Memory scanning for words versus categories. *Journal of Verbal Learning and Verbal Behavior*, 1971, *10*, 522–527.

Kennedy, R. A., & Wilkes, A. Analysis of storage and retrieval processes in memorizing simple sentences. *Journal of Experimental Psychology*, 1969, *80*, 396–398.

Kennedy, R. A., & Hamilton, D. Time to locate probe items in short lists of digits. *American Journal of Psychology*, 1969, *82*, 272–275.

Klatzky, R. L., & Atkinson, R. C. Memory scans based on alternative test stimulus representations. *Perception & Psychophysics*, 1970, *8*, 113–117.

Klatzky, R. L., Juola, J. F., & Atkinson, R. C. Test stimulus representation and experimental context effects in memory scanning. *Journal of Experimental Psychology*, 1971, *87*, 281–288.

Morin, R., DeRosa, D., & Stultz, V. Recognition memory and reaction time. *Acta Psychologica*, 1967, *27*, 298–305.

Naus, M. J. Memory search of categorized lists: A consideration of alternative self-terminating search strategies. *Journal of Experimental Psychology*, 1974, *102*, 992–1000.

Naus, M. J., Glucksberg, S., & Ornstein, P. A. Taxonomic word categories and memory search. *Cognitive Psychology*, 1972, *3*, 643–654.

Perfetti, C., & Goldman, S. Discourse memory and reading comprehension. *Journal of Verbal Learning and Verbal Behavior*, 1976, *15*, 33–42.

Reber, A. A., & Anderson, J. R. The perception of clicks in linguistic and nonlinguistic messages. *Perception & Psychophysics*, 1970, *8*, 81–89.

Ross, J. R. *Universal constraints on variables*. Unpublished doctoral dissertation, M.I.T., 1968.

Shedletsky, L. *Effects of some clause variables on memory-scanning*. Unpublished doctoral dissertation, University of Illinois, 1974.

Simon, H., & Newell, A. *Human Problem Solving*. New Jersey: Prentice-Hall, 1977.

Slobin, D. I. Grammatical transformations and sentence comprehension in childhood and adulthood. *Journal of Verbal Learning and Verbal Behavior*, 1966, *5*, 219–227.

Sternberg, S. High speed scanning in human memory. *Science*, 1966, *153*, 652–654.

Sternberg, S. Retrieval of contextual information from memory. *Psychonomic Science*, 1967, *8*, 55–56.

Sternberg, S. Memory-scanning: Mental processes revealed by reaction-time experiments. *American Scientist*, 1969, *57*, 421–457.

Sternberg, S. Memory scanning: New findings and current controversies. *Quarterly Journal of Experimental Psychology*, 1975, *27*, 1–32.

Straub, R. O. *Serial learning and representation of a sequence in the pigeon*. Unpublished doctoral dissertation, Columbia University, 1979.

Straub, R. O., Seidenberg, M. S., Bever, T. G., & Terrace, H. S. Serial learning in the pigeon. *Journal of the Experimental Analysis of Behavior*, 1979, *32*, 137–148.

Swanson, J. M. & Briggs, G. E. Information processing as a function of speed versus accuracy. *Journal of Experimental Psychology*, 1969, *81*, 223–229.

Tanenhaus, M. *Linguistic context and sentence perception*. Unpublished doctoral dissertation, Columbia University, 1977.

Tanenhaus, M., & Carroll, J. The clausal processing heirarchy and nouniness. In *Papers from the parasession on functionalism*. Chicago: Chicago Linguistic Society, 1975.

Tanenhaus, M., Carroll, J., & Bever, T. Sentence-picture verification models as theories of sentence comprehension: A critique of Carpenter and Just. *Psychological Review*, 1976, *83*, 310–317.

Townsend, D. J., & Bever, T. G. Inter-clause relations and clausal processing. *Journal of Verbal Learning and Verbal Behavior*, 1978, *17*, 509–521.

Townsend, D. J., Bresnick, J., & Bever, T. G. *Two ways of searching portions of active memory*. Unpublished manuscript, 1979.

Wanner, E., & Maratsos, M. *On understanding relative clauses*. Unpublished paper, Harvard University, 1971.

Wickelgren, W. A. Context-sensitive coding, associative memory, and serial order in (speech) behavior. *Psychological Review*, 1969, *76*, 1–15.

Wilkes, A. L., & Kennedy, R. A. Relationship between pausing and retrieval latency in sentences of varying grammatical form. *Journal of Experimental Psychology*, 1969, *79*, 241–245.

Wilkes, A. L., & Kennedy, R. A. The relative accessibility of list items within different pause-defined groups. *Journal of Verbal Learning and Verbal Behavior*, 1970, *9*, 197–201. (a)

Wilkes, A. L., & Kennedy, R. A. Response retrieval in active and passive sentences. *Quarterly Journal of Experimental Psychology*, 1970, *22*, 1–8. (b)

Williams, J. D. Memory enesmble selection in human information processing. *Journal of Experimental Psychology*, 1971, *88*, 231–238.

Wingfield, A., & Klein, J. F. Syntactic structure and acoustic pattern in speech perception. *Perception & Psychophysics*, 1971, *9*, 23–25.

III ATTENTION AND PERFORMANCE

5 Mental Chronometry and the Problem of Consciousness

Michael I. Posner
University of Oregon

Hebb's book, *Organization of Behavior* (1949) had an important influence on experimental psychology. Hebb tried to provide a basis for the integration of physiological and perceptual (subjective) languages for discussing the nature of thought. The problem of the relationship of brain and mind has been a puzzle since Descartes. Whereas Hebb's book served to focus the attention of psychologists on the goal of developing a scientific analysis of conscious processing, there were several difficulties present at the time Hebb wrote that he could not fully overcome.

First, as Hebb recognized, there were strong inhibitions in 1949 even to the discussion of subjective concepts within scientific psychology. Hebb put the problem with respect to use of the words "conscious" and "voluntary" as follows (Hebb, 1949):

> These two terms are not in good standing in modern psychology, and yet they refer to an important psychological distinction.... It is not important whether one is to continue using the words conscious and voluntary in psychological discussion; it *is* important to have the distinction to which they refer made explicit, and to be able to deal with it theoretically [p. 144].

Second, although Hebb's book discussed mental life, both in relation to assemblages of neurons and in terms of subjective experience, there remained a very large gap between the two languages. How could the discrete firings of individual neurons be mapped into the stable perceptual world of our subjective experience?

Third, there was a lack of methods, within the capability of experimental psychologists, for conducting day-to-day investigations that might convert the goal of relating brain and mind into the empirical procedures that form the foundation of science. Obvious approaches to Hebb's theory, such as clinical observations on neurological patients, neurochemistry, or developmental studies of primates, were not readily available to most experimenters.

These problems have been reduced during the 20 years since Hebb's book was written. Mental life in general and consciousness in particular are popular areas of investigation these days. New books deal with the evolution of consciousness in phylogeny (Jerison, 1973; Sagan, 1977) and with its putative development in historical times (Jaynes, 1977). There is much discussion of altered states of consciousness such as those induced by hypnotism (Hilgard, 1977), drugs (Tart, 1969), brain damage (Gazzaniga, 1970), and sleep (Luce, 1971). Hilgard (1977) argues that the widespread use of the term *consciousness* has not arisen from scientific theories or empirical analysis but from the intensity with which a new generation has become concerned with private experience. Confronted with students so interested in questions of the alteration and expansion of consciousness, it is no longer helpful to deny the relevance of psychology to the issues involved. Unfortunately, the wide popular literature discussing consciousness has not provided the kind of consistent definitional and theoretical framework for which Hebb called, nor has it produced sets of consistent experimental methods in which empirical questions concerning consciousness could be answered.

As I hope to make clear in this chapter, studies of the performance and cognition of normal human subjects (e.g., Broadbent, 1958; Posner, 1978) have provided a third language that has proven instrumental in bridging the large gap between physiology and subjective experience. The langauge of information-processing skirts the difficult issue of how the physical energy of neural transmissions can be converted to mental experience by discussing both areas in the more neutral terms of information flow. Both the highly conscious and directed experience involved in solving complex problems and the more automatic sensory processing involved in our contact with the world around us can be discussed as instances of information-processing operations. Information-processing language can be used to refer to complex neural networks specialized in dealing with different aspects of a signal, as well as the subjective experiences that may relate to the activation of such networks. Although the term *consciousness* did not appear in early works employing the information-processing approach, closely related issues of selective attention (Broadbent, 1958) played a prominent role in such models from the very start. More recently, some investigators have been interested in the relation between the mechanisms involved with selective attention and our focal awareness of the presence of a stimulus (e.g., Posner, 1978).

Perhaps a more important feature of the information-processing approach is that it gives rise to a variety of experimental techniques for the investigation of problems related to an understanding of consciousness. These techniques are employed in an effort to observe the time course of information flow in the nervous system. I term them collectively "mental chronometry" (Posner, 1978). Some of these techniques such as the use of reaction time and changes in accuracy with the duration of a stimulus event require careful measurement of performance. Other methods such as the recording of time-locked electrical activity from the scalp or the measurement of changes in the firing rates of cells following a stimulus event do not involve any explicit measurement of task performance. The use of both performance and physiological measures in related situations (see Posner, 1978, for a review) force on the investigator the need to translate from the languages of experience to the languages of brain activity. Chronometric methods can be used to separate forms of information processing, of which the person being studied is unaware, from those that give rise to conscious experience and can be reported by the subject. It is this particular application of mental chronometry that is discussed in this chapter.

In this chapter I examine whether the new climate of interest in the study of consciousness, the information-processing langauge, and the use of chrono- metric techniques are sufficient to allow realization of the goal of a scientific analysis of consciousness. To do so, it is first necessary to get a clearer idea of what might constitute scientific analysis of consciousness.

Popular uses of the term *consciousness* are quite varied. For example, the term has been used to indicate an individual's attitude toward a problem as in the phrase "raising a person's consciousness about some issue." A more scientific use refers to a level of alertness varying from deep sleep to active concentration. No single definition is likely to involve all uses of the term. I believe the core of the concept involves subjective awareness. We have in the center of awareness at any given moment only a small part of the stimuli arising from sensory organs or potentially available in memory. Our focus of attention tends to shift rapidly from object to object so that awareness expands as we take a larger time scale. However, at any given instant the focus of our conscious processes is rather narrow, and it is this narrow focal point with which we are concerned. Often, but not always, awareness is indexed by a verbal report. Limiting the definition of consciousness to awareness does not do much to reduce the complexity of the concept. A still more restricted idea of consciousness involves only self-awareness or a feeling of oneself as a sentient being. This feeling, although often an important part of being conscious, seems to me to be a bit too restricted as a full definition of the term. It may be that the difficulty of isolating this one aspect of awareness contributes to the feeling that a scientific analysis of awareness is impossible (Stent, 1975).

I feel that the concept of consciousness within experimental psychology may play something of the same role as the concept of life in biology or matter in physics. No scientist would expect a theory that fully explains concepts like life and matter, but rather one hopes to develop an explanatory network that elucidates understanding of those aspects of the concepts most amenable to analytic treatment. Physics and biology have made progress in the development of theories that relate to matter and to life, even though the concepts remain ill-defined and not fully explained. Most objective observers would agree that a knowledge of scientific theories related to the concepts of matter and life is a necessary part of understanding them, even though the observer may also argue that relevant aspects of the problem remain outside scientific analysis.

Writers who deal with the nature of consciousness do not feel similarly impelled to know about or consider the contributions of experimental psychologists to the question of normal states of consciousness before writing about the splitting, expanding, or altering of consciousness. My concern in this chapter is to further the conviction on the part of the open-minded reader that we psychologists know something about the concept of consciousness within the normal mind and have techniques available to learn more.

Many of the most exciting findings related to the nature of consciousness have occurred in clinical settings that are not accessible to most experimental investigators. For example, the important finding of Penfield and Roberts (1959) purporting to activate detailed memories by temporal lobe stimulation uses neurosurgical patients. These results cannot be duplicated on a routine basis in the experimental laboratory for obvious ethical reasons. The observations of Sperry (1969) and of Gazzaniga (1970) on the split-brain patients, which has done much to popularize the functional dissociation between the left and right hemisphere, cannot be directly pursued by experimental investigators unable to obtain split-brain subjects. Findings based upon the use of hypnotism are somewhat more available to experimental investigations, but only a small part of the population apparently can produce the automatic writing that Hilgard (1977) argues brings him into contact with events of the unconscious mind beyond the awareness of the subject. The neuropsychological findings Weiskrantz (1977) has recently reviewed concerning amnesia, dyslexia, and visual neglect are also difficult observations to make outside of major medical centers with special populations of brain-injured persons. Nonetheless, these findings are on the cutting edge of science and have given impetus to the idea that conscious processes can be dissociated, at least in special states, from other forms of information processing.

Until the observations suggested by these findings can be tested routinely in laboratories throughout the country with normal human minds, however, there will be an inhibition in accepting them. We will not know to what extent the observations made in pathological or altered states should be applied toward the development of a core theory of consciousness as it occurs within the normal person. Without studies of the normal person we cannot tell which clinical results reflect unique properties of a special state and which are based on general properties of mind that are revealed more completely in the special state. Too often, clinical findings have been used to support crude dichotomies between pathological and normal processes. I believe experimental studies of normal subjects already allow us to relate, and even sometimes to anticipate, the occurrence of some of the findings that arise from dissociations produced by cardiovascular insult, the surgeon's knife, or the hypnotist's will.

In the balance of this chapter I review some evidence employing chronometric techniques and information-processing language. I hopefully show that there has already been considerable progress toward a science of consciousness with the limited goals I have outlined. I examine three propositions: first, that consciousness can be dissociated from more general forms of information processing; second, that there is a separate mechanism underlying subjective experience; third, that there are separable dimensions of this conscious mechanism. In each of these areas, I outline the relationship between dissociations found in chronometric studies with normal humans and the more exotic dissociations found in certain special neurological or psychological states.

CAN CONSCIOUSNESS BE DISSOCIATED FROM INFORMATION PROCESSING?

There have been suggestions (e.g., Bindra, 1970) that consciousness is coincident with all information processing or is the sum total of all internal processes intervening between stimulus and response. These suggestions were natural when cognitive studies were just developing as a reaction to extreme behaviorism because there was little prospect at hand of a more detailed analytic account of internal mental processes. Current cognitive research suggests this holistic view can be replaced by an emphasis upon a variety of internal information-processing subsystems that can be experimentally isolated from one another even though they are integrated in actual thought.

Information theory teaches that dividing the possible alternatives in half contributes one bit of information. The recent popular literature on consciousness has shown a strong tendency to develop one-bit theories. Much work of the split-brain contrasts a language-dominated left hemisphere with a more intuitive holistic and spatial right hemisphere. Hilgard's (1977) book on the division of consciousness deals with two separate observers emerging in response to painful stimuli in the hypnotic state.

As I see it, the most challenging common proposition to result from both the split-brain and the hypnotic work is that an outside investigator can obtain information from processes that are unconscious and thus not available to the person from whom the information is elicited. In the case of the split brain, right hemisphere information can be conveyed to the experimenter by the left hand, apparently without the left hemisphere being aware of it. In the case of the hypnotic syndrome, Hilgard argues for a hidden observer able to respond by automatic writing outside of the consciousness of the subject.

Is it possible for experiments on normal human subjects operating in their usual modes to allow the psychologist to obtain information that is unconscious to the subject involved? The answer seems to be yes, at least in some circumstances. Some evidence for this comes from the processing of ambiguous words. If a subject is given a sentence like, "The boys were throwing stones at the bank," two interpretations are possible. Under most circumstances, the subject is aware of only one of those two meanings. The meaning the subject reports can be influenced by information (e.g., the word "river") arriving simultaneously on an unattended ear, which cannot be separately reported (MacKay, 1973). If a subject is asked to respond to a word related to an unselected meaning (e.g., money), it can also be shown that the efficiency of processing that word is increased due to its relationship to the prior sentence, even though the person is not aware of the second meaning of the sentence (Conrad, 1974). This latter finding suggests an automatic spread of activation from a concept of which the subject is aware (e.g., "bank" in the sense of "river") to related concepts of which the subject is not aware (e.g., "bank" in the sense of "money"). Spreading activation among semantic units of this sort is well documented in the psychological literature (Collins & Loftus, 1975; Posner & Snyder, 1975). What is impressive about these studies is not that *some* information processing occurs outside of the subject's awareness (no one would doubt that retinal or motor reflexes occur outside of consciousness). Rather it is the fact that complex meanings are derived by the subject's nervous system of which the subject is not aware but which affect responses in ways that can be communicated to the observer. This fact is similar to the claims made in the split-brain and hypnotism work.

Chronometric analyses of tasks such as reading and reporting names of words and pictures give rise to models in which information can be represented in physical, phonetic, and semantic information-processing systems (LaBerge & Samuels, 1974; Posner, 1978). Studies indicate that each of these systems can be isolated from the others in the sense that subjects can respond to information in one code independently from information derived in another code. For example, when asked to respond if two letters are physically identical (e.g., AA), subjects are not slowed by their highly over-learned nominal identity (e.g., Aa). It is wrong to view the systems dealing with these codes as serial stages in the processing of information. Instead they should be thought of as complex isolable subsystems, which deal with information in a particular code.

Studies of the spread of information from one of these systems to another suggest that information can flow automatically along pathways linked by habitual associations. Thus, the presentation of a word outside of the subject's attention can activate the habitual pathways to which it has been linked by prior experience.

These results may not sound revolutionary, but they require that activation of the meaning of familiar words occurs outside of the conscious attention of the subject. Thus, activation patterns can affect responses when the subjects themselves are not aware of them. Of course, subjects can become aware of the meaning of a word, its phonetic representation, or its visual form. As in the case of split-brain patients, however, evidence favors access by the experimenter to information outside of the subject's current consciousness. Thus, normal persons given the proper experimental conditions and a sensitive enough technique of analysis can provide model systems for exploring the dissociations found in cases of brain injury.

IS THERE A SEPARATE
CONSCIOUS MECHANISM?

How is our consciousness related to the complex pathways activated by words? It seems most natural to suppose that some sort of brain system or mechanism is involved in the operations that produce conscious awareness. This view is not without considerable dispute even within cognitive psychology. Neisser (1976) says:

> Recent years have witnessed an intensive search for these "internal mechanisms" at both the psychological and the physiological level.... So far, the search has been in vain, and no separate mechanisms of attention have been found. In my opinion, that is because none exist [p. 80].

Indeed, Neisser argues that the quest to find a separate mechanism of consciousness within the overall information-processing system is rather silly. He says:

> In writing *Cognitive Psychology* a decade ago, I deliberately avoided theorizing about consciousness. It seemed to me that Psychology was not ready to tackle the issue, and that any attempt to do so would lead only to philosophically naive and fumbling speculation. Unfortunately, these fears have been realized; many current models of cognition treat consciousness as if it were just a particular stage of processing in a mechanical flow of information. Because I am sure that these models are wrong, it has seemed important to develop an alternative interpretation of the data on which they are based [p. xii–xiii].

Let me first point out that the notion of a separate mechanism of consciousness does not require strict brain localization. Indeed, one of the major accomplishments of Hebb's (1949) formulation is to allow us to consider the possibility that mechanisms with important psychological consequence may not be strictly localized in the brain. What then should be taken as evidence for the existence of a separate mechanism?

One fundamental, widely held proposition concerning consciousness is that it is unified. Suppose we take seriously this idea of the unity of consciousness. The idea produces a very simple consequence. When a unified system is involved in the processing of information, it should be less available to handle any other information. If we can determine exactly when subjects start to have trouble handling an item inconsistent with the current content of consciousness, we would have evidence concerning the time that item reaches the unified system posited to underlie conscious processing.

Support for this viewpoint comes from dual-task studies (Posner, 1978). A primary task involving simple processing such as matching pairs of successive letters or mental addition is combined with a secondary task of responding rapidly to an auditory signal or reporting the presence of a target in a brief flash. Attention to the primary task is measured by the degree of interference produced in the secondary task in comparison to performance on the secondary task alone. These studies indicate that any processing of the primary task that produces active awareness of the stimulus event also shows clear interference with performance on the secondary task. Such interference is, of course, often closely related to the production of overt responses to the primary task, but it can also occur in mental events not associated with responses. Because dual-task methods have occasioned a number of objections having to do with specific problems of coordinating two tasks, it has been useful to develop methods that do not require two separate tasks.

In one such method (Posner & Snyder, 1975) subjects are given a single prime letter followed after a varying interval by a pair of letters. They are to respond "yes" if the letter pair is identical (e.g., AA) and "no" if the two items of the pair differ. In one condition, subjects are not given reasons to attend to the prime, and in another they are given reasons to attend closely to the prime. The striking effects are these: When the prime matches the letter pair, irrespective of whether or not the subject is given an incentive to process the prime, a clear facilitation in time to match the pair of letters occurs over conditions where no prime is given (benefit). This follows from the notion that regardless of the subject's intention the prime activates an internal pathway that can then be reactivated more rapidly and efficiently.[1] On the other hand, the activation of a pathway by a prime does not reduce the efficiency of processing an item that fails to match the prime (cost). As long as the processing systems involve automatic flow along parallel pathways, no

---

[1]The automatic facilitation of processing speed has been confirmed by many experiments involving repetition of stimulus events. Although attended effects can be involved in repetition, there is much evidence that facilitation can occur even when the probability of repetition is low, and when subjects are not aware of the possibility of a repetition (Posner, 1978).

negative consequences of presenting a prime letter will occur. By contrast, when the subject begins to attend consciously to the prime there is interference with any letter pair that fails to match the prime. Such costs in processing letters that mismatch the prime are obtained only in the conditions where subjects are induced to attend to the prime and then only after a delay of 300 msec or more following the prime. These findings suggest that the consciousness of the prime begins to influence the processing of an unexpected item approximately 300 msec after its input in the conditions of this experiment.

These results have been confirmed and extended in a rather impressive way by an experiment recently reported by Neely (1977). In Neely's experiment, subjects are to decide whether or not a string of letters make a word. Prior to getting the string they receive a single category name as a prime. Their task is to either attend directly to the category of the prime or to switch their attention to an arbitrarily associated category (e.g., if they are primed with "animal," they are to expect a body part). In some conditions the letter string is a member of the original primed category, whereas in others it is in the associated category to which subjects are to switch attention. Finally, the string may come from quite a different category. When subjects are not required to switch categories, costs (increased response times to strings in a nonprimed category) and benefits (reduced response times to strings in the primed or associated category) of the prime build up asymmetrically with benefits accruing somewhat faster than costs, just as in the letter match study described previously. When subjects are required to switch attention to a new category but the string occurs in the original category, an early benefit (when subjects are presumably thinking of the original category) becomes a cost after the switch has occurred. These results show the critical time-locking of both the activation of unattended pathways and of switches of conscious attention.

There are many more experimental results and qualifications that could be cited, as there would be in any active scientific area. It is unnecessary to deal with the details of any experiments except to argue that they indicate that conscious attention to an item has important consequences on measures of information processing available to the experimenter.

Instead of such experiments, could the subjects have reported when they first became conscious of the stimulus event? The answer is no. According to our analysis, the subject's awareness developed approximately 300 msec after the occurrence of the input. The subjects would not be able to tell us reliably how their awareness of a signal related to their overt responses. The introspective accounts that subjects give of our experiments do correspond with theory at a general level. Subjects generally say when a prime has poor validity that they do try to ignore it. However, this does not mean they are truly unaware of the prime on every trial.

One of the advantages of the detailed experimental analysis of the time course of conscious processing is to allow a transition in our notion of consciousness from a dichotomous to a continuous process. Although our measurement of consciousness requires the notion of a unified system that will show some interference between signals, it is also true that the more active effort subjects put into attending to one event the longer it takes them to disengage attention from it and switch to another event (Klein, 1977; LaBerge, 1973). If the experimenter can control the details of the subject's commitment to one event, chronometric analysis can provide a quantitative measure of the degree of conscious involvement by observing the subject's ability to shift to another event. This kind of detailed analysis has the potential of changing purely dichotomous analyses present in much of the work on consciousness into a more detailed and quantitative analysis.

DIMENSIONS OF CONSCIOUSNESS

Thus far I have tried to establish the existence of a conscious mechanism separate from many complex information-processing operations and to suggest that psychological manipulations can be used to examine accrual of information outside of consciousness. In one sense this serves as an answer to Neisser's argument about the lack of evidence of mechanisms of attention. However, as Neisser argues, the mere dichotomization of information processing into automatic processes that occur outside of consciousness and the conscious mechanism is not a very satisfactory goal for research. One would want to discuss the properties and organization of a consciousness mechanism in order to show that a framework developed from chronometric results can provide more than a static division of processing into two parts. I would like to describe some efforts along these lines.

At least from the time of Boring (1933) psychologists who thought about the nature of consciousness argued that one should deal with how our conscious attention is directed toward some source of relevant information. Consider the findings of Sokolov (1963) concerning the orienting reflex. According to Sokolov's idea, the orienting reflex consists of a constellation of internal and overt activity including movement of the head and eyes toward a stimulus, changes in vasodilation, EEG blocking, etc., all of which are closely associated with the subject's awareness of that stimulus. Which aspects of the reflex precede and which follow awareness? This issue is not considered by Sokolov. The orienting reflex confounds aligning the sensory organs (e.g., moving head and/or eyes) in the direction of the stimulus with the processes of detection that allow the subject to become aware of the existence of the stimulus. In this sense "orienting" as used by Sokolov involves both directing conscious attention toward the external environment and awareness of the signal resulting from orienting.

Hilgard (1977) argues that hypnotism can loosen or break the connection between attention in the sense of monitoring the external environment and attention in the sense of the appraisal or awareness resulting from that monitoring. It is of interest to know whether these two functions of consciousness are in any sense separate in normal functioning. Can we dissociate orienting the conscious mechanism to an event from the content or results of that orienting? I have tried to break this question down into three subquestions. The first deals with the separation of orienting from detecting for very simple stimuli—points of light in a dark field. The second deals with dissociations between the commitment of consciousness to an event and the appearance of the content of that event in consciousness. The third deals with dissociations between the different content or codes available from the same sensory stimulus. Because of the complexity of each type of experiment, it is only possible for me to illustrate some conclusions and indicate generally the type of experiment on which my conclusions are based. More documentation is available elsewhere (Posner, 1978) on the details of these experiments.

CAN DETECTION BE SEPARATED FROM ORIENTING?

When subjects have consciously detected a stimulus, they presumably can generate any arbitrary response requested by the experimenter. We use as an indicant of detection a simple key-press response which the subjects are instructed to make when they become aware of a light flash. Detection, so defined, is not coincident with all information-processing. Rather, it is evidence that the processing of a signal has reached the unified system we have argued underlies consciousness. It is possible that subjects are able to make a limited set of responses, for example, orienting the eyes and head toward the stimulus prior to their detection (awareness) of the stimulus. At first it may seem strange that we can respond to a stimulus before we are aware of it, but there is no logical paradox in supposing that some response can be made prior to a signal reaching the unified mechanism that allows us to make nonhabitual responses.

If one examines overt orientation such as a movement of the eyes, the issue is quite simple. Everyone would acknowledge that we could orient our eyes in the direction of a potential stimulus before the stimulus is actually presented. We might simply respond to the suggestion to look in a particular direction. When the stimulus is presented we can then detect it. It also seems possible that the occurrence of a stimulus might produce an eye movement prior to our conscious awareness of the details of the event.

The issue is more complex when overt orienting of head and eyes is prevented and subjects can only orient covertly by attention to a chosen place in space. In that case, whatever orienting takes place is a property of the mechanism of attention itself. If only covert orienting is allowed, is it possible to separate the orienting of attention from our awareness of the signal?

Our experiments (Posner, 1978) involve calling the subject's attention to a position in space by providing a cue about where the imperative stimulus will occur. We do not allow the subjects to move their eyes. On most occasions, we place the imperative stimulus at the expected position; on others we place it at another position. Covert orienting improves the efficiency with which one can detect an event at the expected place in the same way overt orienting by eye or head movement does. Because covert orienting, like overt orienting, can take place prior to a signal, it can be separated from detection. Orienting may be considered as an aspect or dimension of consciousness separate from detection.

We find the line of sight plays no special role in orienting for the purposes of detecting large changes of luminance. If the subject's attention is drawn to a peripheral position the costs (increase in reaction time) of receiving an unexpected event in the fovea are the same as would be the case for an unexpected peripheral event when attention is foveal. This symmetry is true only for luminance detection and not when acuity is demanded. When acuity is needed, the fovea does play a special role, as most sensory theories suggest. These results show that conscious processing of visual stimuli is not locked to the fine anatomical structure of the visual system. It fits with the idea of a single central attentional mechanism rather than independent mechanisms for each sensory modality.[2]

Our ability to separate orienting from detection chronometrically shows that these internal processes are in some sense dissociable.[3] It provides a model experimental system for investigation dissociations that have long been reported within certain clinical syndromes. In a recent paper, Weiskrantz (1977) reviews studies of patients with visual scotomas (lesions) who are unable to see an event that occurs within the blind area. If forced to move their eyes to a signal within the blind area, they are able to orient with greater than chance accuracy to the unseen event. This remarkable dissociation between orienting and detection in clinical cases fits very well with the chronometric dissociation we have been able to obtain under laboratory conditions in normal subjects. There is more than can be said concerning the details of our

---

[2]This experimental task provides one way of testing our ability to split orienting between two different positions in visual space. We have conducted experiments to determine if one can simultaneously turn attention to two places in space. We have found that subjects can easily control the size of a contiguous area to which they will orient but have very little if any ability to split orienting to separate positions separated by areas of lower priority.

[3]There is another reason to suppose a separation of the direction of consciousness from detection. Hillyard and Picton (1978) have shown separable components of the evoked cortical potential are related to each of these senses of the term. Although both orienting and detecting may draw from a common pool of capacity, as has been suggested also by Hilgard (1977), they also seem to have several dissociable components as indicated by the reaction time results reported here and by Hilgard's data.

analysis of orienting and detection (Posner, 1978), but I hope this is sufficient to indicate that chronometric results can provide evidence related to the dissociation of orienting and detecting.

DISSOCIATING CAPACITY FROM CONTENT

The work in which we are engaged is continually surprising. I hope I have been able to convey both the sense that there is order lying behind these experimental results and the sense of excitement as we learn new things about internal mechanisms from chronometric experiments. Until recently, I believed that once the act of turning conscious attention towrd a particular event was accomplished, attentional capacity was inextricably associated with the content of that event. Thus I felt that as soon as subjects began to attend to an event we would pick up evidence from all chronometric techniques suggesting that their capacities were invested in the particular information present in that event. I was, therefore, vey surprised when it became possible to dissociate the general capacity of attention from the specific information that is to form the content of that attention. I am afraid the abstract language here is difficult to follow, and I need to present the experiment for you to understand both our puzzlement and our excitement at this potential separation of content from capacity.

The results are due to experiments by McLean and Shulman (1978) conducted as part of their master's theses. Their study combines the dual task method (see page 102) of measuring attention demands with the priming technique previously described. The essence of the experiment is quite simple. The task is to determine if two letters are physically identical. Prior to each letter pair there is a priming letter. Because the prime usually predicts the letter pair, subjects are induced to turn their active attention to the prime. Two different methods of gauging the subject's active attention to the priming event are employed. One method examines reaction time to an auditory tone that occurs on some trials following the priming event. Interference with a tone that follows a priming letter is measured and compared to tones that occur following a neutral visual warning signal. By subtracting reaction time to the auditory signal following a prime from the reaction time to this signal following a neutral warning, one gets the effect on tone processing of directing attention to the prime letter. One can also compare the reaction time to a letter pair that fails to match the prime with reaction time to the same pair following the neutral warning signal. This is the cost in letter matching discussed earlier (pages 102-103) in this chapter.

The results show a striking difference in the time course between these two measures. The measure of general capacity as indexed by interference with tone processing indicates the subject's attention is directed toward the letter as early as we probe (100 msec) and this interference declines by 500 msec. On the other hand, specific costs of processing a letter pair that fails to match the prime are minimal at 100 msec and build up over time just as has been described previously (page 103).

There may be several explanations for McLean and Shulman's results, but they certainly force qualification upon the theories in which the content of attention is totally associated with the limitations in capacity. One explanation of the result is based upon the concept of funneling. Suppose that as subjects pay attention to the prime they first tend to exclude stimuli that are quite different (e.g., occur in another modality), and as they invest attention on the letter prime they finally exclude even those stimuli of the same class (e.g., other letters) that are not identical to the prime. This funneling theory sounds perfectly plausible, but it is not consistent with the date. If it were true, one would expect interference with the auditory probe to continue to be high while interference with the letter pair begins to grow. This is not the case. Instead, we obtain an interaction in which the interference with the probe tone drops off.

McLean and Shulman (1979) propose that it takes time for the capacity invested in a stimulus to build up a detailed expectancy-producing interference with unexpected letter pairs. It is as though capacity requirements are reduced once the subject has successfully developed a hypothesis relating to the letter. The use of the term "hypothesis formation" in this instance is also puzzling. Why should it be that subjects have to build an active hypothesis concerning a letter that is in fact present in front of their eyes? We know that subjects need no great active attention in order to show facilitation from the letter. Why should it be that only when they build an active hypothesis do they show cost to other letters? McLean and Shulman propose that an active expectancy of the letter must be constructed before subjects find it maximally useful in matching. Because of the close similarity between this experiment and those of Neely (1977) cited earlier, it seems unlikely that the kind of hypotheses studied here is limited to the process of matching. The results suggest that we can trace separately the time course of the investment of capacity and the time course of the elaboration of the content of that capacity.

DISSOCIATION OF CONTENT

Can conscious attention be divided among separate contents? Are we capable of focal attention to two entirely separate signals? The answer depends heavily on the criterion one accepts for the division of attention. There is no doubt that we have a general level of awareness of many things at the same time. While I sit at this typewriter I am vaguely aware of my surroundings, but efforts to shift my focal attention away from typing will surely delay the next stroke.

Normal subjects can perform two tasks together, but there will usually be some degree of interference between them. The amount of interference depends on individual task difficulty and their compatibility. At high levels of skill in continuous tasks this interference tends to decline. For example, Shaffer (1975) reports little interference between auditory word shadowing and typing for a highly skilled typist, and a large amount of within-task practice will often eliminate evidence of interference, by some criteria at least (Allport, Antonis, & Reynolds, 1972; Spelke, Hirst, & Neisser, 1976).

One might expect that evidence arising from split-brain or subjects under hypnotic trance would provide convincing evidence in favor of the idea that two streams of activity could occur together without interference. Hilgard, however, reports that hypnotized subjects show large amounts of interference between tasks they perform consciously and tasks of which they report themselves to be unaware. Thus, the hypnotism model fails to produce good evidence of parallel processing.[4] There are some reports that split-brain monkey and human patients are able to carry on two tasks at once without interference (Gazzaniga, 1970), but the evidence on this point is far from convincing.

Even in those cases where two tasks can be carried on without interference, it is difficult to be sure that they both use the mechanism subserving consciousness. If one distinguishes as we have between automatic pathways that do not require active attention and a mechanism that subserves conscious attention, the problem of determining what in any given task requires the latter mechanism is very difficult. One advantage of a quantitative view of consciousness is that one can look for the degree to which commitment of focal attention to one signal interferes with another. For example, one might expect that two signals can be handled simultaneously by methods that do not give rise to detailed reports of focal awareness, whereas they would interfere if the subjects committed themselves thoroughly to one of them.

Because it is often difficult to control the presentation of separate stimuli, perhaps the most elegant demonstration of this point occurs when a single stimulus and task is used, but subjects are dealing with different internal codes of that stimulus. A detailed analysis of how codes can be dealt with independently may help us understand our general ability to divide attention.

---

[4]One interesting aspect of the hypnotism results is that by the usual criterion of chronometric studies, which is interference between tasks, the subjects always seem to be drawing from a common capacity rather than conducting the two tasks in entirely separate systems. Hilgard likens the results to what is obtained in normals when in a memory task they are instructed not to remember some of the items as they try to remember others. There is evidence that the execution of this instruction to forget is not identical to actually forgetting (Bjork, 1970). All of these results suggest that in some ways the hypnotism results do not involve as complete a dissociation between conscious and unconscious tasks as some of the information-processing results.

Consider the presentation of a face that has been associated with a name (Rogers, 1976). Subjects are asked to respond "yes" if the association between the name and face has been previously learned and otherwise "no." The sets of faces and names used in the task are constructed so that they vary in the degree of confusability between members of the set. By determining whether subjects have difficulty with nonmatching pairs when either the faces or the names are similar to the correct answer, it is possible to tell whether the subjects are using a code based on the name or on the face. For example, if subjects expect the name Tom, they will be slower to reject a confusable name like Tim than a dissimilar one like Bob. If the face code is used, rejection of a face that looks like Tom will be slower than one that looks different but has the similar name Tim.

If subjects are given either the name or face first, followed after a second by the other one, the confusability data argue that the match is done entirely in the code of the second stimulus. It is as though the subject's conscious processes are completely dominated by the code the subject expects to be presented. This is what one would expect from a unified conscious mechanism. It is also exactly the introspection that nearly all subjects provide: They say that they actively generate and attend to the code of the expected event.

The important question is what happens when time for generation is insufficient, for example, when both name and face are presented simultaneously? The evidence suggests that the match is done in both codes simultaneously. It appears that the face can contact its name automatically and the name can automatically contact its associated face. These go on in parallel so matches are easily made in both codes. Subjects cannot introspect upon the basis of their matches: They tend to avoid any discussion of the basis for the match. The match appears to be based upon passive activation processes that do not have time to reach the level of clear images in the subjects' minds and thus cannot be reported by them. The parallel processes do not seem to provide evidence for the division of consciousness but for the lack of involvement of consciousness in arriving at many complex judgments.

These findings fit with a viewpoint on the optional nature of conscious process that has been advocated by Logan (1978). According to this view, conscious processing as defined in this chapter deals with the preparation and organization of a speeded task and much less with its execution. When given sufficient time, the subject will carefully prepare an appropriate code for task execution and this code will be available to introspection as a conscious image. Under high time pressure the same codes are activated by stimulus input in an automatic, parallel, and unconscious manner. Certainly the data cited from the Rogers experiment argue that conscious processing is related to a situation when subjects have sufficient time to prepare and organize the appropriate code. Without such preparation the task can be performed but produces neither the single code evidence nor the kind of subjective reports presented when there is time for preparation.

These laboratory results indicate that there are conditions in which a stimulus event can be disassembled into separate codes, both of which enter into a single response without the subject's awareness of the separation. Subjects are simply aware of the appropriate response, even though the experimenter's analyses show it to be based upon independent codes. In Hilgard's (1977) hypnotic studies subjects verbally report no pain even as the manual system writes about the painful feelings. This requires that codes of an event be treated independently by different reporting systems (verbal and manual) and that they be affected separately by the hypnotist's suggestion. It seems possible that further research on dual tasks with normal subjects will reveal the boundary conditions under which hynotic dissociations are most likely to occur. We may already surmise that the automated and untimed nature of the writing response is crucial to its being carried on parallel with the verbal system.

CONCLUSIONS

My working hypothesis is that dissociations obtained in cases of brain injury or hypnotism occur between dimensions of consicousness that can be found to be relatively independent in normal subjects. For example, ability to orient to an unseen stimulus found in cases of occipital scotoma fits with the independence of these functions as dimensions of the consicous mechanisms within the normal subject. Similarly, the types of dissociation found in hypnotism in which an event seems to be interpreted in two opposing ways by different response systems may related to the conditions under which we find separation of codes in the normal subject. Although this hypothesis is more a research strategy than an established principle, I hope it suggests important potential consequences that might arise from a more complete understanding of normal human consciousness.

It is often suggested that the relationship between brain and mind is the most important question facing psychological research. My argument is that in order to construct a science of consciousness it will be necessary to develop model task situations in which the langauges of physiology, phenomenology, and performance can all be brought to bear upon the same problem. The use of normal human subjects in chronometrically controlled tasks seems to be an opportunity for the development of such models. The results arising from vascular insults, neurosurgical preparations, and hypnotism should be related to the findings occurring in normal subjects. A detailed comparison of such results may help us understand both the normal function of human mental processes and the way in which they are disrupted or altered by drugs, neurosurgical intervention, or other means.

ACKNOWLEDGMENTS

This paper was presented in a series of lectures on the Psychology of Thought in honor of D. O. Hebb. The lecture took place March 23, 1978, at Dalhousie University in Halifax. The research described in this paper and its writing was supported by NSF Grant No. BNS 76-18907A01 to the University of Oregon. Mary K. Rothbart and the editors of this volume aided greatly in clarifying this chapter.

REFERENCES

Allport, D. A., Antonis, B., & Reynolds, P.   On the division of attention: A disproof of the single channel hypothesis. *Quarterly Journal of Experimental Psychology*, 1972, *24*, 225–235.

Bindra, D. The problem of subjective experience. *Psychological Review*, 1970, *77*, 581–584.

Bjork, R. A. Positive forgetting: The noninterference of items intentionally forgotten. *Journal of Verbal Learning and Verbal Behavior*, 1970, *9*, 255–268.

Boring, E. G. *The physical dimensions of consciousness.* New York: Century, 1933.

Broadbent, D. E. *Perception and communication.* London: Pergamon, 1958.

Collins, A. M., & Loftus, E. F. A spreading activation theory of semantic processing. *Psychological Review*, 1975, *82*, 407–428.

Conrad, C. Context effects in sentence recognition: A study of the subjective lexicon. *Memory & Cognition*, 1974, *2*, 130–138.

Gazzaniga, M. *The bisected brain.* New York: Appleton-Century-Crofts, 1970.

Hebb, D. O. *Organization of behavior.* New York: Wiley, 1949.

Hilgard, E. R. *Divided consciousness.* New York: Wiley, 1977.

Hillyard, S. A., & Picton, T. W. Cognitive components in cerebral event-related potentials and selective attention. In J. E. Desmedt (Ed.), *Progress in clinical neurophysiology* (Vol. VI). Busel, Germany: Karge, 1978.

Jaynes, J. *The origins of consciousness in the breakdown of the bicameral mind.* Boston: Houghton-Mifflin, 1977.

Jerison, H. J. *The evolution of the brain and intelligence.* New York: Academic Press, 1973.

Klein, R. Attention and visual dominance: A chronometric analysis. *Journal of Experimental Psychology: Human Perception and Performance*, 1977, *3*, 365–378.

LaBerge, D. Identification of two components of the time to switch attention. In S. Kornblum (Ed.), *Attention and performance IV.* New York: Academic Press, 1973.

LaBerge, D., & Samuels, J. Toward a theory of automatic information processing in reading. *Cognitive Psychology*, 1974, *6*, 293–323.

Logan, G. D. Attention in character-classification tasks: Evidence for the automaticity of component stages. *Journal of Experimental Psychology: General*, 1978, *107*, 32–63.

Luce, G. G. *Body time.* New York: Pantheon, 1971.

MacKay, D. G. Aspects of a theory of comprehension, memory and attention. *Quarterly Journal of Experimental Psychology*, 1973, *25*, 22–40.

McLean, J. P., & Shulman, G. L. On the construction and maintenance of expectancies. *Quarterly Journal of Experimental Psychology*, 1978, *30*, 441–454.

Neely, J. H. Semantic priming and retrieval from lexical memory: Roles of inhibitionless spreading activation and limited capacity attention. *Journal of Experimental Psychology: General*, 1977, *106*, 226–254.

Neisser, U. *Cognition and reality.* San Francisco: Freeman, 1976.

Penfield, W., & Roberts, L. *Speech and brain mechanisms.* Princeton, N.J.: Princeton University Press, 1959.

Posner, M. I. *Chronometric explorations of mind.* Hillsdale, N.J.: Lawrence Erlbaum Associates, 1978.

Posner, M. I., & Snyder, C. R. R. Attention and cognitive control. In R. L. Solso (Ed.), *Information processing and cognition.* Hillsdale, N.J.: Lawrence Erlbaum Associates, 1975.

Rogers, M. G. K. *Visual and verbal processes in the recognition of names and faces.* Unpublished doctoral dissertation, University of Oregon, 1976.

Sagan, C. *The dragons of Eden.* New York: Random House, 1977.

Shaffer, L. H. Multiple attention in continuous verbal tasks. In P. M. A. Rabbitt & S. Dornic (Ed.), *Attention and performance V.* New York: Academic Press, 1975.

Sokolov, E. N. *Perception and the conditioned reflex.* New York: Macmillan, 1963.

Spelke, E., Hirst, W., & Neisser, U. Skills of divided attention. *Cognition,* 1976, *4,* 215–230.

Sperry, R. W. A modified concept of consciousness. *Psychological Review,* 1969, *76,* 532–536.

Stent, G. S. Limits to the scientific understanding of man. *Science,* 1975, *187,* 1952–1057.

Tart, C. T. (Ed.), *Altered states of consciousness.* New York: Wiley, 1969.

Weiskrantz, L. Trying to bridge some neuropsychological gaps between monkey and man. *British Journal of Psychology,* 1977, *68,* 431–445.

6 The Limits of Cognition

Ulric Neisser
Cornell University

I deeply appreciate the opportunity to participate in this lecture series, organized in honor of Donald Hebb. Hebb's work has had an enormous and beneficial impact on psychology; he may have done more than any other single individual to bring us out of the Dark Ages. Unfortunately, advancing past the Dark Ages is not enough. History records that the Dark Ages were followed by the Middle Ages, which had problems of their own. During the Middle Ages, people continued to believe a lot of things that were not true and put their faith in an unnecessarily rigid system of thought. We are still in the Middle Ages of psychology, I think. Many false beliefs are widely accepted, including particularly the belief in a rigid and mechanical mental system whose properties need only be discovered by enterprising researchers. Thus, Hebb has left us with a great deal to do.

Everyone is limited in what they can do and understand and be aware of. What is the nature of those limitations? Are they permanent maxima all of us have in our heads or just properties of the degree of skill and training that a given individual may have achieved at a given time? Are they the inevitable result of a mechanism that—a mechanism of fixed capacity whose properties psychologists must discover—or are they only characteristic of one particular mental organization that might be entirely irrelevant for another task? What is the relation between the limits of conscious awareness on the one hand and of mental activity on the other, and more generally between consciousness and thought?

Although I have written about these questions before (Neisser, 1976a), I am not entirely sure of any of the answers. The problems are difficult, at least for me. To my surprise, however, many other psychologists seem to find them easier than I do, or even believe that they have already been solved. There is a rather wide contemporary consensus on one set of answers: a set based on a modish analogy between minds and computers. Just as a computer has a "central processing unit" that can handle only a few bits at a time, so the mind is thought to have a central processor with a similarly fixed capacity. The mechanism can be bypassed for some mental operations—especially simple ones—but not for all. The central processor has been variously described as an "attention centre" that can activate only one "code" at a time (LaBerge, 1975), as "controlled processes (that are) tightly capacity-limited...(and) utilize short-term store" (Schneider and Shiffrin, 1977, p. 3), as a "brain mechanism of limited capacity" (Klein, 1976, p. 147), and so on. It is often suggested that this central system is consciousness itself (Klatzky, 1975, p. 84; Posner, 1973, p. 138). But although my uncertainty may prevent me from putting forward definitive hypotheses of my own on these issues, it does not prevent me from forming an opinion on this all too general consensus. I believe that it is wrong. The mind does not work as today's computers do; consciousness is not a window on the workings of a particular stage of information processing. There is no single central bottleneck through which all thoughts must pass. Human thinking often does exhibit a kind of "center plus margin" structure (Neisser, 1963b), but it is optional, the result of strategy rather than anatomy. The experiments described here were designed to test the fixed-central-limit hypothesis and, if possible, to refute it. In addition, they serve to illustrate a different approach to human capacities and limitations, relating them to changing skills rather than to configurations of hardware.

The notion that the brain is a limited-capacity information processor is so firmly entrenched today that I am often asked whether I can possibly be serious in disputing it. There can be no doubt, after all, that mental activity consists of handling information. Didn't Shannon prove 30 years ago that every channel has a limited "capacity" for information? He did, but there is no reason to believe that his theorem has any implications for human performance. The research of the last 20 years has shown that information rate, in terms of bits per second, is not a very good predictor of human ability. Such phenomena as the span of immediate memory, the understanding of speech, or the reading of prose depend on subjective organization in a way that the capacity of a telephone line does not. Moreover, no one has succeeded in relating the sheer size of the brain—say, the number of neurons or connections it may contain—to any particular limit on performance (although it may be true that organisms with larger brains carry out what are in some sense more complicated activities). Finally, the brain *changes,* not only with maturation but also with learning, so that whatever limits it may have had at one point in development or practice need not apply to another.

The question of capacity looks very different if we consider it from the perspective of biology rather than of engineering; if we regard the mind as something living and growing (which it is) rather than as a machine (which it is not). Every organism begins with a set of genes that endow it with a range of potentialities. What actually happens to the organism—what it becomes—then depends on the succession of environments in which it finds itself. In some environments it will die, in others it grows "normally," and in still others it develops in unusual or atypical ways. A seed is not a mechanism and does not have a capacity. To be sure, the plant that grows from the seed is ordinarily limited in size as in other respects; daffodils don't get to be as tall as oaks. But these limitations are the combined result of the plant's genetic endowment and of the medium in which it grows. What is impossible in one environment may be the norm in another. Moreover, a change in the environment may produce radical changes in the organism at any time in its life so that the notion of "capacity" can *never* be applied to it sensibly unless certain assumptions about the environment are made as well. The same thing is true of the mind. It is no more nearly a mechanism than a seed is, or than an organism is. It has potentialities, but no capacity.

Psychometricians—the psychologists who study and attempt to measure traits like intelligence—have long had some inkling of this. They have been trying for three quarters of a century to measure people's intellectual endowment and to separate out the genetic from the environmental sources of variation in intellectual performance. To be sure, their success so far leaves something to be desired. In part, this may be because they have been interested almost exclusively in school performance and in the puzzlelike test items that predict that performance. There may also be deeper problems: Perhaps potentialities are not the kind of things that lend themselves to measurement at all. But whereas I have sometimes been critical of the psychometric enterprise, I am even less enthusiastic about current efforts to incorporate the mechanistic concepts of information processing into intelligence tests. Those concepts are based on such an inadequate notion of mental life that they are likely to do more harm than good.

Just as all organisms grow and change, so do mental abilities. Cognitive development and learning are embarrassments to theories of information processing. Such theories apply best to the short-run performances of adult subjects in well-defined tasks that are fully understood from the beginning; tasks in which people are made to behave as much like computers as possible. Mechanistic models often give good accounts of such behavior, but they are much less satisfactory as descriptions of developing skills. This difficulty is predictable, and in fact I predicted it some time ago (Neisser, 1963a). It seemed to me then that attempts to produce so-called "artificial intelligence" would succeed only up to a point. There seemed no prospect of a satisfactory digital model for the processes of cognitive development and change or for the human ability to combine disparate activities and implement multiple goals. So far, events have borne me out (Neisser, 1976b). Computers do display certain kinds of learning and they do solve complicated puzzles, but they don't exhibit fundamental cognitive changes; they do not undergo the kind of restructuring that Piaget called "accommodation." No contemporary computer program experiences radical changes of organization as a result of interaction with the environment, as people do when they grow up or practice any skill for a prolonged period.

The effects of practice are especially important—and have been especially neglected—in situations where people must combine two different activities. Although studies of dual-task performance have usually found decrements due to interference, this may be partly because the experimenters have rarely given their subjects extensive practice. One really does feel a little like a limited capacity channel when one first tries to combine a new activity with an old one. If you have learned to drive, you can probably remember a stage of practice when you could not tolerate the slightest distraction. It was quite impossible to talk and drive at once: Talking made you forget to depress the clutch at the right time or interfered with your judgment of the flow of traffic. Later, these difficulties disappeared. The experienced driver can easily talk as he drives, and if he is a psychologist he can probably talk, drive, and reflect on the fact that he is combining them as well.

This achievement is not unique. Skilled musicans can sight-read at the piano while they shadow a passage of prose (Allport, Antonitis, & Reynolds, 1972), and experienced secretaries can type from copy at high speed while carrying on a conversation. How can these accomplishments possibly be reconciled with the notion of limited capacity or with the idea of a central processing unit through which all information must pass? The most common—and most interesting—attempt to deal with such combinations makes use of the concept of *automatism*. Two separate activities can only be conducted together, it is argued, if at least one of them has become automatic. The concept of automaticity is an appealing one, because it makes contact with a familiar introspective experience. In some of these cases, some of the time, we are *aware* of only one of the activities. Perhaps, then, the one of which we are *not* aware is being conducted in some simpler and inferior way that doesn't require central capacity at all. The introspective part of this argument is interesting, and I return to it later. The complexity part is simply wrong, however. Experiments conducted by Elizabeth Spelke, William Hirst, and others at Cornell have shown that activities need not be simple, meaningless, or automatic in order to be successfully combined.

The inspiration for our experiments came from a study carried out in the 1890s by Gertrude Stein and her collaborator Leon Solomons at Harvard (Solomons & Stein, 1896). They were interested in a phenomenon that was (and is) called "automatic writing." In automatic writing, one puts a pencil in one's hand, rests it on a piece of paper, and then tries to let it alone. Sometimes it writes. Clinicians occasionally use automatic writing in the hope that it will reveal unconscious processes, and hypnotists have used it to study divided consciousness (Hilgard, 1977). In order to train themselves to write automatically, Solomons and Stein began by copying words at dictation while they were reading stories. On some trials, Stein would read a story and Solomons would dictate words to her one at a time. On other trials, they exchanged roles. Eventually, they reached a marvelous stage of the experiments in which Stein read one story aloud while Solomons read another, and each copied down what the other was saying. Later on they turned to automatic writing proper, in which no one dictates anything; the subject reads a story only to avoid attending to his pencil-holding hand. It turned out that what is written spontaneously under these conditions is not very interesting; at least it is not interesting to me. Gertrude Stein seems to have liked it.

Because this experiment was conducted in the 1890s, it was not very sophisticated in terms of methodology. Solomons and Stein do not report their reading speeds, or the degree to which they understood what they were reading, or how fast the words were dictated. The only substantial finding, in their view, was that the act of writing dropped out of consciousness after practice. Even this was not a very robust result. Downey and Anderson replicated the experiment in 1915 and reported the opposite outcome: The writing did *not* drop out of consciousness. When Spelke, Hirst, and I approached the problem, we decided that we would not be our own subjects and that we would not rely primarily on introspective observations.

In our first experiment (Spelke, Hirst, & Neisser, 1976), we hired two Cornell undergraduates for a semester. In the opening phase of the study, Spelke and Hirst (who bore the major responsibility for most of the work I describe here) trained the subjects for an hour a day. During this time, the subjects sat at a table and read short stories. Their right hands, holding pencils, rested on stacks of yellow unlined papers. Words were dictated as they read. The subjects copied each word as soon as it was dictated; the experimenter gave them the next word as soon as they had finished writing the one before. They did not look at their hands. When they reached the bottom of a page, they put it to one side and began a the top of the next one. Each subject started a stopwatch when he began a story and stopped it when he had finished; by counting the number of words in the story we could calculate reading speeds. We also devised comprehension tests for each story consisting of specific questions about various significant points. The subject took these tests, in written form, as soon as he had finished reading; his comprehension score was the percent of questions answered correctly. (Later on we developed more elaborate comprehension tests, to be described below.)

When the subjects began their training, they found it impossible to read and write simultaneously. It is difficult indeed: Whenever a word is dictated one tends to stop reading long enough to copy it, and then tries to read a little before one must deal with the next word. One must choose between reading very slowly and pushing ahead without understanding anything; neither alternative seems satisfactory. Nevertheless the subjects made progress, and after 6 weeks they were reading with full comprehension at their ordinary speed. Each day they were given control trials in which they read without taking dictation, as well as the experimental trials in which they copied words. By the end of the training phase they were reading and comprehending equally well under both conditions.

At that point, we began to introduce certain changes in the procedure. The first thing we wanted to know was whether they were writing "automatically." Did they understand the meanings of the dictated words? Without warning the subjects, we incorporated a series of related words into a dictation list. One of our lists consisted of 20 "means of transportation": trolley, skates, truck, horse, airplane, tractor, car, rocket, bike, taxi, scooter, jet, trailer, subway, tank, feet, ship, cab, tricycle, van. The subjects dutifully wrote them all down and gave no sign of realizing that they had come from a single category. Nor, on the next day, did they notice that certain strings of dictated words actually formed sentences. But on the third day of these tests, when the experimenter dictated words that all *rhymed,* both subjects broke into broad smiles after the third or fourth rhyming word and commented on it. They were asked whether they had noticed the semantic relations presented on the preceding days, and they said they had not. On this basis, it was reasonable to conclude that their writing had been automatic indeed. They evidently hadn't known what the words meant.

At that point in the experiment, Spelke and Hirst explicitly asked the subjects to attend to the meanings that they had previously ignored. They were told that from time to time a series of dictated words would come from the same category, or would form a sentence; they were to report whenever they noticed it. The subjects followed these instructions and reported virtually all of the sentences and category sets. The new task reduced their efficiency in reading, but only briefly. One subject slowed down a little, while the other read with reduced comprehension, but after a few days of practice they returned to normal. When this happened, we set them a final and still more demanding task. Hirst and Spelke constructed special dictation lists in which all the words were drawn from one or the other of two categories, such as animal names or items of furniture. Instead of copying the dictated word, the subject was to write the corresponding category: either "animal" or "furniture." Both subjects suffered decrements in reading speed or comprehension with this additional demand, but again their performance soon recovered. After six to twelve sessions of practice with this new task, each subject was able to read normally while categorizing words for their meaning.

If this experiment is taken at face value, it seems to show that people can make decisions involving the meanings of words at the same time that they are reading and understanding an unrelated story. Such an achievement challenges the traditional view that all complex activity involves a single channel with a limited capacity. But that view is well established and cannot be overthrown by a single study. In fact, there are several ways to explain our result without abandoning the single channel hypothesis. Two of these explanations deserve particular consideration. The first is based on the possibility of "time-sharing": Perhaps the subjects were not really reading and writing simultaneously, but only switching back and forth. The second depends on the assumption of "automaticity." It can be argued that determining the meanings of words does not require a very high level of mental activity. Perhaps it is the kind of thing that can go on outside the central channel, automatically. A number of recent studies have been interpreted as evidence for just such a view (e.g., Lackner & Garrett, 1972; MacKay, 1973) although other interpretations of these studies are possible (Neisser, 1976a). We have conducted several additional experiments to explore the role of time-sharing and automaticity in the reading-while-writing task. I describe them rather briefly here. A fuller account appears in Hirst, Spelke, Reaves, Caharack, and Neisser (1980).

Is it really possible that our subjects were switching a single attention channel back and forth, between reading and taking dictation? The time-sharing hypothesis can be formulated in two different ways, one of which is plausible and testable whereas the other is essentially an act of faith. It is testable if one takes the switching seriously, treating it as involving psychologically meaningful amounts of time and as related to the structure of the activities being switched. Without these assumptions, the hypothesis becomes untestable: One can always postulate a high enough rate (e.g., every microsecond) to explain any apparent instance of simultaneous activity. Modern time-shared computers are so fast that they seem to be responding to all the users at once even when they are actually answering one at a time. It is sometimes suggested that people do this also, but such an assertion amounts only to a metaphysical bias, contributing nothing to our understanding of real activity.

In contrast with speculations about high and undetectable switching rates is a very plausible conception of time sharing that is rooted in what is known about the process of reading. Our subjects were reading short stories written in ordinary English prose by ordinary writers. As everyone knows, such stories are *redundant*. One need not read every word in them to "get the gist" or to answer comprehension questions. It could well be argued that our subjects were taking advantage of the redundancy of the stories to switch away from time to time; on those occasions, they could devote their full attention to the words they had to copy. If atttention switching occurs under voluntary control, a reader might be able to switch just when his eyes were resting on relatively redundant words anyway. To test this possibility we conducted a transfer experiment with material of two levels of redundancy. The less redundant material was taken from the *Encyclopaedia Britannica* or the *Encyclopedia of the Social Sciences;* the more redundant consisted of the short stories we had been using already. We reasoned that people who had learned to copy words while reading short stories, by using the redundancy of the stories to switch back and forth, would encounter a good deal of difficulty when they first ran into Encyclopedia selections. The skills previously developed for writing while reading would fail; the subjects would lose the gist of the Encyclopedia article if they switched at the rate that they had been during the stories.

There were eight new subjects in this experiment, divided into two groups of four. The most important group was trained to copy words at dictation while reading short stories, as our first subjects had done. The second group, run for control purposes, started directly with the Encyclopedia. Each group was trained to criterion and then transferred to the other type of material. They were trained in daily 1-hour sessions like the earlier subjects, and reached criterion in 7 to 10 weeks. "Criterion" meant that they were reading just as fast and as well while taking dictation as normally. To be even more sure of this, we devised a more sensitive sort of comprehension test. Instead of asking questions based on the whole story or article, the experimenters chose a single paragraph and went through it line by line, sentence by sentence. They made up one cue for each sentence in the paragraph. If the paragraph included the sequence "He led the girl to the window; there she saw the garden spread before her; the azaleas were in bloom," the subject might be asked "Where did he lead the girl? What did she see? What was in bloom?" and so forth. Because the critical paragraph is selected at random from a story or article many pages long, such a test is very demanding. No one obtains perfect scores, so we avoided ceiling effects in the measurement of comprehension.

As each of the subject in the story group appeared to reach criterion, so that he or she seemed to be reading as rapidly under experimental as under control conditions, they were shifted to a 1-week session of careful testing. Each day they read two stories by the same author—one with writing and one without writing. Strict comprehension tests were used to compare performance in the two conditions. When this procedure had ensured that the subject was really reading equally well under both conditions, he or she was shifted to the other kind of material. The subjects who had been reading stories now encountered Encyclopedia selections for the first time. The strict tests were continued, to see whether they would have difficulty in combining this less redundant kind of reading with taking dictation. As it happens, three of the four subjects transferred their skill immediately. They were able to read the *Encyclopedia of the Social Sciences* while copying words just as they had been able to read stories by Katherine Mansfield while copying words. We concluded that they had not been using the redundancy of the story texts to accomplish the task, but had really been reading and writing at once. The fourth subject *did* have difficulty in transferring. It is probably important that she was the fastest reader of the group. Her basic reading speed was around 400 words a minute (the others were all below 300), so it is likely that she was accustomed to taking advantage of redundancy as she read. She apparently did this in the first phase of our reading and writing experiment too, but could not continue it with the less redundant encyclopedia. She had to learn a new way to write while reading, which required several more weeks of practice.

This study indicates that insofar as the time-sharing hypothesis is testable, it is mostly wrong. Reading and writing together need not be based on the redundancy of the text, though it may be. The data from three of our subjects indicates that the two activities were genuinely simultaneous and not simply being alternated.

Our other experiment was much more difficult to conduct, and is perhaps more interesting from a theoretical point of view. It dealt with the possibility that the copying tasks used in the first study were simply not demanding enough to test the single-channel hypothesis. Perhaps one can note and report the meanings of words "automatically," without central processing. Several contemporary cognitive models assume that knowledge of word-meanings is stored in a mental "lexicon" where it can be directly accessed by verbal stimuli. The operation of the lexicon is assumed to be outside of conscious awareness. If these models are right, our subjects' achievements are not to be wondered at. They may have devoted all their processing capacity to the stories they were reading, and handled the dictation task in an entirely automatic way.

Theoretical possibilities like these make it difficult to set up a definitive test of the limited-capacity hypothesis. That hypothesis insists that two non-automatic activities cannot be conducted at once. But how can we be sure that an activity is nonautomatic? What characteristics of an activity define "automaticity"? Unfortunately, most currently popular definitions are not very helpful. Posner and Snyder (1975), for example, suggests three "indicants" of automaticity. Two of them are the traditional introspective ones (lack of intentionality and absence of consciousness), and are therefore very difficult to apply: The unreliability of introspection has plagued work on attention for a century. The third defines activities as automatic if they do not interfere with central processing. This is circular: It ensures that all noncentral activities will be automatic by defining them as such and leaves no empirical question to be resolved. LaBerge (1975) and Schneider and Shiffrin (1977) have made much the same suggestion: In their view, a process is automatic if it requires no attention. With such definitions as these, the notion of automaticity cannot be used to explain anything.

The only conception of automaticity that does not beg the question is one based on the nature of the activity itself. An automatic process is one that is habitual, simple, and situation-specific, requiring no new integration of information. (Schneider & Shiffrin may have had this in mind in suggesting that automatic responses are made to "particular input configuration(s)"; 1977, p. 2.). It seemed to Hirst, Spelke, and me that if the distinction between central and automatic activities was to play any useful role in information-processing theory, the automatic ones had to be simple. In particular, it should be impossible to grasp new and complex ideas automatically. We therefore resolved to determine whether it is possible to copy and understand *sentences* that are dictated as one reads a story. It is hard to see how such an achievement could be reconciled with the limited-capacity theory. If the hypothetical central processor is not even needed for novel sentences, it is not needed at all.

For these reasons, we began a new experiment with subjects who copied whole sentences as they read. They started with three-word sentences. The experimenter would dictate "Boys play ball," wait for the subject to finish writing it, dictate "She walked homeward," "Do elephants fight?" and so on, as the subject continued to read. Our plan for the experiment included two phases. We first intended to bring the subjects to criterion; i.e., to train them until they were able to read with normal speed and comprehension while copying sentences of this kind. In the second phase, we planned various tests to determine whether they understood the sentences they were copying. As it turned out, this was a difficult plan to execute. The first pair of subjects never got to Phase II. They worked an hour a day, 5 days a week, for nearly a year without reaching criterion. After 8 weeks of direct practice with three-word sentences we began to try various other tasks, but nothing succeeded. In the last few weeks we even tried to teach these subjects the same task of copying single words at dictation that nine other people has mastered by that time, but without success.

It is hard to be sure of the reason for their failure. One possibility that we had to entertain seriously was that they didn't succeed because the task was impossible. Subsequent work, to be described later, has eliminated that alternative. But if the task *is* possible, why didn't our subjects reach criterion? Were they just the wrong sort of people? They seemed as intelligent and as cooperative as anyone else. Perhaps the most plausible explanation is that we adopted unfortunate training procedures. Perhaps we should not have begun their training with full sentences, or conducted memory tests for the dictated material in the early phase of the experiment. Whatever the reason, we were eventually forced to give up on these subjects. Fortunately we did not have to abandon the experiment as a whole, because two subjects who had been in the redundancy experiment during the same period of time were willing to go on. We rehired two of them and started dictating.

This time, we did not present sentences at the beginning. Instead, we started with strings of three randomly chosen unrelated words dictated one after the other. The switch to sentences came only after the subject had reached criterion with unrelated words. This seemed to work better: One subject reached criterion on the strings in about 10 weeks. The other dropped out, but we were able to replace him from an unexpected source. While these studies were being conducted, we were also running some small pilot experiments with other subjects. In one of these, the subjects were asked to copy *numbers* as they read stories rather than copying words. To our surprise, one of the participants in this study (but only one) was able to do this on the first day. She said it was easy. So we tried her on words. In 1 week she mastered what had taken everybody else 6 weeks or 10. After that accomplishment, we could hardly resist trying her on three-word strings. After 3 weeks she had reached criterion on that task as well, and we finally had two subjects to go on with. It is worth mention that this subject, Arlene, had worked for several years as a secretary before becoming a graduate student in psychology. She believes that her skill with our dual task was the result of her experience as a typist; for example, she can easily type from copy while carrying on a conversation.

When Arlene joined Mary, our veteran from the redundancy experiment, we had two subjects who could copy strings of dictated words as they read stories. Comparison with control trials assured us that they were, in fact, reading with their normal comprehension and speed. We therefore shifted both of them from the random strings to three-word sentences; each reached criterion on this task also. Before concluding the first phase of our study, we tried to determine whether they could also master longer sentences and perhaps even sentences of variable length. (This would be necessary if we wanted to consider dictating real stories instead of sentence lists; few literary works are written entirely in three-word sentences.) As it happened, neither subject could cope with the variable-length condition successfully; the lack of a consistent rhythm may have disturbed them. After experimenting with such sentences for some time, we decided to move on to the second phase of the study while the subjects were still available and willing. In the second phase, we used the longest sentences at which each subject had already reached criterion. This length was three words for Arlene and five words for Mary.

Phase II consisted of three kinds of tests, all devised to see whether our two subjects genuinely understood the meaning of the sentences they were copying. The main test (to be described below) was a recognition probe based on relations among consecutively dictated sentences. The two subsidiary tests were more direct, though less demanding. They were based on familiar differences between the effects of sentences and random strings. For example, sentences are easier to copy. Control subjects taking dictation without reading make many more copying errors with random strings than with sentences. The reason is rather obvious. The meaning and redundancy of a real sentence can often disambiguate homophones (or misheard words); random strings have no such advantage. A subject who hears "He was flying the plane" is unlikely to spell the last word "plain." When "plane" appears in a random string, however, there is no way to distinguish it from "plain" at all. This copying advantage can only appear if the subject *understands* the sentences, however; in a foreign language they would just be random strings. Thus it can serve as a test for understanding. Would the sentence-copying advantage appear in our subjects? It did. In 400 five-word sentences copied while reading, Mary made only 8 errors. In an equal number of random strings, there were 55. A similar difference appeared in Arlene's copies of three-word strings and sentences. Thus, both subjects were treating the sentences as something more than a random assortment of words. They were taking advantage of the semantic, or at least the syntactic structure of the sentences they wrote down.

The second of our subsidiary tests was based on accuracy of recall rather than of copying. After copying 30 sentences or 30 random strings, the subjects were given the first noun of each sequence as a recall cue. If one of the sentences was "the princess loved the garden," for example, the recall cue would be "princess." Control subjects find this task relatively easy when genuine sentences have been presented, and much harder in the case of random strings. The same thing was true of Mary and Arlene. They too were far better at recalling words from sentences than words from random strings, even though they had been reading a short story while copying the to-be-remembered material. These results again suggest that our subjects were understanding what they copied. It is worth noting, however, that they recalled considerably less of *both* kinds of material than control subjects did. Mary, for example, recalled only 30 of 600 potentially recallable words from five-word sentences on this test. This compares favorably with the 2 words she recalled from random strings, but it is not much by absolute standards. Perhaps it would be appropriate to conclude that although the subjects did understand the sentences, they did not deal with them in an entirely attentive way. I will return to this issue later.

Our third test of understanding was the most complex. Although I am presenting it last, it was actually administered first. We wanted to conduct it while the subjects were completely unsuspecting, i.e., when they had no reason to believe they would be asked anything at all about the dictated material. The technique itself is a variation on a method devised by Bransford and Franks (1971). The subjects are presented with 30 sentences, which form the basis of a subsesequent recognition test. The memory material is not chosen at random; it consists of 10 sets of three sentences that are related to each other in meaningful ways. Each sentence triad tells a miniature story: "We had dinner for eight. It was last Saturday night. Bob and Jane couldn't come." After all 10 triads have been presented, the subjects are given 30 more sentences in the recognition test: They must say whether each one had been presented earlier or not. Some of the test sentences are *old,* having been actually drawn from those previously presented ("We had dinner for eight"). These old sentences demand a *yes* answer. Other test sentences, however, are merely *implied* by the mini-story without having been presented literally: "The dinner was last Saturday," for example. A subject who responds *yes* to this sentence is committing an error, but it is a meaningful one. His "false recognition" apparently stems from his understanding of the story line that was created by the triad of sentences taken together. As a control, the recognition test also contains non-implied *new* sentences like "Bob had dinner Saturday night." These new sentences provide a base rate for the chance occurrence of false recognition. A subject who "recognizes" substantially more *implied* than *new* sentences is demonstrating that she understood the meanings of the sentence triads as she heard them.

We presented this type of test to our subjects for 10 days in a row. On the first of these days, the subjects were not warned that anything unusual was about to happen. They settled down as usual, reading a story as they copied sentences. In this case, however, the dictated material consisted of specially prepared triads like those described above. After the 30th sentence, reading was interrupted and the subject took the recognition test, indicating for each test sentence whether she believed it had been literally dictated before or not. The responses were given in the form of confidence ratings: *1,* if the subject was sure the sentence had been dictated; *2,* if she was less sure; and so on down to *6,* if she was sure it had *not* been dictated. This first test caught the subjects by surprise; they had never been asked to remember the dictated material in any way before. On the next 9 days they were warned that recognition tests would occasionally be given but were asked not to prepare for them in any way. Instead, they were to continue reading and taking dictation just as they had been doing before.

The overall results were clear-cut. Both of our subjects found the *implied* sentences more "familiar" than the *new* sentences, even though neither type had been presented before. This effect was just as pronounced on the first day of testing as for the average of all 10 days, so it cannot have been due to deliberate preparation for the recognition test. It follows that our subjects must have understood what they were copying. Indeed, they understood it well enough to draw inferences spanning several consecutive sentences. This achievement seems incompatible with any definable notion of automatic processing.

To determine whether our subjects had an entirely "normal" grasp of the dictated material, we ran a number of control subjects as well. For 10 days the controls copied the same dictation lists and were given the same recognition tests as the experimental subjects. The only difference was that the controls were not asked to read stories as they copied, and indeed would have been unable to do so. Of course, the control subjects also showed the Bransford–Franks effect: They found the implied sentences more familiar than the new ones. Interesting, however, they exhibited the effect at a higher overall level of familiarity. Mary and Arlene rarely gave ratings of *1* to any sentence, old or new. *Nothing* seemed very familiar to them, although the new sentences were even more unfamiliar than the implied ones. The controls exhibited no such reluctance to use high ratings, especially for genuinely "old" sentences. Despite this difference—and despite one other difference to which I return below—there can be no doubt that our experimental subjects grasped the meanings of the sentences and of the minature stories that had been dictated to them. In a genuine sense, they were reading and writing simultaneously: following two independent trains of thought at the same time.

Their achievement raises a number of theoretical questions. Its implications for models involving a limited central capacity are obvious: That assumption must be abandoned or at least sharply modified. But what approach to the problem of attention can we substitute for it? One possible lead appears if we ask a somewhat different question. Simultaneous reading and writing is indeed possible. Why, then, is it so difficult? Why did several subjects completely fail in their attempt to copy sentences while reading, and even the successful subjects take so long to master the task? Why do most people need weeks of practice before they can combine normal reading with copying even single words?

The basic source of difficulty, I believe, is the one mentioned by Donald Hebb in his own contribution to this book. Subjects must discover how to keep the two activities separate: If they interpenetrate, they are bound to become confused. To see the nature of the difficulty, consider an experiment in which *one* subject is asked to read while *another* subject takes dictation. No one would be surprised that this is possible, but what is easy about it? It is true that the two subjects may have twice as much central capacity as one, but I doubt that this is the decisive factor. Even two rather simple-minded subjects would be able to accomplish their joint task if the material were not too difficult. The key point, I think, is that the verbal thinking in the reader's brain would not intrude upon the verbal thinking in the writer's, and vice versa. When *one* brain must carry out *both* activities, however, confusion can easily result. This is not really just another way of talking about "capacity." The subject's problem would not be made easier by enlarging their brains or their memory spans. Indeed, split-brain subjects might have some advantage over normal ones in this task, if they could somehow arrange to do one of the tasks in each hemisphere. Such individuals could substitute an anatomical differentiation for the functional one accomplished by our subjects.

On this interpretation, the principal task in reading while writing is to distinguish the two streams of available information. It would have been easier for our subjects if the two activities had been less similar. Thinking and breathing, sight-reading music and shadowing, walking and chewing gum are readily combined: The two components of each pair are very different from each other. Carrying on two separate verbal activities presents a much more difficult problem. In understanding a sentence, the reader or listener must relate later words to earlier ones: verbs to their nouns, pronouns to their referents. To understand a paragraph, one must use ideas that have already been established in order to understand new ideas. If one has two verbal trains of thought going on at once, there is a considerable risk that an idea from A may be used in interpreting B, leading to complete confusion. This confusion can only be prevented, I think, by attending closely to the features that distinguish A from B throughout. Some of these "features" are contextual: The continuing coherence of the story certainly helps to identify its elements. I rather doubt that this is enough, however. It seems likely that the simple stimulus difference between our two sources of information was also very important: One was printed while the other was spoken. Over the course of the experiment, the successful subjects may have learned to attend to this difference in a more effective way and use it to help them distinguish between the two activities.

These considerations suggest that understanding what one reads or hears is a matter of picking up the right information, not of processing it through the right structure. Understanding requires considerable skill even under normal conditions. New skills must be developed for our dual task, to capitalize on the information by which the two messages can be distinguished. When this information is reduced, the task must become still more difficult. I do not know if a person could ever learn to follow two independent *spoken* streams of speech: two prolonged parallel conversations at the famous psychological cocktail party, for example. If it turns out to be impossible, however, the impossibility should not be ascribed to a *capacity* limitation in the listener. It would result from a lack of information adquate to specify which conversation is which.

This discussion of the limits of cognition cannot be complete without some consideration of the question of consciousness itself. It is reasonable to ask whether our subjects were *aware* of the stories as well as of the words they were copying at the same time. We did ask, of course. Unfortunately, the answers were not consistent. The subjects sometimes said yes, sometimes no, sometimes maybe. Arlene, our most skillful subject, often reported relatively full awareness: She was not only conscious of reading and of writing but also reflected on the fact that she could do both so easily. But there were also many occasions when subjects said they had been completely oblivious to the dictated sentences and to the act of copying them. Moreover, one sharp difference between experimental and control subjects in the implied-sentence recognition test concerned awareness rather directly. All the control subjects soon noticed that the dictated sentences were arranged in related groups of three, but neither experimental subject ever made this observation. Arlene and Mary were both surprised when this structure was pointed out to them after the tenth day of testing. Thus it seems that they picked up the relations between the sentences without actually being aware that they were doing so. Dual awareness does not seem necessary for the conduct of the dual task. Nevertheless it it sometimes present, at least in a limited form. What are we to make of this?

Let us first consider occasions on which a subject is *not* aware of the dictated material, or its meaning, although the data show that she has understood it. Such occasions are not really surprising. Psychologists have known for a long time that most of the work of thinking is unconscious. At the turn of the century, the Wurzburg introspectionists systematically tried to report the processes by which they produced categorical responses or solved problems, but they failed. Their work stands as conclusive evidence of the fundamental inaccessibility of the machinery of thought. Innumerable accounts of the creative process by scientists and poets give the same testimony: "The idea just came to me out of nowhere." Certain modern social psychologists have recently rediscovered this fact and announced once again that experimental subjects cannot give a good account of the causes of their judgments and preferences (Nisbett & Wilson, 1977). There is no reason to be suprised: Freud knew all about it.

Although complex processes do not have to be conscious, they need not be entirely unconscious either. We often know *what* we are doing, although we may not know just *how* we are doing it. Why are some subjects aware of the secondary activity whereas others are not? It depends, I think, on their introspective abilities. Introspection is a skill too. In fact, it is a skill not unlike those that we have studied in our experiments: a skill of doing two things at once. One must simultanteously carry out an activity and think about carrying it out. Like any other combination of skills, this is hard to do when one first tried it. That is why the introspective reports of young children are so inadequate: they haven't yet learned how. The same reason explains why it's hard to think about the placement of one's feet as one is walking upstairs. The attempt tends to make one stumble, especially at first. But one need not always stumble: Practice at "walking while thinking about it" will improve performance. One can learn to do something and introspect on it, just as one can learn to read and take dictation at the same time.

One further complication remains to be considered. Doing two things at once and being aware of doing them both (as Arlene was) must bring them into a relationship. This relationship might easily lead to the very sort of interpenetration that would prevent the individual from carrying out the tasks at all. Such a disaster can be avoided only by developing a more complex, hierarchical mental structure, in which each activity has a specified part. In that case, however, the two activities will seem (consciously) as if they were somehow unified or single. They will have become integrated, like the point and counterpoint of a musical composition. A skilled listener can hear both voices at once, but when he does so, they are heard as parts of an integrated piece of music. Thus when dual consciousness is finally achieved, it turns out to be single after all.

If this is the true state of affairs, the frequently observed "singleness of consciousness" has nothing to do with any capacity limitation. To put it bluntly, what we are aware of is just what we are aware of. Even when it stems from two environmental sources or is defined by an experimenter as comprising two different tasks, to experience both at once is to unify them. This achievement depends on discovering and taking advantage of some aspect of the two task structures in order to treat them together. It is not a simple achievement, but people can do it. The singleness of consciousness actually testifies to the very opposite of a cognitive limit: With increasing skill, one can discover forms of coherence in information structures that once seemed entirely independent. And, as we have seen, the equally solid fact that some activities are conducted *without* awareness provides no evidence of those elusive limits either. Highly complex activities can be carried out unconsciously as well as consciously, separately as well as together.

What, then, are the limits of cognition? I believe that they are not set by the fixed size of any mechanism of the mind, whether conscious or otherwise. Our limitations, when they do not simply reflect the stubborn facts of the environment, are just instances of things that we have not yet learned how to do.

REFERENCES

Allport, D. A., Antonitis, B., & Reynolds, P. On the division of attention: A disproof of the single channel hypothesis. *Quarterly Journal of Experimental Psychology*, 1972, *24*, 225–235.

Bransford, J. D., & Franks, J. J. The abstraction of linguistic ideas. *Cognitive Psychology*, 1971, *2*, 331–350.

Downey, J. E., & Anderson, J. E. Automatic writing. *American Journal of Psychology*, 1915, *26*, 161–195.

Hilgard, E. R. *Divided consciousness*. New York: Wiley, 1977.

Hirst, W., Spelke, E. S., Reaves, C. C., Caharack, G., & Neisser, U. Dividing attention without alternation or automaticity. *Journal of Experimental Psychology: General*, 1980, *109*, 98–117.

Klatzky, R. L. *Human memory: Structures and processes*. San Francisco: W. H. Freeman, 1975.

Klein, R. M. Attention and movement. In G. Stelmach (Ed.), *Motor control: Issues and trends*. New York: Academic Press, 1976.

LaBerge, D. Acquisition of automatic processing in perceptual and associative learning. In P. M. A. Rabbitt & S. Dornic (Eds.) *Attention and performance V*. New York: Academic Press, 1975.

Lackner, J. R., & Garrett, M. F. Resolving ambiguity: Effects of biasing context in the unattended ear. *Cognition*, 1972, *1*, 359–372.

MacKay, D. G. Aspects of the theory of comprehension, memory, and attention. *Quarterly Journal of Experimental Psychology*, 1973, *25*, 22–40.

Neisser, U. The imitation of man by machine. *Science*, 1963, *139*, 193–197. (a)

Neisser, U. The multiplicity of thought. *British Journal of Psychology*, 1963, *54*, 1–14. (b)

Neisser, U. *Cognition and reality.* San Francisco: W. H. Freeman, 1976. (a)

Neisser, U. General, academic, and artificial intelligence. In L. Resnick (Ed.), *The nature of intelligence.* Hillsdale, N.J.: Lawrence Erlbaum Associates, 1976. (b)

Nisbett, R. E., & Wilson, T. D. Telling more than we can know: Verbal reports on mental processes. *Psychological Review,* 1977, *84,* 231–259.

Posner, M. I. *Cognition: An introduction.* Glenview, Ill.: Scott, Foresman, 1973.

Posner, M. I., & Snyder, C. R. R. Attention and cognitive control. In R. L. Solso (Ed.) *Information processing and cognition.* Hillsdale, N.J.: Lawrence Erlbaum Associates, 1975.

Schneider, W., & Shiffrin, R. M. Controlled and automatic human information processing: I. Detection, search, and attention. *Psychological Review,* 1977, *84,* 1–66.

Solomons, L., & Stein, G. Normal motor automatism. *Psychological Review,* 1896, *3,* 492–512.

Spelke, E., Hirst, W., & Neisser, U. Skills of divided attention. *Cognition,* 1976, *4,* 214–230.

IV MENTAL REPRESENTATION

7
On Weighing Things in Your Mind

Allan Paivio
University of Western Ontario

We often find ourselves "weighing things in our minds" before making a behavioral choice. We may choose a meal in a restaurant by imagining the alternatives and deciding what most appeals to us. We may mentally select the shorter of two routes when driving home. Having forgotten to bring the worn-out washer, we choose from the various sizes in the hardware store on the basis of memory. Some washers are "obviously" too large or too small, and they are quickly rejected. Others are in the right "ball park" and, after some vacillation, we decide to play safe by taking home more than one size. These are familiar experiences, involving simple cognitive acts. But their psychological interpretation is apparently far from simple, judging from the amount of research and theoretical debate that has been directed recently at their laboratory counterparts.

What kinds of mental entities are being evaluated in such tasks? Are they images, as some of the examples suggest? Or are they simple words, as though we know that a mouse is small and an elphant big because we habitually speak of them in such terms? Alternatively, perhaps the knowledge is neither imaginal nor verbal, but consists instead of some kind of abstract data base, of which the experienced images and words are epiphenomenal expressions that play no causal role in behavior. Again, what is the nature of the comparison process that operates on the mental entities whatever their form? In a more descriptive vein, how fine are the memory discriminations that individuals are able to make, how similar are they to their perceptual analogues, if any, and how do they relate to other cognitive abilities? These are the kinds of questions that I explore in this chapter. First, I present a brief overview of the area as an experimental problem, including a summary of the principle findings and theoretical views. Then I discuss some of our recent research on individual differences in relation to mental comparisons.

GENERAL RESEARCH BACKGROUND

Mental comparisons were first studied some time ago (e.g., Dashiell, 1937), but current interest in the problem began with Moyer's (1973) investigation of size comparisons as a problem in memory psychophysics. He presented his participants with pairs of animal names and asked them to choose the one that was larger in "real life." The pairs were constructed from the names of seven animals ranked according to size, so that some pairs differed greatly in size (e.g., *cat-moose*) whereas others differed less (e.g., *moose-cow*). The interesting result was that the reaction time to make a decision varied inversely with the size difference: the larger the ordinal difference, the faster the decision. This inverse function was a logarithmic one, similar to that obtained when individuals compare stimuli that differ on some perceptual dimension, such as size or length. The important difference is that Moyer's study involved a kind of memory psychophysics, where the critical attribute is varied symbolically rather than perceptually. Moyer and Bayer (1976) accordingly referred to the psychophysical function as the *symbolic distance* effect.

The effect is very general, having been observed in comparison with numerical magnitudes (Moyer & Landauer, 1967) and judgments of names of objects on such dimensions as angularity-roundness (which is rounder, a *book* or a *toaster*?), brightness (which is darker, a *cucumber* or a *lime*), pleasantness (which is more pleasant, a *butterfly* or a *baseball*?), and value (which costs more, a *house* or a *ship*?), (Paivio, 1978b, 1978d). Others have obtained the effect for the time dimension (Holyoak & Walker, 1976), animal intelligence (Banks & Flora, 1977), and ferocity (Kerst & Howard, 1977). Note that such dimensions as size and roundness are concrete and continuously variable perceptual attributes of the referent objects, whereas such characteristics as pleasantness and value are more abstract, not directly reflected in a simple perceptual correlate. The symbolic distance effect has even been obtained for the purely linguistic attributes of rated pronounceability and frequency (familiarity) of words (Paivio, 1978b). Why the distance effect occurs with such a diversity of attributes is one of the basic theoretical issues in the area. Other key issues stem from the variable effects of stimulus materials (e.g., pictures as compared to words) and of individual differences among subjects. Such problems are discussed in the context of relevant theories.

THEORETICAL APPROACHES TO
MENTAL COMPARISONS

Moyer (1973) interpreted the symbolic distance effect that he obtained with size comparisons in terms of an analog model, according to which the observer first translates the names into analog representations that preserve size information. The analogs are then compared much as in a perceptual comparison task, resulting in a typical psychophysical function described earlier. Moyer and Dumais (1978) subsequently explicated some of the assumptions of the model and extended it to other dimensions and phenomena. Paivio (1975) also proposed an analog approach based on a dual coding theory of memory and thought. The theory assumes separate but interconnected systems for the processing of verbal and nonverbal information. Some of the main assumptions are schematically presented in Fig. 7.1. The two systems consist of organized, information-processing structures resulting from perceptual-motor experience with language and with the world of nonverbal objects and events. Processing of linguistic units accordingly

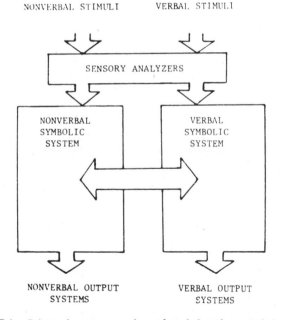

FIG. 7.1. Schematic representation of verbal and nonverbal symbolic systems showing their connections within input and output mechanisms and with each other.

involves activation of representations ("logogens") in the verbal system, whereas processing of nonlinguistic information consists of the activation of representations ("imagens") in the nonverbal image-generating system. Through associative experience involving both classes of events, referential relations are established between the systems, so that words can arouse images, and perceptual objects, qualities, and activities can be named. Imagens are assumed to be perceptual analogs in the sense that they "contain" information concerning perceptual appearances and other attributes that are highly isomorphic with the perceptual objects themselves; that is, activation of the memory representations in the form of conscious images involves a perceptual experience comparable to that evoked by the perceptual objects themselves. This is not to say that we are always conscious of the activity of imagens, but when we are, their perceptual attributes are particularly salient. By contrast, logogens do not in themselves "carry" any information that is directly related to the nonverbal world. They do so only by virtue of their associative connections with the image system, which permits a kind of digital-to-analog translation. Logogens are, however, linguistic analogs in the sense that they must map onto the attributes of the linguistic events that they represent; that is, the internal structure of logogens must correlate with the acoustic and motor patterns of the units of language.

The application of the model to comparison tasks is straightforward. Presentation of a pair of words such as *cat* and *toaster* together with the question "Which is larger?" results in activation of logogens corresponding to the stimulus words and the comparative, larger. The nouns activate imagens corresponding to *cat* and *toaster* and the comparative guides the comparison process and behavioral choice. The difficulty of the choice depends on the relative size difference between the two imagens, which is experientially determined and parallels the difficulties encountered in a perceptual comparison task. That pushes the mystery of the comparison process back to the perceptual level, where a number of theoretical alternatives are available (Pike, 1973).

The preceding analysis, in which comparisons are assumed to be based on perceptual memory representations of the referent objects, does not preclude the possibility of comparisons based entirely on verbal information. As mentioned at the outset, animals such as elephants are typically called large whereas mice and ants are usually considered small. These verbal habits could be the basis of the decision, at least in some instances. Moreover, such a mechanism could account for the typical symbolic distance effect simply in terms of differential associative strengths linking the two stimulus terms of the verbal associate (large or small). Certain experimental designs, involving repetition of experimental items within a list, provide for the possibility of a differential build-up of associative connections between stimulus terms and the verbal associate within the experiment itself. Paivio (1975) designed an experiment to minimize the influence of these variables in a comparison task. The symbolic distance effect appeared despite such controls, thereby reducing the plausibility of the verbal associative approach as a sufficient explanation of the phenomenon. That verbal processes can nonetheless contribute to the effect under certain circumstances has been demonstrated by Kosslyn, Murphy, Bemesderfer, and Feinstein (1977).

A more abstract version of the verbal approach has been proposed by Banks (1977). In brief, Banks's model is based on the assumption that subjects associate each stimulus item with some kind of linguistic-semantic code and then compare these codes. The codes are based on information in semantic memory stored in an abstract format (propositions, features, etc.). An "availability principle" assumes that the more similar two items are on the comparison dimension, the longer it will take to find information in a semantic memory that will permit the generation of discriminative codes. For example, two items far apart on the size dimension may be coded "small" and "large," which would enable the participant to discriminate the items on the size continuum. Two items that are relatively close together on the dimension might both be initially coded as "large," and discrimination would not be possible. Accordingly, the information search continues until differentiating codes such as "large" and "larger +" can be generated. The distance effect is obtained because two large (or small) items require a longer search time before distinguishing codes can be generated. The semantic coding model accounts for the symbolic distance effect as well as a number of other phenomena that is only touched on here. We shall see that it does not account for certain findings that are easily predicted by the dual-coding model.

THEORETICALLY CHALLENGING EXTENSIONS OF THE COMPARISON TASK

One of the obvious predictions of the dual-coding model is that comparisons on concrete attributes should be faster with pictures than with words as stimuli. This is because pictures are assumed to have more direct access than words to the imagens on which the comparisons are based (see Fig. 7.1.). The reverse would be predicted from a verbal associative hypothesis, because the verbal associates would occur more quickly with words than pictures. An unelaborated version of Banks's semantic coding model includes no assumptions that would permit a directional prediction to be made. The dual-coding prediction was strongly supported in the case of size (Paivio, 1975) and other comparisons considered later. A converse prediction is that comparisons on linguistic attributes, such as the relative pronounceability of picture names and printed words, would be faster with words than with pictures because the comparison presumably would be based on the properties of logogens, which are more directly accessible by means of verbal stimuli. This simple prediction has also been confirmed (Paivio, 1975). A further expectation is that a Stroop-like conflict should be observed when perceptual information contrasts with memory information concerning the dimension on which the comparison is being made. Thus, it should take longer to judge which of two pictured objects is larger in real life when the size relation in the picture is incongruent with real life size then when it is congruent. This is precisely the result that was obtained in experimental tests of the hypothesis (Banks, 1977; Paivio, 1975).

A variant of the size congruity-incongruity paradigm provided a particularly strong test of the predictive power of dual-coding theory. The theory leads to the prediction that the Stroop-like conflict obtained with memory-size comparisons should be reversed when the observer is asked to make a relative depth judgment of the pictured objects, that is, to determine which object looks farther away. This follows from the simple fact that objects known to be larger appear to be far away when pictured smaller than those known to be small. The expectation was strongly confirmed (Paivio, 1975). The contrasting effects obtained in the size and depth judgment tasks are particularly interesting because both require the subject to take account of perceptual and memory size information. Thus, the same representational information mediated contrasting behavioral effects when the demands of the task were altered. Taken together, the contrasting effects provide compelling evidence for the modality-specific nature of the representational systems used in the comparison process. For example, the Stroop-like conflict presumably occurred because perceptual size information conflicted with visual memory information concerning the real-life size of the pictured objects, resulting in a response conflict.

The set of results just described are all consistent with dual coding and with analog models in general (e.g., Moyer & Dumais, 1978) but not with other current approaches to mental comparisons. As already mentioned, faster comparison times for pictures than words is a problem for any verbal coding approach. Banks (1977) accommodated the picture-word difference and the Stroop-like conflict into his model by the ad hoc assumption that pictures have more direct access than printed words to the abstract informational base that determined semantic coding. Further ad hoc assumptions would have to be added, however, in order to account for the slower comparison times for pictures than words when a linguistic dimension such as pronounceability is involved. Moreover, it is difficult to see how the semantic coding model would account for the reversal of the conflict effect when observers are required to make relative depth judgments of pictured objects varying in size.

The findings from a number of other studies are similarly consistent with the basic assumptions of the dual-coding approach. One of these (Paivio, 1978a) involved comparisons of mental clocks. Subjects were asked to think of two analog clocks showing different times, such as 3:20 and 7:50, and to choose the time in which the hour hand and minute hand would form the larger (or smaller) angle. Note that because the times were presented numerically, the task requires a digital-to-analog transformation. A computational procedure could be used to arrive at the correct answer, inasmuch as minutes are related to hours by multiples of 5, and this ratio is faithfully reflected in the relative positions of the two hands of a clock. However, few subjects would be expected to work out the relationship and its implications for the comparison task, whereas all had extensive experience with visual clocks, relying accordingly on imagery to perform the task. This assumption was confirmed by a postexperimental questionnaire in which subjects overwhelmingly reported relying on imagery to perfom the task.

Several experiments yielded smooth symbolic distance effects in which longer comparison times were associated with small angular differences. Of particular interest was an experiment in which some subjects were presented digital pairs, others a digital time paired with a drawing of an analog clock showing the two hands at a particular time, and a third group with two drawn clocks. A simple prediction from the imagery-based dual-coding position is that the comparison times should be faster for the mixed digital-analog condition than for the digital-digital condition because in the former case, only one clock time required transformation into a visual analog form. The prediction would be reversed if one assumes that the task is done verbally or by means of a computational procedure, because the transformation into a verbal or numerical code should take longer when the subject is presented a visual clock than when both times are available as numerals. The results clearly supported the prediction from the imagery position. In addition, the comparison times were fastest for the perceptual condition in which subjects were presented the two visual clocks. This would be expected from any theoretical viewpoint, so it is not a crucial observation in the present context.

The assumption that subjects could nonetheless preform the clock comparison task using a computational strategy was tested in an unpublished follow-up experiment. Subjects were first taught and had practiced on the computational strategy for determining which of two times involves the larger angle. Some subjects were then presented digital-digital pairs and others digital-analog pairs in the experimental task. The expectation was that the digital-analog condition would now yield slower comparison times than the digital-digital, contrary to the results obtained in the experiment previously described. This was dramatically confirmed. These contrasting findings are particularly interesting because they indicate that the clock comparison task can be performed either imaginally or by an abstract verbal (mathematical) procedure. In the absence of special instructions to the contrary, however, imagery appears to be the preferred mode of processing.

The clock task is rather unique, and it could be argued that the results do not establish the generality of the imagery strategy with mixed perceptual and symbolic pairs. To do so, the study was replicated in principle using angularity-roundess comparisons. Subjects received pairs of items that differed in roundness according to normative ratings previously obtained from a different group. The pair members were presented as words, as pictures, or as mixed picture–word pairs. The results are shown in Fig. 7.2, where it can be seen that comparison times decreased systematically from word–word, to picture–word, to picture–picture conditions. Like the analogous results from the clock comparison experiment, the angularity-roundness data are just what one would expect from a dual-coding viewpoint, assuming that comparisons on concrete attributes are ordinarily performed on modality-specific perceptual memory representations.

Thus far, the discussion has centered on findings that seemed to be unequivocally favorable to dual-coding theory. Another set of general findings requires some modification or elaboration of that approach. The symbolic distance effect has been obtained with abstract dimensions such as pleasantness and monetary value (Paivio, 1978d) as well as intelligence and ferocity of animals (Banks & Flora, 1977; Kerst & Howard, 1977). Because the effects are assumed to be mediated by analog representations, which somehow represent values on a continuous dimension, the question arises as to the nature of such analogs when the information is abstract rather than perceptually concrete. The problem appears to be compounded by the fact that comparison times on pleasantness, value, and animal intelligence in the foregoing studies were found to be faster for pictures than words. In the case of intelligence judgments, Banks and Flora (1977) argued that the finding is inconsistent with the dual-coding idea that faster comparisons with pictures means that the processing is mediated by representations in the imagery system. Because the attribute is abstract, the comparison would have to be based on verbal representations according to dual coding. As it was not, Banks and Flora proposed instead that the finding is consistent with their semantic coding hypothesis, given the additional assumption that this abstract coding system is accessed more quickly through pictures than words.

I have alternatively proposed (Paivio, 1978d) that the findings may call into question the interpretation of attribute abstractness and the manner in which such properties are psychologically represented, rather than necessarily being

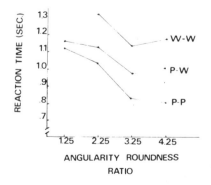

FIG. 7.2.   Angularity-roundness comparison time for word-word (W–W), picture-word (P–W), and picture-picture (P-P) pairs varying in the ratio difference in rated angularity-roundness.

inconsistent with dual-coding theory. The general argument is that such attributes as pleasantness, value, and intelligence are primarily characteristics of things rather than words or are based on learned reactions to things. Thus roses are pleasant, diamonds are expensive, and things are smart because of their intrinsic sensory properties or behavior, or events associated with either. We know these characteristics because they are part of our memories of the objects and events. The properties are abstract by definition, but they belong to concrete objects. To the extent that this is true, subjects in a comparison task would have to access the memory reresentations of the things and their associated properties before they can make the required judgment. Words and pictures alike simply provide access to those representations, but pictures do so more directly, hence the faster comparison times.

The symbolic distance effect might be explained by the further assumption that the abstract properties are represented in a continuously variable form in appropriate sensory-motor systems. Pleasantness, for example, might be based on interoceptive and motor-response systems that mediate affective reaction. These originally would have been learned primarily as reactions to the things themselves, thereby becoming associated with perceptual representations (imagens) corresponding to the visual shapes of the objects. This analysis in principle parallels an earlier one (Paivio, 1971, pp. 149–150) in which it was argued that visual imagery normally includes motor and haptic components. More generally, it is consistent with the idea that verbal and nonverbal (imaginal) representational systems are general symbolic systems that are orthogonal to sensory modalities (Paivio, 1972)—verbal and nonverbal information alike can be visual, auditory, or tactual, and the symbolic systems must have components capable of processing the different types of input.

The theoretical picture is blurred by other recent findings that do not fit neatly into any of the preceding interpretations. These involve memory for color information. Participants in one experiment were asked to indicate which of a pair of items was brighter or darker in real life. Examples of pairs that varied in the degree to which they differed on the dimension are *beet–apple, robin–onion, tire–onion,* and *piano–swan,* in increasing order of brightness difference. The items were presented either as words or as line drawings that did not contain the brightness difference. The results revealed the usual symbolic distance effect but, surprisingly, no picture–word effect emerged. In fact, a significant interaction suggested that the comparison times were actually slightly faster for words than picture pairs when the brightness differences were small, but the word superiority disappeared when symbolic distance increased.

Pictures and words also did not differ significantly in a further experiment done in collaboration with John te Linde, in which subjects compared three items on hue (te Lende & Paivio, 1979). Normative ratings were used to select object names (and pictures) that had stable real-life color attributes. Distance was varied in terms of the number of units separating the items on the color circle following a procedure used in a prior related experiment. The experimental triads consisted of an object name or picture in the center, with a focal color name to the left and right. The subject's task was to choose the color name that most closely represented the typical color of the object. Symbolic distance was varied in terms of the subtractive distance between the location of the object color and each of the two comparison color names on the hue circle. Thus the triad, blue–CARROT–red, represents a relatively large symbolic distance (carrots are typically much closer to red than blue), whereas yellow–PEACH–orange represents a small symbolic distance (some peaches are slightly more orange than yellow). Again, the usual symbolic distance effect was obtained (e.g., reaction times were faster for triplets such as blue–CARROT–red than ones like yellow–PEACH–orange), thereby providing evidence that object color is stored in an analog fashion in long-term memory. However, no picture–word difference occured. On the basis of the logic involved in the case of other attributes, the lack of a picture–word difference in the case of color attributes suggests that such information is represented in a system that is equally accessible to the name and/or pictured shape of an object. I return to a more detailed consideration of this point later. Suffice it to say at this point that the contrasting picture–word effects for different attributes, although theoretically puzzling, are also encouraging because they indicate that the picture–word variable in comparison tasks is sensitive to the form or location of attribute information in long-term memory. Thus, they refute any argument to the effect that picture superiority, when obtained, is simply due to some perceptual advantage for pictures as compared to words, or differential accessibility of pictures and words to some abstract data base. If this were so, pictures should have the advantage in any comparison tsaks.

COGNITIVE ABILITIES AND
MENTAL COMPARISONS

We turn now to individual differences in cognitive abilities, particularly ones that can be clearly identified with the theoretically relevant imaginal and verbal coding systems. A common misconception must be dispelled at the outset. Investigators interested in individual differences in imagery have often asesumed, explicitly or implicitly, that there is some unidimensional skill called imagery ability. This cannot be so, at least within the context of the current dual-coding approach to cognition. Imagery is defined generally as a system that is specialized for processing nonverbal information. It is not restricted to *visual* information processing, although the emphasis tends to be on visual imagery because of the dominance of vision as a perceptual modality in sighted individuals. Even within the visual mode, however, there are many tests that can be interpreted as measures of imagery ability. Guilford's (1967) research on the structure-of-the-intellect model, for example, suggests various figural ability tests that would be relevant, particularly those grouped under cognitive and memory abilities. I have reviewed the general problem in some detail elsewhere (Paivio, 1971) where I concluded that "imagery is a construction based on stored information, and...the storage and the constructive utilization of imagery might constitute different abilities, which emerge empirically on different factors in the study of individual differences. Imagery is conceptually broader, therefore, than the ability concept [p. 492]." The point in the present context is that the imagery system is implicated in different abilities, which will be differentially relevant as predictors of performance on different tasks. Given the mental comparison tasks under consideration here, one cannot be sure on a priori grounds what specific imagery abilities might be most relevant. The same arguments apply , of course, to verbal abilities but the facts that the term encompasses many different specific skills has been more generally recognized than has been the case with imagery ability. The multicomponential nature of imagery ability may be the reason that imagery ability tests have been rather inconsistent as predictors of performance in criterion tasks (see Ernest, 1977; Paivio, 1971, Chapter 14). The situation contrasts markedly with the relatively consistent findings that emerge when imagery is manipulated by means of experimental procedures, such as mnemonic instructions, and variation in the imagery-arousing value of materials.

The uncertain predictions from individual difference variables in past research led me initially to adopt the practical strategy of simply having subjects in the mental comparisons studies complete a battery of individual difference tests without any attempt to preselect people on the basis of test scores. This meant that the number of subjects in individual experiments was often too small to provide conclusive findings in regard to relevant abilities, but the tests did provide suggestive evidence that could be pursued more systematically in follow-up studies. The tests were selected to be conceptually relevant to the functioning of verbal and nonverbal symbolic systems and to prior research involving the dual-coding approach. Thus the key imagery tests consisted of the three spatial transformational ability tests: namely, Space Relations, the Minnesota Paper Form Board (MPFB), and Cube Visualization. The last of these involves a task that was introduced in the early part of the century as a test.of imagery ability. It has been quantified as a figural ability test by Guilford (1967). It differs from the other two spatial tests in that the test is presented entirely verbally, but the subject presumably must use imagery to solve the test items. Each item requires the subject to think of a cube of a certain color and then to imagine it being sliced up into a certain number of smaller cubes. The test calls for answers to questions concerning the number of cubes that have a specified number of faces that contain the surface color. The measure of verbal ability initially consisted only of an association fluency test, which presumably taps verbal divergent thinking (Guilford, 1967). The test is essentially uncorrelated with the spatial ability tests, which correlate moderately among themselves (see Paivio, 1978b, for a more detailed description).

A number of experiments involving comparison of word pairs or pictures on concrete dimensions consistently showed the imagery test battery predicted comparison times, whereas the verbal test did not. Although the relations were not always significant, high imagery subjects generally showed faster reaction times than low imagery subjects. These relations have been obtained for unpublished studies involving size comparisons and shape comparisons (for a summary, see Paivio, 1978c). Significant results were reported for the clock comparison task (Paivio, 1978b), the average correlation between imagery ability and reaction time being –.40 over four different experimental groups. That is, high imagery scores were associated with fast comparison times. The corresponding pooled correlation with verbal ability was zero. These findings add further support to the interpretation that the imagery system plays a dominant role in these tasks. The convergent operations that implicate imagery dominance include a faster comparison time for pictures than for words, (reports from subjects indicating that they relied mainly on imagery during the task), and a faster reaction time for high than for low imagery subjects. Note that the verbal system must also be functional in the tasks: Particularly when the to-be-compared items are presented as words, logogens must be activated before imagery can be aroused. The pattern of findings suggests, however, that the imagery system is primary in the comparison phase itself.

It is particularly interesting that a similar picture emerged in the case of two abstract dimensions. Individuals scoring high on imagery ability had faster comparison times than those with low ability in the case of both pleasantness and value comparisons, with either pictures or words as items (Paivio, 1978d). Verbal fluency again showed no significant relation to comparison time, although it did emerge as a significant factor in interaction with imagery in the case of pleasantness comparisons. The fastest reaction times on the average were obtained by subjects who scored high on both imagery and verbal ability, whereas the other three combinations of the two abilities did not differ significantly among themselves. This suggests that verbal ability may play a more important part in pleasantness comparisons than in the other tasks considered up to this point. Until more data are available on the problem, however, it does not seem worthwhile to speculate about the possible reasons for the difference. Apart from the interaction, these findings are consistent with the imagery interpretation suggested earlier: Although pleasantness and value are abstract dimensions, they are nonetheless characteristics of things, and reaction time will be facilitated by any factor that makes the nonverbal memory representations more available or accessible. High imagery ability ensures availability of such representations, and pictorial stimuli enhance their accessibility.

It is important to note that these results do not simply represent a general superiority of high imagery subjects in all comparison tasks. If that were the case, one might well argue that the correlations reflect some general ability, such as intelligence, which happens to correlate with the imagery tests. Such an argument is countered by the fact that imagery ability did not correlate with comparison times on verbal attributes such as word (or name) familiarity or pronounceability. Verbal associational fluency fared somewhat better as a predictor in these tasks, although less research has been done on them than on some of the other attributes and the conclusions must remain tentative, particularly in regard to individual differences.

Other comparison tasks have yielded some surprises in regard to individual differences. One of these involved comparisons of animals on relative intelligence (which is more intelligent, *dog* or *rat*?). Recall that Banks and Flora (1977) found the typical symbolic distance effect for comparisons on this dimension and also observed that reaction times were faster for pictures than for words. In the earlier discussion of this finding, I suggested that intelligence, like pleasantness and value, is an attribute of living things and that subjects must access the representations of those things in order to decide which member of a pair is smarter. If this is true, subjects should predominantly report using imagery to do the comparisons, and those who score high on imagery ability tests should have faster comparison times than those who score low. Marc Marschark and I recently tested these implications in an unpublished study in which we systematically replicated the Banks and Flora experiment using a somewhat modified design. Banks and Flora used a relatively small number of animals ranked for intelligence, so that each item was presented a number of times, but paired with different partners. In addition, each subject received blocks of both picture and word pairs, in counterbalanced order. We instead used a much larger set of items arranged into independent pairs, and different groups of subjects received pictures and words. Following the experimental task, subjects filled out a questionnaire concerning the strategies used during the task and also completed a battery of individual difference tests. To our chagrin, none of the imagery and verbal ability tests correlated significantly with comparison time, although Space Relations showed an appropriate trend in that high scorers tended to be faster than low scorers ($r = -.32$) when pictures served as items. Even more surprising was the fact that we failed completely to replicate the Banks and Flora picture–word effect. Reaction times did not differ for the two classes of material. These findings suggested that imagery played a less dominant role in this task than in other comparison tasks discussed. The postexperimental questionnaire results were also consistent with that conclusion in that subjects reported relying about equally on verbal mechanisms and imagery in order to decide which animal of a pair was more intelligent. We have not entirely resolved these contradictory observations, but we were able to clarify them through some additional observations.

We had added a picture vocabulary test (Ammons & Ammons, 1948) to our test battery. This was included because it is purported to be a "quick" test of intelligence, but it is also specifically relevant to the dual-coding approach because the task requires transfer from pictorial to verbal information. It turned out that the test scores correlated significantly with mean comparison times but only for the group of subjects that had received pictures as items ($r = -.57, p < .002$, as compared to $-.03$ for the word group). This observation suggested that subjects who score high on the picture vocabularly test benefited from pictures in the comparison task, either because they were skilled at identifying pictured objects or because they were adept at labeling them. That ability was irrelevant in the case of the word condition because the identifying names were equally available to all subjects. The anaylsis also implies that absence of a picture–word effect in the overall analysis simply obscured an underlying interaction between vocabulary test scores and type of material. This was confirmed by a further analysis, which showed that high scorers on the picture vocabulary tests were faster with pictures than words, whereas the reverse was the case for low scorers.

The analysis in terms of the availability of identifying labels for pictures also suggested a possible basis for resolving the differences between our results and those of Banks and Flora (1977). Banks and Flora obtained reaction times that were generally faster for pictures than words using a within-subjects experimental design. We accordingly conducted a second experiment in which we replicated the important features of their experiment, including using the same pairs and testing each subject with both pictures and words in counterbalanced blocks of trials. Under those conditions, we also obtained faster reaction times for pictures than words, but this effect was attributable entirely to the second trial block. That is, the pictorial superiority was due to subjects who first compared animal names and then switched to pictures of animals on the second block. These subjects showed a sharp decrease in reaction times from word to picture conditions. The subjects who received pictures first showed no decrease when they subsequently compared names.

In general, these results indicate that the prior experience with name comparisons primed picture processing more than picture comparisons primed subsequent name processing. The differential transfer effect could have been on the coding of the to-be-compared units, or the comparison process itself, or both unit coding and comparison. If unit coding was the important factor, the interpretation might be that comparisons are facilitated by dual coding, and that prior experience with names primes dual coding of pictures more than picture comparisons prime dual coding of words. If the effect is primarily through the comparison process, however, the interpretation might be that word comparisons provide practice at generation as well as comparison of the relevant imagens. Pictures subsequently activate the same imagens and comparison processes more directly. Initial picture comparisons provided no practice with the generation and comparison of images to words, so that subjects essentially began word comparisons without relevant priming. This interpretation is consistent with the observation that the average reaction time and the pattern of reaction time over trials were similar for subjects who received words on the different blocks of trials.

These suggestions are quite speculative at this time and others could be readily suggested, but I do not pursue these speculations here.

The important general point concerning intelligence comparisons is that the task implicates dual coding, but in quite a different way than in the comparison tasks discussed earlier. Pleasantness and value comparisons, for example, yielded picture–word effects and correlations with cognitive abilities, which suggested that imagery plays a primary functional role, and verbal processes a necessary but secondary role in the task. In the case of intelligence comparisons, main effects of the picture–word variable and of imaginal and verbal abilities were absent. The experimental and individual difference data suggest instead that the primary determinant of performance was the linkage between the image of a referent object and its identifying label. This seems to place the theoretical emphasis on the relationship or connection between imaginal and verbal systems, rather than on their individual functional capacities as measured by the spatial and verbal tests used in these studies. Nonetheless, the availability of the image system seems especially important even in this task, because comparisons became faster with pictures than words, rather than vice versa, given prior experience with their names.

Anomalous findings also occurred in another comparison task, and these, too, remain to be adequately resolved. The findings involved comparisons of memory objects on brightness and hue. As mentioned earlier, neither attribute showed any general picture–word difference, and an interaction even suggested that the comparison, when difficult, may be faster with words than pictures, contrary to theoretical expectations. Moreover, we have found no consistent correlation between color comparison time and individual differences in cognitive abilities. Apparently the representation of color differs in some important way from the representation for concrete attributes, such as shape and size, as well as abstract ones, such as pleasantness, value, and intelligence.

On the basis of the logic applied to the results of other comparison tasks, the results for color suggest that such information is about equally accessible to pictures and words. Theoretically, this implies that memory information for color, despite its perceptual origin, is not stored any more closely with memory representations for the shapes of objects than for their names. This conclusion seems to be consistent with neuropsychological findings reported by De Renzi & Spinnler (1967), who observed that aphasics with normal color perception showed disturbances in their memory for object color even when the color memory task did not explicitly require color naming. This suggests that verbal mechanisms are implicated somehow in the processing of long-term memory information concerning object color.

My tentative interpretation of the contrasting findings from different tasks involves a theoretical distinction between *intrinsic* and *associative* properties of internal representations (Paivio, 1978b). The assumption is that pattern or form is the essential, intrinsic property of both imagens and logogens. The pattern may be either spatial or temporal in the sense that activation of the internal representation by symbolic stimuli results in spatially or temporally organized perceptual or motor responses, analogous to those evoked by the external events themselves. Associative properties, on the other hand, are not intrinsic aspects of the "core" representation of an object or verbal unit considered in isolation, but are found in their relation to other units or reaction systems. Thus, even the concrete property of size can be viewed as an associative or relational attribute of objects. A tiny model of an elephant, for example, can be recognized accurately as long as it has the appropriate shape. The relative size is known either verbally ("elephants are big") or contextually —that is, in relation to other known objects. The attributes of pleasantness, value, and intelligence are associative in the sense that they involve interoceptive and motor response associated with imagens. The associative information is accessed given prior activation of an imagen together with contextual information (e.g., verbal instructions) that specify which associative attribute is relevant to the task. I now suggest that color, too, may be an associative rather than an intrinsic attribute of objects. Thus, although yellow is a prototypical characteristic of bananas, they also come in varying shades of green or brown. Moreover, many other things are also yellow, and the identification of a banana depends on its having the right shape as well as color. In fact, subjects can reliably name black and white outlined drawings as bananas from the shape alone. In the absence of shape, they are not likely to do so to a shapeless yellow spot on a piece of paper. What all of this amounts to is the idea that color, though perceptually concrete and specific, is highly variable in its linkage with particular shapes in the perceptual world. It is therefore an abstract attribute of things in the sense that it can be varied or removed (abstracted out) without destroying the identity of most objects. This variable, nonintrinsic nature of the color attribute was demonstrated by the considerable difficulty we had in coming up with a pool of items that have consistent color characteristics. Objects like flowers are indeed brilliantly colored, but few flowers come in only one hue. Moreover, the same colors may be shared by objects other than flowers. It would be convenient, therefore, for the brain to abstract color out of the shape of an object and store each attribute in a separate memory system, or to store multiple exemplars of classes of objects that come in variable colors. This analysis may provide a basis for explaining the apparently equivalent psychological distances between memory colors and verbal and object representations with which they are associated. If the internal representations of colors and object shapes are separate, for example, they may develop independent connections with the names of the objects, so color attributes are equally accessible from line drawings and printed names of objects. Such speculative ideas remain to be tested.

MENTAL COMPARISONS PREDICTED FROM COGNITIVE ABILITIES

Richard Harshman and I recently undertook a large scale individual-difference approach to the structure of verbal and nonverbal cognitive abilities, including mental comparison tasks, which may ultimately clarify some of the preceding problems. The battery of tests included tests designed to be indicators of left or right hemisphere functioning, according to information from prior research (Harshman, Crawford, & Hecht, 1976). The study is incomplete, and I cannot make any firm statements here concerning the differential contribution of left and right hemispheres to task performance. However, I can give an overview of the general research design and discuss some of the findings that are particularly relevant to dual-coding theory. The study involved group administration of a large test battery to university students over a period of several hours on separate days. All tests were administered twice so that test reliability could be taken into account in the analyses. The ability tests sampled verbal and figural abilities. The former included the Inference Test (1962), which presumably measures abstract verbal reasoning, as well as word fluency, expressional fluency tests from Guilford's (1967) battery of tests. The nonverbal tests included Space Relations, the MPFB, and a perceptual closure test. Group versions of the size comparison and clock comparison tasks were also included. These were constructed so that a given test page contained a series of pairs, which differed by a relatively constant amount on the dimension involved. Thus, in the case of size comparisons, a page contained pairs of names of animals and objects so that the symbolic size difference was, on the average, relatively slight on one page, medium on another, and large on a third. The subject's task was to circle the larger member of each pair. The resulting score was the number of correct choices in a fixed time period per page. Similarly, the clock comparison task involved pairs of digital clock times, with four size differences as samples of four different pages. This procedure yielded the typical symbolic distance effect in that, for both dimensions, the number of correct comparisons increased as the symbolic distance increased. Thus we could safely assume that the group version of the mental comparison tasks yielded results that were generally comparable to those obtained in the individual reaction time experiments.

Correlational analyses were then performed on the cognitive ability and mental comparison test scores. The latter included both slope scores and mean scores over all symbolic distances. I discuss only the latter because they yielded the stronger relations and because they are more comparable to the analyses performed in the context of the earlier experimental studies. The most pertinent results emerged from a multiple regression analysis in which the subjects' symbolic comparison times were predicted from the ability tests. Table 7.1 shows the stepwise regression predictions of, and simple correlations with, size comparison scores. Four of the tests correlated significantly with size comparisons, but only two of these contributed significantly to the multiple correlation. The best predictor was the Inference test, followed by Space Relations, and then Word Fluency. Thus both verbal and nonverbal (presumably imagery) abilities contributed to performance on the size comparison task. The positive role of imagery is consistent with the earlier conclusions (Paivio, 1975) based on several variants of the size comparion task involving pictures as well as words as astimuli. The novel contribution of the present results is that they implicate verbal abilities in the size comparison task more clearly than was done by the earlier findings, although it was always assumed that the verbal system is essential to task performance, particularly when words serve as stimuli.

The pattern of results was slightly different for the clock comparisons task. Table 7.2 shows that space relations was now the best predictor of comparison scores, with the Inference test ranking second. No other test contributed significantly to the prediction. Thus, the imagery system appears to dominate

TABLE 7.1
Stepwise Regression Predictions of Size Comparison
RT (N = 105)

Test	Multiple r	Simple r
Inference test	.44[a]	.43[a]
Space relations	.49[a]	.35[a]
Word fluency	.52	.26[a]
MPFB	.54	.33[a]
Ideational fluency	.54	.01
Closure	.54	.10
Expressional fluency	.54	.07

[a]$p < .05$, two-tailed.

TABLE 7.2
Stepwise Regression Predictions of Clock Comparison
RT (N = 105)

Test	Multiple r	Simple r
Space relations	.35[a]	.35[a]
Inference test	.40[a]	.29[a]
Word fluency	.41	.16
Ideational fluency	.41	.15
Closure	.42	.06
Expressional fluency	.43	.04
MPFB	.43	.18[a]

[a] $p < .05$, two-tailed.

in this task with an additional contribution from verbal reasoning. This could mean either that numerals are in some sense less verbal than words, for which there is evidence from perceptual laterality studies (see Paivio, 1971, p. 116), or that the symbolic comparisons themselves depend more strongly on imagery in the case of the clocks than the size comparisons tsk. Clarification of these correlational differences involving the two tasks will require additional studies. For example, the size comparison task involved only words and it is possible that a somewhat different pattern of correlation would emerge if pictures served as items, particularly in view of the dual-coding assumption that pictures have more direct access to the nonverbal cognitive system. The clock comparisons task could also be made more nonverbal by presenting the pairs in a mixed digital-analog clock form.

Interpretations of the cognitive processes involved in the comparison task will also be aided by the addition of comparisons with other dimensions. One extension that we are currently investigating involves shape comparisons, in which subjects are asked to indicate which of a pair of named objects is rounder (or more angular). This is interesting for a number of reasons. First, the clock comparison task was originally introduced because it seemed to be a completely objective approach to size comparisons. The angle formed by the hands of a clock can be large or small and comparisons of two clock times might be based only on the angle or sector size differences. However, clock times differ also in shape (small angular differences involve a more pointed shape formed by the two hands than does a larger angular difference). Perhaps subjects can base their comparisons of clock times either on shape or size differences, or both. Which cognitive strategy is chosen may depend on individual differences in the pattern of relevant abilities as well as on experimental conditions that bias strategies in one way or another. We are encouraged to pursue this line of thinking because, to our initial surprise, performance scores on the group version of the size and clock comparison tasks were not strongly correlated. If it turns out that performance on the clocks task correlates more highly with shape comparisons than with size, it would mean that subjects are generally biased in favor of shape information when shape and size covary, as they do in the case of analog clocks. The results are not yet available for the telling, but I have mentioned the line of reasoning involved to give some appreciation of the potential breadth of the comparison task as a general took for investigating precisely how we go about weighing things in our minds.

It already seems apparent from the studies reviewed here that mental comparisons can be based on different symbolic processes, depending on the precise attributes being compared. Successful evaluation and comparison of highly concrete perceptual characteristics, such as the angular properties of analog clock times, apparently depend heavily on modality-specific perceptual-spatial memories. Others, like pleasantness, intelligence, and even size appear to require considerable verbal as well as perceptual memory processing. Within the latter group, subtle distinctions emerge, so that evaluating the relative intelligence of animals seems to depend more on the strength of the connection between verbal and perceptual memory information than on the availability of either class of information alone. In the case of at least one class of perceptual information, color, we are not yet in a position to say anything about the pattern of cognitive abilities that contribute to task performance. Finally, although the universality of the negative relation between reaction time and the magnitude of the difference on any dimension—the symbolic distance effect—indicates that the values of the memory attributes very continuously, or at least by relatively small and systematic discrete steps characteristic of analog systems, the nature of that analog information remains uncertain. In some isntances, it appears to be clearly perceptual in the exteroceptive sense, whereas in others it may be based on interoceptive or proprioceptive reaction systems. Still others may be based on systems that are relatively abstract and modality-free.

I have suggested elsewhere (Paivio, 1978e) how Hebb's (1949, 1968) cell-assembly theory might provide the basis for a neuropsychological model of such an abstract representational system. According to that approach, abstract information would be represented in higher order cell assemblies that develop out of lower order ones. The latter represent perceptual information in a relatively concrete (analog?) form. The higher order assemblies are constructed on the basis of features that have been abstracted out of specific perceptual events. Such abstract information may be relatively amodal, but it retains its association with the lower order perceptual systems from which it originated. Assuming that this is the case with such abstract attributes as pleasantness and value, it would explain why mental comparisons on those dimensions are faster with pictures than words as stimuli. The abstract dimensional information is represented in higher order assembly systems, which are more closely associated with the lower order perceptual assemblies activated by pictures than they are with verbal assemblies. A little reflection will make it clear that this is essentially a paraphrase of my earlier analysis of the problem in terms of intrinsic and associative attributes of imagens and logogens: Intrinsic attributes correspond to lower level assemblies; associative (and relational) attributes correspond to higher level assemblies. The match would be complete if one assumes in addition that the higher level assemblies include, or have connections with, interoceptive and motor assemblies that represent such properties as affective value (pleasantness) of specific objects. The representations would have to be sufficiently fine-grained to produce the symbolic distance and other effects observed in mental comparison studies. Cell-assembly theory is general enough to accommodate such assumptions, but a detailed model of that kind is yet to be realized.

REFERENCES

Ammons, R. B., & Ammons, H. S. *Full-range picture vocabulary test.* Missoula, Mont.: Psychological Test Specialists, 1948.

Banks, W. P. Encoding and processing of symbolic information in comparative judgments. In G. H. Bower (Ed.), *The Psychology of learning and motivation* (Vol. 11). New York: Academic Press, 1977.

Banks, W. P., & Flora, J. Semantic and perceptual processes in symbolic comparisons. *Journal of Experimental Psychology: Human Perception and Performance,* 1977, *3,* 278–290.

Dashiell, J. F. Affective value-distances as a determinant of esthetic judgment-times. *American Journal of Psychology,* 1937, *50,* 57–67.

De Renzie, E., & Spinnler, H. Impaired performance on color tasks in patients with hemispheric damage. *Cortex,* 1967, *3,* 194–217.

Ernest, C., H. Imagery ability and cognition: A critical review. *Journal of Mental Imagery,* 1977, *1,* 181–216.

Guilford, J. P. *The nature of human intelligence.* New York: McGraw-Hill, 1967.

Harshman, R. A., Crawford, H. J., & Hecht, E. Marihuana, cognitive style, and lateralized hemispheric functions. In S. Cohen & R. C. Stillman (Eds.), *The therapeutic potential of marihuana.* New York: Plenum, 1976.

Hebb, D. O. *The organization of behavior.* New York: Wiley, 1949.

Hebb, D. O. Concerning imagery. *Psychological Review,* 1968, *75,* 466–477.

Holyoak, K., & Walker, J. Subjective magnitude information in semantic orderings. *Journal of Verbal Learning and Verbal Behavior,* 1976, *15,* 287–300.

Inference Test. Princeton, N.J.: Educational Testing Service, 1962.

Kerst, S. M., & Howard, J. H., Jr. Mental comparisons for ordered information on abstract and concrete dimensions. *Memory and Cognition,* 1977, *5,* 227–234.

Kosslyn, S. M., Murphy, G. L., Bemesderfer, M. E., & Feinstein, K. J. Category and continuum in mental comparisons. *Journal of Experimental Psychology: General,* 1977, *106,* 341–375.

Moyer, R. S. Comparing objects in memory: Evidence suggesting an internal psychophysics. *Perception & Psychophysics,* 1973, *13,* 180–184.

Moyer, R. S., & Bayer, R. H. Mental comparisons and the symbolic distance effects. *Cognitive Psychology,* 1976, *8,* 228–246.

Moyer, R. S., & Dumais, S. T. Mental comparison. In G. Bower (Ed.), *Psychology of learning and motivation.* New York: Academic Press, 1978.

Moyer, R. S., & Landauer, T. K. The time required for judgments of numerical inequality. *Nature,* 1967, *215,* 1519–1520.

Paivio, A. *Imagery and verbal processes.* New York: Holt, Rinehart & Winston, 1971.

Paivio, A. Symbolic and sensory modalities of memory. In M. E. Meyer (Ed.), *The Third Western Symposium of learning: Cognitive Learning.* Bellingham: Western Washington State College, 1972.

Paivio, A. Perceptual comparisons through the mind's eye. *Memory and Cognition,* 1975, *3,* 635–647.

Paivio, A. Comparisons of mental clocks. *Journal of Experimental Psychology: Human Perception and Performance,* 1978, *4,* 61–71. (a)

Paivio, A. Dual coding: Theoretical issues and empirical evidence. In J. M. Scandura & C. J. Brainerd (Eds.), *Structural/process models of complex human behavior.* Leiden: Nordhoff, 1978. (b)

Paivio, A. Imagery, language, and semantic memory. *International Journal of Psycholinguistics,* 1978, (c)

Paivio, A. Mental comparisons involving abstract attributes. *Memory and Cognition,* 1978, *6,* 199–208. (d)

Paivio, A. The relationship between verbal and perceptual codes. In E. C. Carterette & M. P. Friedman (Eds.), *Handbook of perception. Vol. IX: Perceptual processing.* New York: Academic Press, 1978. (e).

Pike, R. Response latency models for signal detection. *Psychological Review,* 1973, *80,* 53–68.

te Linde, J., & Paivio, A. Symbolic comparison of color similarity. *Memory & Cognition,* 1979, *7,* 141–148.

8 The Lingua Mentis and Its Role in Thought

Peter W. Jusczyk
Bruce Earhard
Dalhousie University

> *The mass of our thinking vanishes forever, beyond hope of recovery, and psychology only gathers up a few of the crumbs that fall from the feast.*
>
> —William James

"What is the nature of thought?" As evidenced by the diverse collection of essays in this book, there are differing opinions as to how this question ought best be answered. Some, like Posner (Chapter 5), believe that we might best proceed by studying the nature of the information-handling capacities of the organism. Others, like Krueger and Osherson (Chapter 9) strive to formally characterize the nature of concepts knowable by humans. In the end, no single approach can suffice, as the nature-of-thought question requires answers on a number of levels. In this chapter, we consider the nature of thought from another perspective, that of a "Lingua Mentis," or language of thought. In what follows, some of the potential characteristics of the Lingua Mentis and its role in thought are examined. Some consideration is also given to the possible ramifications that this notion might have for the way in which cognitive processes are studied.

WHAT IS THE "LINGUA MENTIS" AND WHY IS IT NECESSARY?

Just what do psychologists mean by the term Lingua Mentis? In what sense is there a *language* of thought? Do they mean *language* in the sense of a natural language, and if so, which one? If psychologists do mean language in the sense of natural language, then it is safe to assume they do not mean that a particular natural langauge serves as a basis for thought for all people everywhere. (So much for the ancient dispute of whether the language is Phrygian or Egyptian.) However, there is a second possibility, namely that the particular natural language an individual acquires serves as his Lingua Mentis. There are several interesting consequences of this position. First, before language is acquired, there is either no Lingua Mentis or quite a different one. Either way, thought before and after language acquisition should be qualitatively distinct. Indeed, several notable psychologists, such as Vygotsky (1962) and Bruner (e.g., Bruner, Olver, & Greenfield, 1966), have argued that this is the case. A second consequence of the Lingua-Mentis-as-the-native-language position is that it commits one to the Whorfian view that speakers of different natural languages think differently as a result of differences between the languages. But surely any strong form of this Whorfian hypothesis is false.[1] Putting stylistic considerations aside, we are able to translate the thoughts expressed in one language into thoughts expressed in another language. *If* speakers of different natural languages think differently, the origins of the differences are likely to be cultural and not specifically linguistic.

If the Lingua Mentis is not a natural language, then how might it be analogous to a language? Consider what a language is. It is a means of representing one's ideas so as to communicate them to others. Thus, the Lingua Mentis may be a means of representing ideas to oneself. It would serve as a medium in which information gained from different sensory modalities can be represented and integrated. Yet, if representation is the sole property shared by the Lingua Mentis and natural languages, then the analogy between the two is quite weak. However, there are other structural features of natural language that may be paralleled in thought. For example, all natural languages are composed of a finite set of elements whose permissible combinations are tightly constrained by rules.[2] If our analogy holds, then a similar organization should characterize the Lingua Mentis. Namely, there exists a finite set of elemental units (concepts) and a set of rules that combine them in some ways, but not in others.[3] So, whereas "bachelor" may strike one as a permissible combination of conceptual elements, "nonretachelor" (i.e., something that means either a man who has never married, or a nonreturnable bottle[4]) seems to be an unnatural and nonpermissible combination of

---

[1]Our purpose is not to make the case against the Whorfian hypothesis here. If arguments about its circularity are not convincing (e.g., Dale, 1976), then Rosch's (1973) demonstrations of the Danis' ability to learn color terms not found in their natural language should be.

[2]Of course, the elements here may occur at a number of levels, e.g., phones, words, and so on.

[3]For the time being, questions of the size and nature of concepts will be left open.

[4]We have coined this term to designate Savin's (1973) unnatural concept.

conceptual elements. Moreover, as with natural languages, at least some of the rules of the Lingua Mentis must be of the type to allow it to transform one state into another. Thus, problems as diverse as mental rotation and multiplication require transformations from an initial state to a final state in order to achieve solution.

It seems unlikely that the Lingua Mentis could bear a much stronger similarity to natural language than the one just outlined. After, all the Lingua Mentis must serve as the medium for representing nonlinguistic information as well as linguistic information. Therefore, it must be flexible enough to accommodate such diverse calculations as those essential to constructing spatial maps or visualizing faces in addition to ones necessary for comprehending speech or acquiring language. Thus, tying one's conceptualization of the Lingua Mentis too strongly to natural language may render it incapable of representing (except, perhaps, with great inefficiency) the nonlinguistic aspects of cognitive functioning.

We believe that the picture outlined here is consistent with other notions of the Lingua Mentis in psychology. Although the term "Lingua Mentis" is not often employed, the notion that a uniform system of representation underlies thought has received a great deal of attention recently. Thus, proponents of computer-based similations of cognitive processes have argued for an underlying propositional-based system of representation that can handle information presented visually or verbally (e.g., Rosenberg & Simon, 1977). Others, such as Pylyshyn (1973), and Anderson and Bower (1973), have commented that a propositional network provides the base for the construction of visual images. Similarly, Bransford, Franks, and their associates have stressed the importance of an underlying tacit knowledge system for cognitive processes (e.g., Bransford & McCarrell, 1974; Franks, 1974). Moreover, researchers in the area of semantic memory, such as Norman and Rumelhart (1975) and their colleagues, have proposed similar kinds of representational networks to encode information gathered through the various modalities. Finally, in a most important book, Fodor (1975) has argued at length that a consideration of a "language of thought" is necessary for understanding cognitive processes. Although the various formulations of the system underlying cognitive representations (or "Lingua Mentis" in our terms) may differ in detail, they are highly similar to each other in spirit. The goal behind such work on representational systems appears to be directed toward the development of a single theory of the structure of thought. Such a theory would: (1) claim that there exists a single system underlying cognitive representations; (2) specify the nature and type of the elemental units, the possible combinatorial rules, and the permissible types of transformation in the system; and (3) specify the relationship between mental representations and various types of cognitive processes. Let us for convenience refer to such a theory as the "Lingua Mentis Theory."

What benefits do we derive from the Lingua Mentis Theory? Perhaps, the best way of answering this question is to consider some alternative conceptualizations of mental representation. There are, it would seem, only two alternatives to the notion that we possess a single representational system. On the one hand, we might assume that there are no representations at all. Proponents of this view (e.g., Skinner, 1977) would hold that representations are unnecessary appendages to psychological theories, and that all cognitive processes can be explained via the appropriate physiological or behavioral mechanisms. On the other hand, we might assume that there is no single system of representations but rather multiple systems, which are probably modality specific. Thus, there might be separate systems for verbal and visual information as Paivio (1971) has argued, and even additional ones to deal with touch, smell, and so on.

The first of these two alternatives, namely that representations do not exist (or that they are merely epiphenomena), strikes us as completely untenable. Without question, people can and do use mental representations such as internal spatial maps and are able to mentally transform sentences into paraphrases. Any reader who doubts the existence of any kind of representation may have his skepticism dispelled by considering Fodor's (1975) excellent commentary in his introductory chapter to *The Language of Thought*. In what follows we confine our remarks solely to the issue of whether there is a single system or multiple systems of representation.

THE LINGUA MENTIS VERSUS
MULTIPLE SYSTEMS OF REPRESENTATION

In light of recent discussions concerning the nature of the representational system (e.g., Anderson, 1978; Bever, 1975; Kosslyn & Pomerantz, 1977; Paivio, 1978; Pylyshyn, 1973), the second alternative, viz. that there are multiple systems of representation, needs to be considered more seriously. We begin by examining just what is implied by the claim that there are multiple systems of representations. Two interpretations are possible. On the one hand, what is being claimed may amount to no more than the fact that humans have the capacity to mentally represent information in a variety of ways. Posed in this fashion, the claim is nonspecific as to whether different systems of representation could draw from a common pool of information but simply operate in different ways to construct representations. We refer to this interpretation of the multiple-systems-of-representation claim as the *weak version*. The alternative version of the claim asserts that the various systems of representation are largely independent. Not only is it the case that each system of representation employs its own specialized operations, but the elements it applies them to are distinct from those used by the other systems.

We designate this position as the *strong version* of the multiple systems of representation claim. We believe that the strong version of the claim is the only one that poses a threat to Lingua Mentis Theory. Therefore, we discuss this version and in the process of doing so demonstrate how the weak version is actually consistent with Lingua Mentis Theory.

Can the mind be composed of a set of different representational systems, each of which is independent and unique? Bever (1975) has raised this possibility; however, there are difficulties with this approach. A major problem confronting advocates of multiple independent representational systems is to explain how comparisons between the various representational systems of different modalities are achieved. How, for example, are we able to select by touch, from a number of objects concealed from sight, one which is identical to a cube that we view in front of us? From the point of view of the Lingua Mentis Theory, it is assumed that visual and tactile representations have a common or single expression in the Lingua Mentis, and thus identity judgments can be made. If no Lingua Mentis is assumed, then there can be no underlying core representation, and recourse has to be made to other devices to explain such cross-modality matching capacities. Bever (1975) has contended that the cross-modality matching problem can be solved by a model that employs multiple independent systems of representation (what he calls a "Federated Faculties Model"). His proposed solution is that each modality assigns its own independent and distinctive representation to input, but that, in addition, any given representation in one modality is capable of being mapped into or onto any other representational modality by some form of unidirectional mapping process. Thus, presumably a visual representation resulting from looking at a wooden cube can be mapped onto a tactile representation produced by manipulating the cube in one's hand.

The inadequacies of such a formulation become evident when we attempt to understand just how one representational faculty could be mapped onto another. We can start by taking Bever literally and assuming that the act of mapping is such that there is a relatively precise projection of one representational faculty onto another; that is, all essential features of the object being considered are preserved in the movement from one representation to another. But can such a position be taken seriously? Assume we are looking at a solid cube set at an angle on a table in front of us, and at the same time are required to manipulate an object by touch behind our back, which (unknown to us) is a cube indentical to that which we are seeing. How does the mapping of representational structures onto one another proceed so that we may know whether we are dealing with same or with different objects? The "seen" cube has only seven corners (the eighth is out of sight), but the "touched" cube has eight. The difference in the number of features to be mapped in the two different representational formats can be reconciled only if one has recourse to an interpretive process that specifies the properties of perceived cubes. It is by such an interpretive process that it can be determined that for cubes positioned at an angle, one corner is normally not visible. But to posit an interpretive system is to admit that there is no straightforward mapping. This is tantamount to assuming what Bever's proposal endeavors to avoid, i.e., than an underlying interpretive structure to translate between modality specific representations, or a Lingua Mentis, is required.

If one takes a less literal interpretation of Bever's mapping claim and assumes that there need not be a feature-by-feature matching process or any other form of correspondence required when representations from one modality are mapped into or onto another, the situation worsens. One is left with the possibility that there will be one visual representation produced by looking at an object such as a cube, and another different visual representation produced by mapping the effect of tactile manipulation of the cube into the visual modality. How is one to decide whether two different objects are represented by the two representations or whether (as in this case) both represent the identical object? Whatever Bever's assumptions about the mapping process, the conclusion is the same; recourse must be made to some sort of underlying interpretive structure of Lingua Mentis.

Although it should be apparent from the foregoing discussion that cross-modality matching operations cannot be carried out without recourse to a Lingua Mentis, this has not deterred a number of investigators from advancing a strong version of the multiple systems of representation claim. It is to a consideration of these efforts that we now turn. Many of the most serious attempts to advance the *strong version* of the multiple systems of representation claim have taken the form of dual-coding models (e.g., Anderson, 1978; Kosslyn & Pomerantz, 1977; Paivio, 1971, 1978). For example, Paivio (1978) has argued that

> cognitive behavior is mediated by two independent but richly interconnected symbolic systems, that are specialized for encoding, organizing, transforming, storing, and retrieving information. One (the *image system*) is specialized for dealing with perceptual information concerning nonverbal objects and events. The other (the *verbal system*) is specialized for dealing with linguistic information. The systems differ in the nature of representational units, the way the units are organized into higher order structures, and the way structures can be reorganized or transformed [p. 379].

There are two aspects of Paivio's description that are of particular interest. The first is that the systems are specialized for storing information. This implies that information processed by the image system is stored in a different form than information processed by the verbal system. The second is that the systems differ in the *nature* of representational units. Thus, the units for the image system are "perceptual isomorphs or analogs" and those for the verbal system are "discrete entities corresponding to the functional units of language." Both of these assertions are antithetical to the Lingua Mentis view that ultimately all information one receives is coded into a common format and stored in this form. It must be stressed at this point that Lingua Mentis Theory does not deny the existence of "perceptual isomorphs or analogs" nor "discrete entities corresponding to the functional units of language." Both must certainly exist. What we are denying is that they are the basic representational units. We submit that perceptual isomorphs and linguistic entities are the result of different types of operations being applied to units chosen from a common set of elements. Thus, Lingua Mentis Theory is completely compatible with the view that there are different subsystems of operations that are specialized for generating imagined or verbal constructs for use in different task situations.

Supporters of the dual-coding approach believe that experimental evidence demands the existence of independent imaginal (or nonverbal) and verbal systems with different types of representations units. Evidence cited in support of this hypothesis comes from an array of studies impressive in their diversity. Included are the following: (1) neurophysiological evidence to the effect that nonverbal and verbal abilities are localized in different hemispheres (Kimura, 1973); (2) studies demonstrating modality specific interference (e.g., Atwood, 1971; Brooks, 1968); (3) studies showing that verbal and nonverbal abilities are factorially independent (e.g., Paivio, 1971); (4) studies of mental rotation (e.g., Cooper & Shepard, 1973); (5) the results of reaction time studies requiring identity matches (e.g., Posner, Boies, Eichelman, & Taylor, 1969); (6) picture–word comparison studies (e.g., Paivio & Begg, 1974); and (7) studies of mental comparison (e.g., Paivio, Chapter 7, this book). The conclusion that emerges from this set of studies is that nonverbal materials are processed differently than verbal materials. The question is whether this conclusion is sufficient to support dual-coding models and all their assumptions (in particular, those claiming that the systems are specialized for storing information and that they differ in the nature of their representational units). We think not. To be sure, an indication that nonverbal materials are processed differently than verbal materials is *consistent* with dual-coding theory, but it is also consistent with a number of other theories including the Lingua Mentis Theory. To see why this is so, let us trace the implications of each set of findings in support of dual-coding theory:

1. *Neurophysiological evidence suggests that verbal and nonverbal abilities are localized in different hemispheres.* It is difficult to know what to make of this evidence because what is localized may merely be the processes for operating on verbal or nonverbal materials. That is, finding that the left hemisphere deals principally with verbal material and the right hemisphere with spatial material tells us no more than this. It does not allow us to decide

whether the specialization is in the operations or the underlying representations. Thus, one need not resort to the postulation of distinct (modality-specific) representational systems to account for this kind of evidence. A view such as Lingua Mentis Theory that assumes a single underlying representational system, which may be operated on in different ways, would suffice equally well.

2. *Studies demonstrate the existence of modality-specific interference.* Again, these studies are inconclusive as to the form in which information is stored. The results of these studies can be explained by the fact that different operations are involved in processing verbal and nonverbal materials. Modality-specific interference stems from the fact that the same set of operations are required for performing two different verbal (or nonverbal) tasks. When, on the other hand, a verbal task is paired with a nonverbal task, the interference between the two tasks is apt to be much less because the operations needed to perform each task are chosen, for the most part, from different sets. For example, subjects in Brooks' (1968) experiment found it very difficult to simultaneously image a block letter and point to various spatial locations designating appropriate responses to questions about the letter. It is likely that this difficulty arose because there is a great deal of overlap between the operations used in imaging and those required for determining spatial locations. This is evident from the fact that subjects had little difficulty in employing the pointing task in conjunction with a simultaneous verbal task.

3. *Verbal and nonverbal abilities are factorially independent.* Someone who has verbal ability is one who has an aptitude for manipulating verbal materials. Similarly someone who has imagery ability is one skilled in manipulating visual materials. The very nature of this activity suggests that what is involved in each instance is a facility for applying an appropriate set of operations to solve a particular problem. We suggest that differences in verbal and nonverbal abilities reflect nothing more than the different degrees to which individuals can apply operations to verbal and nonverbal materials.

4. *Studies of mental rotation are frequently cited as evidence that some information must be stored as images.* In defense of this position, its supporters (e.g., Kosslyn & Pomerantz, 1977; Paivio, 1976) point to the relationship that exists between the degree to which the figure must be rotated and the subject's decision times. The further the figure must be rotated, the longer are the subject's decision times. Supporters of the dual-coding position attribute this result to the fact that the image is stored in a cannonical orientation and that matches to the test stimulus are made only when the mental image is rotated to correspond to the orientation of the test stimulus. According to Kosslyn and Pomerantz (1977), the mental rotation process is belived to "mimic the sorts of gradual transformations that occur when one physically manipulates objects [p. 68]."

It is indeed possible that in order to solve a mental rotation problem one might gradually transform the orientation of a mental image of an object so as to correspond to that of the test stimulus. However, the fact that subjects may employ such a strategy does not entail that they have stored information about the object as an *image*. In fact, Shepard (1978) himself is noncommital as to whether the underlying stored representation is imaginal or propositional. We would argue that the image is produced by applying certain operations to information stored in a propositional format.[5]

5. *Reaction time studies requiring identity matches provide support for dual-code models.* According to Paivio (1978), these studies "provide strong evidence for at least two kinds of representations: one containing information corresponding rather directly to visual-spatial patterns, and the other, to language [p. 386]." This statement is certainly correct. The work of Posner and his colleagues (and in particular, Posner, Boies, Eichelman, & Taylor, 1969) suggests that given sufficient time and information, subjects will *generate* the appropriate perceptual information to provide an identity match to a subsequent visual stimulus. The key here, of course, is the word "generate." By applying the appropriate set of operations to the information they receive, subjects are able to create a suitable visual image to match to the test stimulus. Note that in order to explain Posner's findings, there is no need to resort to an account that says we store a visual image of the letter. In fact, the nature of the results would seem to dictate otherwise, because rapid matches to test stimuli occur only when subjects are given sufficient time between the prime and the test item. Presumably, the length of the interval reflects the time necessary for subjects to generate visual images from information stored in a propositional format. Although we recognize that one could also argue that the interval is actually indicative of the time necessary to call up a stored visual image, these reaction time studies do not prove that one stores visual images.

6. *Picture–word comparison studies are considered to be another basis of support for the dual-coding model.* These studies bear a great similarity to those discussed previously. Although there are many variants, the basic task consists of trying to match one stimulus to another. Often, the two items are presented successively (e.g., Pavio & Begg, 1974), and the subject must search through an array of targets to locate the matching stimulus. The two items that subjects are required to match may be pictures, words, or a combination

---

[5]It is worth noting at this point that we are not denying that an image is a type of mental representation. We believe that an image constitutes a means of representing information that we have stored in an underlying propositional format. Similarly, sentences are a means of representing such information. However, the representations engendered when we form images or sentences are temporary, serve a particular purpose at the time, and do not constitute the form in which we represent stored information.

of both types of materials. Although it has frequently been observed that matches to pictures are faster than matches to words (e.g., Paivio & Begg, 1974 (Exps. I & II); Paivio, 1975), this is not always the case (e.g., Paivio & Begg, 1974 (Exp. III)). In fact, there appears to be considerable flexibility with respect to the kind of representation subjects employ in these tasks. This is evident from the performance of some of Rosch's (1975) subjects. Rosch extended the comparison paradigm by preceding the comparison stimuli (presented simultaneously) with a priming stimulus. Sometimes the priming stimulus was related to the comparison pair and sometimes it was not. Her work shows that in some instances a very abstract representation of the meaning of a particular cognitive category can serve to facilitate the comparison process. For example, priming with the word "fruit" speeds the judgment that "apple" and "banana" are members of the same category. Moreover, she also demonstrated that given a sufficient interval between the prime and the comparison pair, subjects were able to generate representations that facilitate performance on either picture or word comparison pairs.

It seems clear from these studies that subjects may employ different kinds of representations in order to succeed on the comparison task. Just what kind of representation subjects will employ is dictated by a number of factors including the amount of time available and expectations about the mode (verbal or visual) in which the comparison stimuli are likely to appear. Again, the fact that benefits accrue to the prime only when subjects are given sufficient time before the onset of the comparison pair suggests that the representations subjects employ are the result of applying certain operations to the information at hand. That subjects are able to strategically deploy such representations does not require that these representations already be stored by the subject. Rather, such modality-specific representations may be generated on the spot for use in a particular task.

7. *Studies of mental comparison are also cited by Paivio (1978) as a source of evidence for the dual-coding position.* The task here requires subjects to compare two objects along some experimenter-defined dimension. The time necessary to make such comparisons has been shown to vary inversely with the degree to separation of the items along the dimension (i.e., as the amount of separation increases, the decision time decreases). This phenomenon is referred to as the *symbolic distance effect* (Moyer & Bayer, 1976). This effect has been demonstrated for judgments over an incredibly wide variety of psychological dimensions including numerical magnitudes (Moyer & Landauer, 1967), size (Moyer, 1973), brightness (Paivio, 1978), value (Friedman, 1978; Paivio, 1978), animal intelligence (Banks & Flora, 1977), time (Holyoak & Walker, 1976) and many more. The fact that the symbolic distance effect occurs for such a variety of judgments suggests tht it is a byproduct of the mental comparison process. The question is what, if anything, do such studies have to say about the nature of mental representation?

Given the diversity of dimensions for which the symbolic distance effect is observed, it seems more parsimonious to treat it as a consequence of the operations employed during the comparison process. In some instances (e.g., size comparisons) one may construct an imagelike representation to facilitate comparisons. But under other circumstances (e.g., decisions regarding animal intelligence) the representations employed may not be imagelike. Again, there is no necessity for any of the information to be stored as images. Instead, it is likely that the diversity of information one has about an object is stored in an abstract format. In fact, finding distance effects across a wide range of concrete and highly abstract domains is just the kind of result expected by Lingua Mentis Theory. That is, there appears to be a particular structure (or rule-ordered list) by which magnitudes are coded. For an interesting experimental analysis along these lines, see Friedman, 1978.

Paivio (Chapter 7, this volume) has also argued that another aspect of the results of mental comparison studies supports the dual-coding model. He points to the fact that decision times for concrete objects varying along perceptual dimensions (e.g., size) are faster when subjects are presented with pictures, rather than names, of objects. Conversely, comparisons involving linguistic attributes are made more swiftly when words, as opposed to pictures are presented. Paivio believes that these results support the dual-coding model because in the former case pictures are assumed to have more direct access than words to the representations on which the comparisons are based. Just the opposite is true for the latter case. Perhaps, such predictions do fall readily out of the model (although we see no strong a priori reasons that necessitate such assumptions). There are, however, several other instances in which picture–word differences are observed that are not easily explained by a dual-coding model. In particular, comparison times for pleasantness (Paivio, 1978), value (Paivio, 1978), and animal intelligence (Banks & Flora, 1977) have all been found to be faster with pictures than with words. It is difficult to imagine why seeing pictures of animals should help subjects make decisions about their relative intelligence. In fact, in some cases such information might even be misleading, e.g., bears versus whales. Moreover, for most of us, information about the relative intelligence of animals probably comes through reading rather than direct experience. In order to account for these results, Paivio is forced to make a number of post hoc assumptions such as the following: "The properties are abstract by definition, but they belong to concrete objects. To the extent that this is true, subjects in a comparison task would have to access the memory representations of the things and their associated properties before they can make the required judgment. Words and pictures alike simply provide access to those representations, but pictures do so more directly, hence the faster comparison times [p. 142, this volume]." Further stretching of the model is necessary in order to explain the occurrence of the symbolic distance effect for these dimensions. Thus, he suggests that pleasantness "might be based on interoceptive and motor-response systems that mediate affective reactions." Even if Paivio were correct in this last assumption, it would not entail that the representation to which pleasantness becomes attached must be an image. Finally, an even more troublesome problem for the dual-coding model is the finding that at least two perceptually based dimensions, brightness and hue, appear to be more (brightness) or equally (hue) accessible by words than by pictures. With all the model's emphasis on the usefulness of the imagery system for dealing with perceptual properties, one would have expected the opposite result for such perceptual features of concrete objects. In order to handle this kind of result, Paivio is forced to assume that color is stored as an attribute in a separate memory system and is equally accessible from line drawings and names. But the decision to treat color this way, and not to treat other physical attributes such as size in a similar fashion, is determined only by consideration of the pattern of results of the experiments. It has no strong independent motivation.

In summary, then, we do not think that any of the seven areas of research reviewed here provide persuasive evidence for the claim that there are independent systems for permanently storing information and that these systems differ in the nature of their representational units. We have tried to show how in each instance the facts can be accounted for by a model that postulates a single underlying abstract representational system for storage together with a set of operations that allow for the generation of temporary structures (representations). In the next section, we elaborate on some of the inconsistencies and inadequacies of dual-coding models, which make them unsatisfactory in accounting for the nature of representation.

CAN A DUAL-CODING MODEL
NOT BE PROPOSITIONAL?

In a recent paper, John Anderson (1978) compared a dual-coding model to a propositional model. He attempted to demonstrate that, owing to the unspecified nature of the processes attached to representations, both models could be made to account for exactly the same set of experimental results. The conclusion Anderson draws from this observation is that it may not be possible to establish whether an internal representation is pictorial or propositional. Given Anderson's claims for the equivalence of the two types of representational systems, it is worth examining the nature of the dual-coding model that he employs.

First of all, he is aware that he must demonstrate that the dual-coding model he proposes is a true alternative to a propositional model. Thus

Anderson (1978) notes: "It is important that the theory I propose be faithful to the Paivio position. If it is, it definitely should be clear that I have not bolstered the power of a picture theory by sneaking in propositions. [p. 252]." Accordingly, he puts forth a model with visual and verbal representations. The visual representations are equated with pictures and the verbal ones with word strings. He then goes on to present an example of a representation in this system. His example of a chessboard in an end-game position incorporates both picture fragments and interpretive statements like the following "knight attacks king," "contains some white pawns," "black can mate," and so on. That such interpretations of pictorial representations are necessary is demonstrated by the fact that pictures have no truth value without an accompanying interpretation. A picture or an image of a person or thing conveys information about many properties simultaneously. Thus, a picture of Oliver Hardy could be used to express a number of different propositions about him such as, "This man is fat," "This man is a comedian," "This man has a mustache," "This man has dark hair," "This man is wearing a derby," "This is a man," and so on. *Without some further interpretation of the picture, we have no way of knowing which of these attributes is being ascribed to the individual depicted.*

Thus, equipped with this type of representation containing both visual and verbal elements, Anderson attempts to show how it is immune from the criticisms frequently directed at dual-coding theories. The problem with his approach here is that he has, in fact, bolstered his dual-coding model by "sneaking in propositions." Anderson seems to think that he has avoided this criticism by dealing with word strings. "What is important is that they [the word strings] not be interpreted as abstract propositions. I think that it is a correct reading both of Paivio's exposition of this theory and of the attacks on it by the propositional camp that nothing in his theory can be considered abstract propositional [p. 252]."[6] Although it is true that there is a distinction between word strings and propositions, word strings, if they are at all meaningful, must express propositions. In general, when propositions, as opposed to word strings or sentences, are spoken of, it is because the

---

[6]We agree with Anderson's reading of Paivio and his critics. There is nothing in Paivio's original analyses of the verbal component that could be directly construed as "abstract propositional." In his research, Paivio has concentrated on specifying functional distinctions between the verbal and imaginal systems. Although this has been a fruitful and productive line of inquiry, this has led him to put aside systemtic consideration of the interpretive mechanisms that must underlie the verbal component of the dual-coding theory. As Kieras (1978) has recently pointed out, the theory has little more to rely on in the way of an interpretive mechanism than to assert that visual and verbal codes are activated. Our view is that consideration of what underlies the interpretation of the verbal component can no longer be put aside. When such consideration is undertaken, the inevitable conclusion is that the verbal component must have a propositional base.

particular phonetic and syntactic characteristics of the sentences that express the propositions are irrelevant. The string "Knight attacks King" must be equivalent to "The King is attacked by the Knight" in Anderson's dual-coding system. Each of these strings serves equally well in the task and does so because the two express the same proposition.

Propositions are very much identified with the sense of sentences. Katz (1972) is quite clear on this point:

> Thus from a theoretical viewpoint, we ought not to suppose that there are two distinct sorts of entities: in virtually all essential respects, talk about propositions and talk about senses of sentences are interchangeable except for perspective. The following considerations make this more plausible. Sentences that do not have a sense–semantically anomalous sentences—cannot be said to express a proposition; sentences that have *n* distinct senses will be said to express *n* distinct propositions; and pairs of sentences that share a sense will be said to express the same proposition [p. 122].

The point is that in order for Anderson's word strings to be interpreted meaningfully at all, they must express a proposition (i.e., have a sense or meaning). Uninterpreted word strings are just acoustic or visual patterns bearing no more information to its user than a string of words in foreign language or group of nonsense syllables. Thus, in order to provide the necessary interpretation for the pictorial elements in his representations that his account requires, Anderson must employ meaningful word strings (and therefore propositions).

Anderson argued that if one insisted upon a propositional component to his dual-coding representations, then "one would be conceding that there is no difference between dual-code and propositional models." This is not quite correct. Although the amount of overlap between the two models is enhanced by the fact that both are seen to involve storage of information in the form of propositions, the dual-coding model still includes an additional and different type of storage in the form of images. The choice between the two models is now reduced to a choice between a propositional model without stored images and one with stored images. Considerations of parsimony dictate that a propositional model without stored images is the more desirable one. In order to justify the selection of the alternative model with its two different types of storage, one would have to demonstrate that the inclusion of imaginal coding makes it possible for the dual-coding model to account for a greater set of facts than a purely propositional model. As we noted in the previous section, such is not the case. The facts do not dictate that information is stored as images; they only require that images can be generated from stored information. For this purpose, one need only assume a single form of permanent information storage (propositional), together with a set of operations that permit the construction of a temporary imaginal representation.[7]

In summary, then, it seems certain that dual-coding models, such as the one proposed by Anderson, do require a propositional component. For only with such a component is it possible to provide an interpretation for imaginal representations. Consequently, one might view dual-coding models as both propositional and imaginal. Although empirical evidence to distinguish this model from a purely propositional model may be difficult to adduce, parsimony in the form of a single underlying code (vs. multiple codes) would seem to favor the latter.

ON SPECIFYING THE NATURE OF THE LINGUA MENTIS

Having argued for the necessity of a representational system such as the Lingua Mentis, we now turn our attention to questions concerning its structure and its role in thought. Ideally, we would like to be able to provide a characterization of the basic elements and operations of such a system. Unfortunately, in many instances, there is not sufficient information available to allow for a definitive statement as to which of a number of alternative conceptualizations provides the correct description. Thus, often the best we can do is to point out some of the issues that must be resolved before an understanding of the Lingua Mentis can be achieved. In what follows, then, we consider three aspects of the Lingua Mentis in some detail. Specifically, we explore: (1) the nature of its basic elemental units; (2) the types and functions of its operations; and (3) its role in cognitive development.

The Nature of the Units

Our starting point for the Lingua Mentis is that it is a system of propositional representations. The propositions themselves are composed of well-formed strings of elements. Our view is that the elements correspond to the set of human concepts. Different orderings of these concepts, then, result in different propositional representations.

To simply say that the basic elements organized into propositional representations are concepts is not terribly revealing unless we can say

---

[7]It bears repeating that we are not denying the existence of imagery or the intrinsic interest of studying the subsystem responsible for our experience of imagery. Rather, our position is that information is ultimately encoded and stored in a more abstract format, i.e., the Lingua Mentis.

something further about what a concept is. This problem has been a vexing one for psychologists and philosophers throughout the ages. However, it is fairly safe to say that the viewpoint that has most strongly influenced psychologists on this matter is the one advanced by Locke and the British Associationists. What Locke proposed was a kind of mental chemistry whereby a small set of primitive concepts (simple ideas) plus some sort of constructive process combine to yield the full repetoire of adult concepts. The primitive concepts essentially formed the innate conceptual endowment for man. These primitive concepts were considered to have a perceptual basis and to be the direct result of the way in which the sensory systems are structured. Thus, environmental stimulation impinging on our sensory systems auto- matically gives rise to certain simple ideas or concepts such as color, sound, heat, and so on. In order to account for the fact that the adult conceptual structure is much richer than such simple ideas, Locke proposed that simple ideas could be combined so as to produce a compound concept. Thus, repeated experience with a particular combination of simple ideas leads to the formation of a compound concept such as table. A point to recognize here is that compound concepts are deemed to be completely decomposable into the primitive elements, simple ideas.

Locke's notion that the set of adult concepts might be reduced to a small set of primitive concepts grounded in perception has been the starting point for most psychological explorations of concepts (although see Rosch, Mervis, Gray, Johnson, & Boyes-Braem, 1976). One can certainly view the literature on "concept formation" in this light. Study after study is based on the premise that the way in which compound concepts are formed is by building them through the association of simple perceptually based concepts. Call the primitive units "features," "attributes," "markers," or whatever you like, the notion that compound concepts are constructed from (and decomposable into) a set of simpler elements has been pervasive in psychology.

The major obstacle for British Associationism was how to deal with the notion of abstract concepts. Because the primitive elements were claimed to have a perceptual basis, abstract concepts could only be accounted for by reducing them to perceptual properties. This is almost certainly a futile task as anyone who has tried to decompose concepts such as "hope," "justice," or "but" into perceptual properties can readily testify.

One way to avoid problems with abstract concepts would be to allow for simple ideas that do not have a basis in perception but instead are nonperceptual. Of course, such a solution was hardly open to the Associa- tionists, given their conviction that human conceptual structure was ulti- mately reducible to perceptual elements. Rather, the view that some abstract concepts might be innately given is much more in line with the position taken by Rationalists such as Kant. Consequently, it is perhaps not surprising that the most systematic attempt to formulate a version of mental chemistry in our own times, Katzian semantics, is couched within a rationalist framework.

In 1963, Jerrold Katz and Jerry Fodor published an article that greatly influenced the thinking of psychologists and linguists alike with respect to the way in which meanings of words are represented. Although Katz and Fodor have long since parted company (see Fodor, Fodor, & Garrett, 1975; Katz, 1977), the ideas expressed in their early paper laid the groundwork for much of Katz's current theory (Katz, 1972, 1977). Of particular importance is the notion that the meanings of words are represented as sets of semantic markers and distinguishers. In essence, the theory argued for the decomposition of a word's meaning into its atomic concepts. However, unlike the Associationist accounts, the markers in Katz and Fodor's theory could designate abstract, nonperceptual concepts as well as perceptual ones. Moreover, another way in which Katz's mental chemistry differs from the Associationist one is in terms of the way in which the simple concepts are combined to form compound ones. Whereas, according to the Associationist account, compound concepts were merely collections of simple concepts having no particular organization, Katzian semantic markers are internally structured such that constraints exist on the possible combinations of simple concepts.[8] Thus, consider the well-worn example of the meaning of the word "good" in an expression such as "a good knife." It seems clear that "good" does not modify all of the attributes of "knife" but only a particular one, viz. its usefulness in cutting. If a knife cuts well, one could, without contradiction, refer to it as "a good knife' even if its handle were chipped or its blade tarnished. The point is that the meaning of "knife" is structured in such a way that "good" applies only to part of its structure, i.e., its effectiveness as a cutting instrument. The only way to alter which portion of the structure that "good" applies to is by introducing an external qualifier, as in the case of "a good knife for throwing," or "a good knife to reflect light with," and so on.[9]

Although Katz restricts himself to the linguistic domain, his analysis of word meaning has widespread ramifications for the study of human conceptual structure. If Katz is correct, then both abstract and perceptually based elements must be included in the set of primitive concepts. Moreover,

---

[8]Of course, we are referring to the markers proposed in the later versions of the theory such as Katz (1972) rather than the original Katz and Fodor (1963) model, which did employ unstructured sets of markers.

[9]To attempt a further explication of the kind of structure present in Katz's concepts would require a description of many of the details of his theory. Because this would take us far afield of the present topic, we refer the reader directly to the source (Katz, 1972) or to the excellent review of that book by Savin (1973).

differences in the essential nature of the primitives themselves would serve to restrict the way in which they could be combined to yield higher order concepts (thus presumably blocking the derivation of such terms as "nonretachelor," "meloncat," or "grue").[10] These aspects of Katz's analysis fit well with our own thinking about the nature of the elements employed in the Lingua Mentis. On the other hand, we have some reservations about some of the other claims he makes. Specifically, we wonder if the set of primitive concepts is appreciably smaller than the number of words in a given natural language and whether all concepts are potentially expressible in language.

With respect to the first issue, it is very difficult to provide a convincing lexical decomposition for many words in English.[11] One often cited example (J. D. Fodor, 1977; Jackendoff, 1977) is the unsuccessful decomposition of color terms such as "red." If one follows a Katzian analysis, then the discovery that something is red always entails its being colored, requiring us to say that the concept of being colored is part of the concept of being red. The difficulty with this is that "red" means more than "colored," and it does not seem to be possible to specify what the other component concept or concepts might be. As Janet Fodor (1977) observes, "For this component to be independent of the coloredness component, it must consist of the concept of redness–but–not –necessarily–coloredness. But there surely is no such concept (or even percept) [p. 150]." Yet without such a component, we have no way of distinguishing "red" from "green," or any other color term.

Were color terms the only problem for decomposition, then perhaps one might pass them off as an anomaly. However, there is a whole host of terms that provide similar sorts of difficulties, namely the so-called "natural kind" terms. The problem with natural kind terms is that they do not lend themselves to a decomposition in terms of essential properties. Take "lemons," for example. What can one say about the essential properties of a lemon? Virtually any of its properties (color, shape, size, odor, taste, etc.) could be changed, and yet it would still be a lemon by virtue of its biological essence. In short, words like "lemon," "tiger," "gold," etc., do not appear to be

---

[10]We defined "nonretachelor" earlier (see Footnote 4). According to Osherson (1978): "An object counts as a meloncat just in case it is a watermelon about to be squashed by a giant pussycat, or a pussycat about to be squashed by a giant watermelon [p. 264].""Grue," of course, is Goodman's (1965) term for "all things examined before [time] t just in case they are green but to other things [i.e., ones examined after time t] just in case they are blue [p. 74]."

[11]In fact, during his colloquium here, Fodor observed that only two words could be so defined—"bachelor" and "kill"—and that the analysis of the latter is incorrect. However, this seems a bit extreme as a number of other words would seem to lend themselves to decomposition, such as "spinster," "lawyer," "wife," and so on. Nevertheless, the general point that good decompositions are hard to find seems well taken.

decomposable into a set of simpler concepts.[12] (For further discussion of this issue see Katz, 1975; Putnam, 1975).

In view of the difficulties attendant in lexical decomposition,[13] some (e.g., Fodor, Fodor, & Garrett, 1975; Jackendoff, 1977) have called for an end to the attempts to reduce all concepts to a finite set of primitives. Instead, one would assume that almost all concepts were irreducible. The number of such simple concepts would then be almost as great as the number of words in any natural language, and perhaps even greater if we allow for the possibility that not all concepts are expressible in language. Were we to adopt this position with respect to the Lingua Mentis, it would simply mean that the number of primitive elements is extremly large. (As we understand it, this is basically the position taken by Fodor, 1975.)

What consequences follow from an abandonment of lexical decomposition? One of the attractions of the earlier approach was that by breaking a word down into its semantic components, it was possible to provide an account for a whole host of phenomena related to word meanings. For instance, reference to the lexical decomposition of the words "king" and "monarch" allows us to predict that the statement "Monarchs are generous," if true, entail that "Kings are generous." Moreover, certain aspects of psychological processing of words appear to be explainable by recourse to their underlying semantic features. Thus, highly associated items on word association tests often share many semantic features. Similarly, certain kinds of speech errors involve the intrusion of items with similar semantic components. Therefore, if we reject the notion of decomposition, then we must find a new way to account for these phenomena. Several suggestions have been offered as to how some of these facts might be accommodated. Fodor, Fodor, and Garrett (1975) propose that entailment relations (including synonymy) might be handled by the use of meaning postulates. These are

[12]Katz (1975) does offer a defense of his position by saying that the necessary semantic markers underlying a word's definition are those necessary to make successful "predictions about the semantic properties and relations of sentences." The problem with this defense is that it makes his theory less a general account of human conceptual structure and more an abstract description of the way in which meaning is structured in a particular langauge (one which need not bear any direct relation to psychological reality).

[13]Experimental evidence employing reaction time measures also suggests that decomposition does not occur during sentence comprehension (Fodor, Fodor, & Garrett, 1975; Kintsch, 1974). However, Katz (1977) has argued, quite persuasively we think, that such tests tap linguistic performance and may not have any direct bearing on linguisitic competence. One could hypothesize that although words are initially mastered by combining their appropriate semantic components, the fluent speaker is able to shortcut the decomposition process by appropriate heuristic devices. Our argument here is similar to the one advanced by Bever (1970a, 1970b) with respect to syntactic processing.

entailment relation that exists between "red" and "colored," one could include a meaning postulate of the form (Red) → (Colored). One difficulty with this solution is that Fodor et al. never make clear what the origins of these postulates are, i.e., whether they are part of innate endowment or if they arise as a result of experience. Judging by Fodor's views on related matters (see Fodor, 1975), we suspect that it must be the former.[14]

The entailment relation is but one of the kinds of semantic relations that exist between words, so any nondecompositional approach must account for the other kinds of relations as well. One suggestion as to how other important relationships that exist between concepts might be accommodated is via the notion of semantic fields (e.g., Jackendoff, 1977; Miller, 1978; Miller & Johnson-Laird, 1976). Proponents of this approach all agree that the notion of semantic field is difficult to define. The basis most often chosen for identifying semantic fields is people's intuitive judgments about the similarity of two words (Miller, 1978): "The greater the judged similarity of meaning, the smaller is the smallest semantic field that contains them both [p. 94]." There are certain kinds of concepts which appear to provide focal points for the organization of semantic fields (e.g., color, motion, possession, etc.). Different concepts, which fall into one of these groupings, are often judged by subjects to be similar in meaning. On the other hand, there are other kinds of concepts that appear to cut across different semantic fields (e.g., space, time, quantity, cause, etc.). Different concepts falling under one of these kinds of headings are not necessarily judged to be similar in meaning—e.g., causative verbs such as *give* ("cause to have") and *kill* ("cause to die") fall under the heading of "cause" but are not intuitively similar in their meaning. The function of this latter type of conceptual organization is assumed to be in providing internal structure for the semantic fields (Miller, 1978).

At this point it is impossible to determine whether semantic fields can provide a viable alternative to decomposition. Details are somewhat sketchy and it remains to be seen if semantic field theory can offer a noncircular account of why people judge two words to be similar in meaning (not simply because they occur in the same field). One would also like to see an explanation as to what factors (innate or experiential) determine the organization of a field.

We suggest that it might be possible to strike some sort of middle ground between an approach that tries to decompose all concepts into primitive

---

[14]A slightly different view of the entailment problem, although one in much the same vein, has been expressed by Jackendoff (1977). The starting point for his analysis is the relationship of hyponymy, which he defines as follows: "If X is a hyponym of Y, every instance of X is also an instance of Y." Commenting further he notes. "The statement 'X is a hyponym of Y' can be taken to mean that it is impossible to determine whether X truly represents a given percept without doing all the mental computation that would be required to determine whether Y truly represents that percept as well. Hyponymy can thus be thought of as a sort of procedural entailment [p. 63]."

elements and one that assumes no decomposition whatsoever. Perhaps only some concepts are decomposable and others are not. An analysis along these lines has been suggested by Schwartz (1977). He draws a distinction between *natural kind* terms, like "lemons," "cats," "water," and what he calls *nominal kind* terms, such as "bachelor," "lawyer," and "sloop." Nominal kinds do not share any particular type of biological or atomic essence. Rather, nominal kind terms are used to group things satisfying a particular description we have in mind. In principle it should be possible to convey this description as a set of primitive conceptual elements, as Katz (1972) has done for "bachelor." Whether this approach will lead to an ultimate resolution of the decomposition issue is not possible to say just yet, but it may be a fruitful direciton to pursue.

The way in which the decomposition issue is resolved will certainly have a bearing on the way in which we think about the Lingua Mentis. One immediate effect will be in terms of the numbers of primitive elements—a reasonably small set or an enormously large one. An additional consequence would relate to the kinds of operations that must be assumed, particularly with respect to the interface between the Lingua Mentis and natural language. Simple mapping operations between conceptual units in the Lingua Mentis and words in natural languages might suffice if decomposition does not occur. More complicated operations might be needed if decomposition does occur in order to account for the relationships that would exist between different component elements. Regardless of the way in which the decomposition issue is decided, the conceptual units of the Lingua Mentis must be internally structured so that "impossible" concepts like "nonretachelor" are excluded from the system. Furthermore, the Lingua Mentis must include both perceptual and nonperceptual elements.

One additional point to consider here is what Katz (1972) has called "effability." It is his contention that "each human thought is expressible by some sentence of any natural language." In order for this to be the case, one would have to allow for a potential mapping from any conceptual unit in the Lingua Mentis to some word in natural language. Without knowing what all of the conceptual elements are, it is impossible to decide this matter. It does seem to us that one might have concepts that are inexpressible in language, such as those that might be expressed in either the visual or musical arts. One way in which this could occur is if there were constraints operating on the mapping rules for the Lingua Mentis to a particular sensory modality. Such constraints might take the form of only allowing concepts having a certain kind of internal structure to be mapped into the particular modality. This view seems at least as plausible as Katz's.

Finally, we need to consider the issue of whether everyone has the same concepts. If primitive concepts are innate, then everyone should possess the same set of primitive concepts. However, individuals may differ in terms of the kinds of propositional structures they may form from these primitives.

Confusion often arises at this point, because the term "concept" is frequently used to cover all attendant knowledge one has about a particular object. Consider, for example, the situation that exists when you say that your concept of oysters differs from mine. Do the concepts themselves really differ, or is there a difference in the kind and amount of additional information that we have about oysters? Surely it must be the latter or else we would not be able to determine whether we were both talking about the same thing. It seems likely that we have a basic shared concept of oysters but that we also build up an extensive personalized representation of them as well. Included in this representation may be facts about the marine existence of the oyster, its relation to other types of shellfish, knowledge of the best methods of digging for oysters, where to find them, how to open them, the best way to prepare them for eating, and certain prejudices about oysters. In addition, one probably has also stored some information regarding personal experiences with oysters. It is clear that one may have available a lot of information about oysters that is not necessary for understanding what an oyster is. Thus, it may be more appropriate to restrict the term concept to the sense of a primitive element, to the aspect that allows one to determine some extension in the real world (e.g., which objects are oysters and which are not).

Operations in the Lingua Mentis

Among those who have argued for the necessity of an underlying tacit knowledge system like the Lingua Mentis, there appears to be agreement on two issues. First, that the proposed system must have a representational capacity rich enough to encompass all possible human concepts. Second, that it must have associated with it a set of computational procedures that serve to construct, transform, or otherwise modify mental representations. The second issue is addressed in this section.

Although nearly everyone might agree on the necessity for computational operations, unfortunately no one has been able to say anything very precisely about the character of these operations. Even Fodor (1975), who has surely made one of the most thorough attempts to elucidate the nature of what we call the Lingua Mentis, is stymied when it comes to describing these computational procedures. The best he seems to be able to manage is the following:

> The intended claim is that the sequence of events that causally determines the mental state of an organism will be describable as a sequence of steps in a derivation if it is describable in the vocabulary of psychology at all. More exactly: Mental states are relations between organisms and internal representations, and causally interrelated mental states succeed one another according to the computational principles which apply formally *to the representations* [p. 198].

Later, Fodor shows that he recognizes the importance of being able to clarify the nature of these operations when in discussing issues for a program of empirical research he lists such questions as, "What kinds of operations upon the formulae of that system can count as computational operations?" and "Which sequences of such formulae constitute 'derivations' in the sense required?".

The chief difficulty with specifying the nature of these operations is that they are necessarily of an abstract general nature and, therefore, are not directly observable. In order to discuss any one of the operations, we are forced to particularize (or in Bregman's, 1977, terms "instantiate") it by giving it a nonabstract representation in words or images. In so doing we may introduce distortions that are a reflection of properties of the mode of expression we have chosen and that are not necessarily part of the operation in the abstract.

Given that this dilemma exists, how might our investigation as to the nature of the operations in the Lingua Mentis be advanced? We have no certain answers here, all we can do is to make some suggestions as to particular lines of inquiry that may prove fruitful.

One direction of research that may yield information about the basic character of computational operations is to look for similarities in the way that we process information acquired via different perceptual modalities. The notion here is that although the structure of a particular modality system constrains the nature of its operations, we may nevertheless uncover instances of universal principles governing human information processing. One of the more interesting attempts to pursue this approach has been made by Bever (1970a, 1970b). He recognized that certain features of language processing may reflect general cognitive constraints rather than particular linguistic ones. Thus, in attempting to explain why doubly center-embedded sentences like "The dog the flea the man freed bit died" are difficult to process correctly, Bever observed that these sentences had analogs in the visual domain, viz. "impossible" figures. Both types of cases seemed to be manifestations of the same general principles that "a stimulus cannot be perceived in two incompatible ways at the same time." With respect to linguistic processing, this principle shows up in the form of a constraint to the effect that a noun phrase in a sentence cannot serve simultaneously as the subject and object of a particular verb. In the visual domain, the principle manifests itself as a stricture that the same segment may not simultaneously end one *kind* of figure and begin another *kind*. Just how successful we will be in uncovering other principles common to linguistic and perceptual processing remains to be seen (although for further suggestions along these lines, see Bever, 1974; Katz & Bever, 1976). Nevertheless, to the extent that we can specify such principles, we will gain some knowledge of the constraints that exist on mental operations.

Another domain in which we might hope to gain an insight as to the nature of the computational operations is that of logical reasoning abilities. The attempt to specify a set of operations underlying human reasoning has a long history in psychology dating back at least to the time of Boole (1854) and continuing today in the work of Braine (1978), Inhelder and Piaget (1958), Osherson (1974a, 1974b, 1975, 1976), Wason and Johnson-Laird (1972) among others. The attraction that the pursuit of general laws of reasoning has to the present concerns is obvious. Our conception that alterations in mental representations are the result of applications of computational operations finds its analog in the way in which logical proofs are derived by the application of successive logical operations. To the extent that we can uncover general laws of reasoning, we will be able to specify more clearly the nature of at least some of these operations that apply to mental representations.

One of the most systematic attempts to specify a set of logical operations underlying some aspect of human reasoning has been conducted by Osherson (1975). He endeavored to provide a psychological model that could account for logical judgments in certain kinds of deductive inference problems employing the expressions "and," "or," "not," and "if...then...". His model included a set of inference rules (operations) along with a set of instructions (the executive) that determined the application of the operations. What is interesting about his approach is that Osherson intended the derivations generated by the model to correspond directly to the mental steps involved in evaluating logical arguments. Thus, the inference rules chosen presumably reflect the operations that subjects utilize in reasoning about these problems. Separate tests of the model were conducted using arguments presented in either an abstract form (e.g., If there is a Z, then there is both a Q and an H) or with familiar content (e.g., Either the dog is asleep or Jane is washing the dishes). Support for the model was obtained in both instances, although the fit was better for abstract arguments. Thus, Osherson can claim a measure of psychological validity for his model. As a further test of the model's generality, he sought to determine whether it could account for judgments about class-inclusion arguments. Unfortunately, there was only a partial overlap between the set of derivations for these kinds of arguments and the earlier ones. Nevertheless, Osherson's work constitutes a reasonable starting point for further investigation of computational operations in the Lingua Mentis. It is certainly one kind of research endeavor that is likely to lead to insights about the operations.

Another line of research that may prove helpful in understanding the nature of the operations is focused on the ways in which representations are deployed in different task settings (e.g., Ozier, 1978). The idea that we may develop particular representations to deal with a class of situations is certainly not a new one. It has many names (e.g., schema, frame, setting, prototype, etc.) and many advocates (e.g., Bartlett, 1932; Goffman, 1974; Head, 1920;

Labov, 1973; Minsky, 1977; Neisser, 1976; Piaget, 1952; Rosch, 1978). For purposes of discussion, the term *schema* is used to refer to all of these notions. Schemas provide us with a means by which we can categorize our experiences. They are developed to take into account regularities that exist across a variety of related situations. By employing a schema to fill in the constancies that occur in a class of situations, one is presumably free to encode only those details deemed to be important on a particular occasion. Schemas can play an important role in explaining how one is able to cope with storage capacity limitations of the brain. Rather than assuming that it is necessary to encode all of the possible information available in a given situation, we need only assume that one stores a few particulars and uses generalized schemas to fill in the background elements. Thus, when one stores information about a particular room, only certain details peculiar to that room need be noted (e.g., the existence of a spiral staircase, a large crack in the ceiling, a parquet floor, etc.), other general properties could be filled in from a scheme (or schemas) that one has about rooms (e.g., that it has an entrance, a floor and a ceiling, four walls, and so on). This point is sometimes overlooked by critics who claim that an enormous number of propositions may be required to represent the information contained in an image. Indeed, one might gain this impression from looking only at the information required for representing a single instance but to do this is to ignore the fact that redundancies exist across a wide variety of situations.

Schemas, like concepts, are not arbitrary. The world is segmented in some ways but not in others. One would like to believe that research focusing on the way in which schemas are generated would reveal something about the nature of the operations in the Lingua Mentis. For instance, might we be able to discover a set of common principles concerning the organization of schemas? If so, then these principles might serve to constrain the types of operations possible in the Lingua Mentis. Regrettably, the only general principle that has emerged at this time is that of "functional utility." More specifically, the fundamental principle underlying the conceptual partitioning of the world is the functional utility of that partitioning for the organism. For example, functional utility dominates Gibson's (1977) theorizing about the way in which perceptual experience is partitioned. Optical information from surfaces, substances, and objects is said to "afford" the organism information about the use to which they may be put (in other words their functional utility). Thus, the information specifies that they may be "graspable," "walk-on-able," "sit-on-able," and so on. Similarly, it can be argued that functional utility underlies the categorical structures analyzed recently by Rosch (Rosch, Mervis, Gray, Johnson, & Boyes-Braem, 1976) who notes: "One purpose of categorization is to reduce the infinite differences among stimuli to behaviorally and cognitively usable proportions. It is to the organism's advantage not to differentiate one stimulus from another when that differentiation is irrelevant for the purposes at hand [p. 384]." In this context, Smith (1979) has suggested that an essential factor in the *development* of classification is the subjective purpose of the classification task. For mature classifiers in laboratory tasks, the purpose is to solve a problem and the useful relation in this context is a criterial property. For young children, however, the purpose is the construction of a category, and the useful relation is wholistic or "family" resemblance (in the sense put forth by Rosch & Mervis, 1976). To preview a conclusion in the following section, the developmentally young and the mature apply different "frames" to classification tasks and each has its own functional utility.

There may be certain heuristic advantages that accrue from viewing schematic structures from the perspective of functional utility. For example, such a view dictates that each species develop a conceptual partitioning reflecting functional utilities central to its survival. But more important, functional utility must be critical for the intelligent management of representations. It is presumably functional utility that determines in any given situation the mode of representation derived from the Lingua Mentis, e.g., whether imaginal or verbal constructs are chosen to deal with a particular problem.[15]

The Lingua Mentis and Cognitive Development

In discussing an underlying propositionally based system of representation like the Lingua Mentis, we have postulated the existence of both a set of primitive elements or concepts and a set of basic operations that are applied to them. One question that arises with respect to developmental concerns is whether there may be any changes or additions to either the set of concepts or the set of operations. It is more or less a direct consequence of our position that any such changes, if they occur at all, could only be the result of maturational factors. To see why this is so, first consider the issue as it applies to concepts and then to operations.

The problem with the notion that one might acquire new conceptual units, *not reducible to existing primitives,* is that no one has been able to specify a mechanism whereby such concepts are abstracted from our environment.[16] We believe that this criticism holds even for what has to be one of the most valiant attempts to deal with this problem, viz. the Hebbian cell assembly. Hebb's (1949, 1968) notion basically states that although any given interaction with an object may give rise to a diffuse pattern excitation over a large population of neurons, there will be a common core of interconnected

---

[15]Fodor (1975) also appears to be committed to this view when he acknowledges that "which representation is assigned is determined by calculations which rationally subserve the utilities of the organism [p. 173]."

[16]It should be clear that the view we are propounding here presents no difficulties for an approach along the lines of Katz (1972) because any higher order concepts could be represented in terms of primitives.

neurons that discharge in response to any experiences with that type of object. Repeated contacts with an object will cause this subpopulation of neurons to become activated as a unit or, in Hebb's terminology, a cell assembly. Concepts of varying orders of complexity are assumed to emerge from combinations of such cell-assembly structures. For example, one's abstract general concept of a triangle presumably arises from the cell-assembly structures that are common to all instances of triangles regardless of their particular features (e.g., shape, size, color, etc.).[17] The difficulty with this solution is in explaining how it comes to pass that a given object always excites a particular subpopulation of neurons. We see no solution other than to assume that the brain is prewired to permit the segmentation and classification of perceptual and conceptual phenomena in this manner.[18] Of course, this is tantamount to admitting that innate properties of brain structure determine whether or not any two experiences are classified as belonging to the same types. Such pre-existing structuring of information has to be a reflection of one's innate conceptual structure. In short, the proposed abstraction process amounts to a direct mapping of the world onto one's existing conceptual structure.

Although from a slightly different perspective, Fodor (1975), too, has pointed out the difficulty that exists for the view that we can acquire new concepts. His argument is essentially that the only model proposed for concept learning involves the projection and confirmation of hypotheses. Because testing a hypothesis requires that one first be able to represent it to oneself, there is a sense in which no new concept can be learned. Rather, one must choose which of several pre-existing concepts best fits the current situation. Thus, once again, concept learning is reduced to mapping from a situation in the world to a concept that one already possesses.[19]

---

[17]Hebb, Lambert, and Tucker (1971) even go so far as to suggest that a concept such as "nounness" arises from a higher order cell-assembly shared by all nouns.

[18]Certainly, the stand we have taken here, because of its nativist assumptions, is not one that would be endorsed by Hebb. He assumes that cell-assemblies representing perceptual and conceptual phenomena can be formed out of a largely unstructured neural network through repeated experience. Our view is that the complexity of perceptual experience requires that *meaningful* segmentation and classification must *precede* the development of such assemblies, and not *follow* them.

[19]To avoid confusion here we should note that Fodor is merely arguing against the possibility of learning new primitives. He is not necessarily arguing against the possibility of combining concepts into a higher order grouping like a sentence, or even a "chunk" in memory. In fact, he suggests that such higher order groupings may have real mnemonic utility.

Finally, it is worth noting that some evidence which might be brought to bear on the issue of whether decomposition to a small set of primitives occurs or not might come from studies of language acquisition. We suggested earlier (see Footnote 13) that adult speakers may be able to shortcut the decomposition process by use of appropriate heuristic devices. However, a language learner may not be able to avoid decomposition during the initial stages of experience with such a word. This might show up in terms of greater processing for words with complex derivations, thus supporting Katz's view.

The argument as to whether new operations, not directly derivable from preceding ones, can be added to the Lingua Mentis is similar in many respects to the previous one. We subscribe to the view that children do not differ from adults in the kinds of basic operations they possess but only in the extent of the domains to which they are able to apply the operations. Our view here is diametrically opposed to the stance taken by Piaget (1950; Inhelder & Piaget, 1958). Piaget has long held that the mental operations that direct the child's thought processes undergo marked changes during development. As Brainerd (1978) has noted: "The mental operation is where cognitive development is *going* in Piaget's view.... Operations are the great 'something' that older children and adults have but infants and younger children do not. [p. 96]." Moreover, Piaget suggests that children acquire different kinds of operations at different stages in their lives (in fact, the major stages of intellectual growth derive their names from the operations, i.e., concrete operational and formal operational).

There is good reason to challenge Piaget's view that children acquire different operations at various stages of cognitive development. First of all, as Fodor (1972) noted: "If the conceptualizations of children are radically different than adults, it is extremely difficult to imagine how children and adults could ever manage to understand one another [p. 87]." More important, there is a growing body of experimental evidence suggesting that children and adults do not differ in the nature of the operations they possess but rather in the range of situations to which the operations can be applied (e.g., Gelman, 1972; Osherson, 1975, 1976; Smith, 1979; Trabasso, Riley, & Wilson, 1975). Osherson's work, in particular, illustrates this point nicely. As we noted in the previous section, he (Osherson, 1975) devised a model to characterize the operations underlying the way in which adolescents (11th and 12th graders) solve deductive inference problems. Next (Osherson, 1976) he tested whether or not the model provided a valid description of the operations underlying 5th graders' solutions to these problems. His results suggested that the children and adolescents did indeed employ the same basic operations. Thus, Osherson's work calls into question Piaget's claim that there is a qualitative difference between the operations employed by children and adults.

Finally, even if there were evidence to support Piaget's contention, the problem of accounting for the way in which additional operations are acquired would still remain. Piaget's suggested mechanism, "equilibration" (roughly, developmental change occurs because one recognizes contradictory or discrepant elements between the present situation and one's conceptualization of it) has been criticized as being more of a description of the process of change rather than an explanation for it (e.g., Flavell, 1977; Fodor, 1975). Moreover, it is hard to imagine how new operations could be learned, because as noted earlier, learning requires being able to represent alternatives within some existing system of representation. Therefore, only two alternatives are left that can account for developmental changes—physiological maturational processes and new combinations of existing operations. In other words, the basic operations of the Lingua Mentis are innately determined.

In conclusion, then, we believe that neither the set of elemental concepts, nor the set of basic operations in the Lingua Mentis develop. Rather, the process of cognitive development consists of building up mental representations of the world. This is accomplished by devising a satisfactory map of the world in terms of operations and concepts that already exist in the Lingua Mentis.

SUMMARY

Earlier we posed the question, "What is Lingua Mentis and why is it necessary?" Our intent was to convince the reader that the Lingua Mentis is a necessary construct central to any theory of thought. We tried to accomplish this by outlining some of the advantages of this position and by considering it in relation to alternative ways of dealing with mental representation. In particular, we contrasted the Lingua Mentis with theories that postulate multiple modality-specific systems underlying mental representation. Our conclusion was that not only is a propositionally based system underlying mental representation (the Lingua Mentis) preferable, but also that a propositional base is presupposed by the alternative view. We then tried to provide something in the way of a preliminary description of the basic elements, structure, and operations of the Lingua Mentis and to speculate about its role in development. We hope that our characterization of the Lingua Mentis has served to persuade the reader of its value in understanding thought.

ACKNOWLEDGMENTS

Preparation of this chapter was aided by support received from the Natural Sciences and Engineering Research Council Canada (A-0282 and A-0142). We also wish to thank the following individuals for their critical comments on earlier versions of this manuscript: Ray Klein, Lynn Nadel, Marcia Ozier, and especially Linda B. Smith.

REFERENCES

Anderson, J. R. Arguments concerning representations for mental imagery. *Psychological Review,* 1978, *85,* 249–277.

Anderson, J. R., & Bower, G. H. *Human associative memory.* Washington, D. C.: V. H. Winston & Sons, 1973.

Atwood, G. An experimental study of visual imagination and memory. *Cognitive Psychology,* 1971, *2,* 290–299.

Banks, W. P., & Flora, J. Semantic and perceptual processes in symbolic comparisons. *Journal of Experimental Psychology: Human Perception and Performance,* 1977, *3,* 278–290.

Bartlett, F. C. *Remembering: A study in experimental and social psychology.* Cambridge: Cambridge University Press, 1932.

Bever, T. G. The cognitive basis of linguistic structures. In J. R. Hayes (Ed.), *Cognition and the development of language.* New York: Wiley, 1970. (a)

Bever, T. G. The influence of speech performance on linguistic structure. In G. B. Flores d'Arcais & J. M. Levelt (Eds.), *Advances in psycholinguistics.* Amsterdam: North-Holland, 1970. (b)

Bever, T. G. The ascent of the specious, or there's a lot we don't know about mirrors. In D. Cohen (Ed.), *Explaining linguistic phenomena.* Washington, D.C.: Hemisphere, 1974.

Bever, T. G. Some theoretical and empirical issues that arise if we insist on distinguishing language and thought. In *Annals of the New York Academy of Sciences, Vol. 263: Developmental Psycholinguistics and Communication Disorders,* 1975, 76–83.

Boole, G. *An investigation of the laws of thought.* London: Walton & Maberley, 1854.

Braine, M. D. S. On the relation between natural logic of reasoning and standard logic. *Psychological Review,* 1978, *85,* 1–21.

Brainerd, C. J. *Piaget's theory of intelligence.* Englewood Cliffs, N.J.: Prentice-Hall, 1978.

Bransford, J. D., & McCarrell, N. S. A sketch of a cognitive approach to comprehension. In W. Weimer & D. Palermo (Eds.), *Cognition and the symbolic processes.* Hillsdale, N.J.: Lawrence Erlbaum Associates, 1974.

Bregman, A. S. Perception and behavior as composition of ideals. *Cognitive Psychology,* 1977, *9,* 250–292.

Brooks, L. R. Spatial and verbal components of the act of recall. *Canadian Journal of Psychology,* 1968, *22,* 349–368.

Bruner, J. S., Olver, R. R., & Greenfield, P. M. *Studies in cognitive growth.* New York: Wiley, 1966.

Cooper, L. A., & Shepard R. N. Chronometric studies of the rotation of mental images. In W. G. Chase (Ed.), *Visual information processing.* New York: Academic Press, 1973.

Dale, P. S. *Language development: Structure and function* (2nd ed.). New York: Holt, Rinehart & Winston, 1976.

Flavell, J. H. *Cognitive development.* Englewood Cliffs, N.J.: Prentice-Hall, 1977.

Fodor, J. A. Some reflections on L. S. Vygotsky's "Thought and Language." *Cognition,* 1972, *1,* 83–96.

Fodor, J. A. *The language of thought.* New York: Crowell, 1975.

Fodor, J. D. *Semantics: Theories of meaning in generative grammar.* New York: Crowell, 1977.

Fodor, J. D., Fodor, J. A., & Garrett, M. F. The psychological unreality of semantic representations. *Linguistic Inquiry,* 1975, *6,* 515–531.

Franks, J. J. Toward understanding understanding. In W. Weimer & D. Palermo (Eds.), *Cognition and the symbolic process.* Hillsdale, N.J.: Lawrence Erlbaum Associates, 1974.

Friedman, A. Memorial comparisons without the "Mind's Eye." *Journal of Verbal Learning and Verbal Behavior,* 1978, *17,* 427–444.

Gelman, R. The nature and development of early number concepts. In H. W. Reese (Ed.), *Advances in child development and behavior* (Vol. 7). New York: Academic Press, 1972.

Gibson, J. J. The theory of affordances. In R. Shaw & J. Bransford (Eds.), *Perceiving, acting, and knowing.* Hillsdale, N.J.: Lawrence Erlbaum Associates, 1977.

Goffman, E. *Frame analysis: An essay on the organization of experience.* New York: Harper & Row, 1974.

Goodman, N. *Fact, fiction, and forecast* (2nd Edition). Indianapolis: Bobbs Merrill, 1965.

Head, H. *Studies in neurology*. Oxford: Oxford University Press, 1920.

Hebb, D. O. *The organization of behavior*. New York: Wiley, 1949.

Hebb, D. O. Concerning imagery. *Psychological Review*, 1968, *75*, 466–477.

Hebb, D. O., Lambert, W. E., & Tucker, G. R. Language, thought and experience. *Modern Language Journal*, 1971, *55*, 212–222.

Holyoak, K., & Walker, J. Subjective magnitude information in semantic orderings. *Journal of Verbal Learning and Verbal Behavior*, 1976, *15*, 287–300.

Inhelder, B., & Piaget, J. *The growth of logical thinking*. New York: Basic Books, 1958.

Jackendoff, R. Toward a cognitively viable semantics. In C. Rameh (Ed.), *Georgetown University Roundtable on Languages and Linguistics 1976*. Washington, D.C.: Georgetown University Press, 1977.

Katz, J. J. *Semantic theory*. New York: Harper, 1972.

Katz, J. J. Logic and language: An examination of recent criticisms of intensionalism. In K. Gunderson (Ed.), *Minnesota studies in the philosophy of science*. Minneapolis: University of Minnesota Press, 1975.

Katz, J. J. The real status of semantic representations. *Linguistic Inquiry*, 1977, *8*, 559–584.

Katz, J. J., & Bever, T. G. The fall and rise of empiricism. In T. G. Bever, J. J. Katz, & D. T. Langendoen (Eds.), *An integrated theory of linguistic ability*. New York: Crowell, 1976.

Katz, J. J., & Fodor, J. A. The structure of a semantic theory. *Language*, 1963, *39*, 170–210.

Kieras, D. Beyond pictures and words: Alternative information processing models for imagery effects in verbal memory. *Psychological Bulletin*, 1978, *85*, 532–554.

Kimura, D. The asymmetry of the human brain. *Scientific American*, 1973, *228*, 70–78.

Kintsch, W. *The representation of meaning in memory*. Hillsdale, N.J.: Lawrence Erlbaum Associates, 1974.

Kosslyn, S. M., & Pomerantz, J. R. Imagery, propositions, and the form of internal representations. *Cognitive Psychology*, 1977, *9*, 52–76.

Labov, W. The boundaries of words and their meanings. In C. -J. N. Bailey & R. W. Shuy (Eds.), *New ways in analyzing variation in English* (Vol. 1). Washington, D.C.: Georgetown University Press, 1973.

Miller, G. A. Semantic relations among words. In M. Halle, J. Bresnan, & G. A. Miller (Eds.), *Linguistic theory and psychological reality*. Cambridge, Mass,: M.I.T. Press, 1978.

Miller, G. A., & Johnson-Laird, P. N. *Language and perception*. Cambridge, Mass.: Harvard University Press, 1976.

Minsky, M. Frame-system theory. In P. N. Johnson & P. C. Wason (Eds.), *Thinking: Readings in cognitive science*. Cambridge: Cambridge University Press, 1977.

Moyer, R. S. Comparing objects in memory: Evidence suggesting an internal psychophysics. *Perception and Psychophysics*, 1973, *13*, 180–184.

Moyer, R. S., & Bayer, R. H. Mental comparison and the symbolic distance effect. *Cognitive Psychology*, 1976, *8*, 228–246.

Moyer, R. S., & Landauer, T. K. The time required for judgments of numerical inequality. *Nature*, 1967, *215*, 1519–1520.

Neisser, U. *Cognition and reality*. San Francisco: Freeman, 1976.

Norman, D. A., & Rumelhart, D. E. (Eds.). *Explorations in cognition*. San Francisco: Freeman, 1975.

Osherson, D. N. *Logical abilities in children, Vol. 1: Organization of length and class concepts: Empirical consequences of a Piagetian formalism*. Hillsdale, N.J.: Lawrence Erlbaum Associates, 1974. (a)

Osherson, D. N. *Logical abilities in children, Vol. 2: Logical inference: Underlying operations*. Hillsdale, N.J.: Lawrence Erlbaum Associates, 1974. (b)

Osherson, D. N. *Logical abilities in children, Vol. 3: Reasoning in adolescence: Deductive inference*. Hillsdale, N.J.: Lawrence Erlbaum Associates, 1975.

Osherson, D. N. *Logical abilities in children, Vol. 4: Reasoning and concepts.* Hillsdale, N.J.: Lawrence Erlbaum Associates, 1976.

Osherson, D. N. Three conditions on conceptual naturalness. *Cognition,* 1978, *6,* 263–289.

Ozier, M. Access to the memory trace through orthographic and categoric information. *Journal of Experimental Psychology: Human Learning and Memory,* 1978, *4,* 469–485.

Paivio, A. *Imagery and verbal processes.* New York: Holt, Rinehart & Winston, 1971.

Paivio, A. Perceptual comparisons through the mind's eye. *Memory and Cognition,* 1975, *3,* 635–647.

Paivio, A. Imagery, propositions, and knowledge. In J. M. Nicholas (Ed.), *Images, perception, and knowledge.* Dordrecht: Reidel, 1976.

Paivio, A. The relationship between verbal and perceptual codes. In E. C. Carterette & M. P. Friedman (Eds.), *Handbook of perception, Volume IX: Perceptual processing.* New York: Academic Press, 1978.

Paivio, A., & Begg, I. Pictures and words in visual search. *Memory and Cognition,* 1974, *2,* 515–521.

Piaget, J. *The psychology of intelligence.* London: Routledge, 1950.

Piaget, J. *The origins of intelligence in children.* New York: International Universities Press, 1952.

Posner, M. I., Boies, S. J., Eichelman, W. H., & Taylor, R. L. Retention of visual and name codes of single letters. *Journal of Experimental Psychology Monograph,* 1969, *79,* (1, Pt. 2).

Putnam, H. The meaning of "meaning." In K. Gunderson (Ed.), *Minnesota studies in the philosophy of science, Vol. VII: Language, mind and knowledge.* Minneapolis: University of Minnesota Press, 1975.

Pylyshyn, Z. What the mind's eye tells the mind's brain: A critique of mental imagery. *Psychological Bulletin,* 1973, *80,* 1–24.

Rosch, E. H. On the internal structure of perceptual and semantic categories. In T. E. Moore (Ed.), *Cognition and the acquisition of language.* New York: Academic Press, 1973.

Rosch, E. Cognitive representations of semantic categories. *Journal of Experimental Psychology: General,* 1975, *105,* 192–233.

Rosch, E. Principles of categorization. In E. Rosch & B. B. Lloyd (Eds.), *Cognition and categorization.* Hillsdale, N.J.: Lawrence Erlbaum Associates, 1978.

Rosch, E. H., Mervis, C. B., Gray, W., Johnson, D., & Boyes-Braem, P. Basic objects in natural categories. *Cognitive Psychology,* 1976, *8,* 382–439.

Rosenberg, S., & Simon, H. A. Modeling semantic memory: Effects of presenting semantic information in different modalities. *Cognitive Psychology,* 1977, *9,* 293–325.

Savin, H. B. Meanings and concepts: A review of Jerold J. Katz's "Semantic Theory." *Cognition,* 1973, *2,* 212–238.

Schwartz, S. P. Introduction. In S. P. Schwartz (Ed.), *Naming, necessity and natural kinds.* Ithaca, N.Y.: Cornell University Press, 1977.

Shepard, R. N. The mental image. *American Psychologist,* 1978, *33,* 125–137.

Skinner, B. F. Why I am not a cognitive psychologist. *Behaviorism,* 1977, *5,* 1–10.

Smith, L. B. Perceptual development and category generalization. *Child Development.* 1979, *50.*

Trabasso, T., Riley, C. A., & Wilson, E. G. The representation of linear order and spatial strategies in reasoning: A developmental study. In R. J. Falmagne (Ed.), *Reasoning: Representation and process in children and adults.* Hillsdale, N.J.: Lawrence Erlbaum Associates, 1975.

Vygotsky, L. S. *Thought and language.* Cambridge, Mass.: M.I.T. Press, 1962.

Wason, P. C., & Johnson-Laird, P. N. *Psychology of reasoning.* Cambridge, Mass.: Harvard University Press, 1972.

9 On the Psychology of Structural Simplicity

Janet Krueger
Daniel Osherson
University of Pennsylvania

INTRODUCTION

Simplicity figures in our choice among competing hypotheses, our reaction to art and metaphor, and our facility with new ideas and information. Abstractly, the brain can be credited with computational routines for assessing simplicity in these contexts. Characterization of these routines would count as a partial characterization of the human kind of intelligence, distinguishing it from other intelligences that reckon simplicity differently.

It seems unlikely that our varied judgments of simplicity rest on a single mental mechanism; otherwise, it would be easier to compare the simplicity of poems and scientific theories. The common properties uniting these diverse intuitions under the term "simplicity" will likely emerge only after an examination of several mental subsystems that reflect it. In this chapter, we examine the hypothesis that one such subsystem is devoted to evaluating the *structural simplicity* of subsets of n-fold Cartesian products, i.e., of sets of n-tuples. To illustrate this terminology, let D be a set (called a *domain*) containing the four elements a, b, c, d. The three-fold Cartesian product of D is the set containing all triples of elements of D, such as $\langle a,a,a \rangle$, $\langle a,b,a \rangle$, $\langle c,d,b \rangle$; every three-term sequence, with or without repetitions, of elements drawn from D, is a member of the three-fold Cartesian product of D. Subsets of the latter set contain zero or more of these triples, e.g., $\{\langle a,a,b \rangle, \langle b,b,c \rangle\}$.

The kind of simplicity under consideration is called "structural" because the nature of the elements comprising a set is irrelevant to the (structural) complexity value assigned to it; only the identity and diversity of the elements appearing in its n-tuples will affect a set's structural simplicity. For example, the sets $\{\langle a,a,a\rangle,\ \langle b,b,b\rangle\}$ and $\{\langle c,c,c\rangle,\ \langle d,d,d\rangle\}$ share the same structural complexity value (with respect to the domain D), although they differ in membership.

To help evaluate the stated hypothesis, we present evidence relevant to the empirical adequacy of a particular theory of structural simplicity. The theory is presented by Nelson Goodman and is developed in Chapter III of Goodman's *The Structure of Appearance* (2nd ed., 1966). The program of research, within which we evaluate Goodman's work, is not one that he would necessarily endorse.

In the following section, we provide an overview of Goodman's theory. Later, additional assumptions are introduced that allow the theory to deduce predictions about the perceived simplicity of certain visual stimuli. We then present these stimuli and describe and discuss the data derived from them. In conclusion, we present a speculation about the connection between the structural simplicity of sets and the "naturalness" of concepts whose extensions are those sets.

GOODMAN'S THEORY

Goodman's theory consists of a list of selected structural properties applicable to sets of n-tuples, along with postulates that assign integral complexity values to such sets on the basis of the properties true of them. These structural properties provide information about: (1) the *arity* of a set of n-tuples (i.e., the value of n); (2) its degree of *self-completeness* (a strengthened form of transitivity); (3) its degree of *symmetry;* and (4) its *regularity* (which concerns the kind of reflexivity the set manifests).

The arity of a set indicates the number of elements occurring in each n-tuple in the set. Thus, a set of pairs has an arity of 2, a set of triples has an arity of 3, and so forth. Pairs of the form $\langle x,x\rangle$ are identity pairs; pairs of the form $\langle x,y\rangle$, where $x \neq y$, are diversity pairs. Identity and diversity sequences are defined analogously for arities greater than 2. For example, the triple $\langle a,a,a\rangle$ is an identity sequence, whereas the triple $\langle a,b,c\rangle$ is a diversity sequence (partial identity and diversity of sequences can be defined in obvious ways).

A set S of pairs is self-complete if and only if it meets the condition: $(x)\ (y)$ $(z)\ (w)\ [(\langle x,y\rangle \in S\ \&\ \langle z, w\rangle \in S\ \&\ x \neq y\ \&\ z \neq w\ \&\ x \neq w) \supset \langle x,w\rangle \in S]$ (i.e., every element that is the left component of a diversity pair occurs with every element that is the right component of a diversity pair as long as the resulting pair is a diversity pair). For example, the set $\{\langle a,b\rangle,\ \langle c,d\rangle,\ \langle a,d\rangle,$ $\langle c,b\rangle\}$ is self-complete, because each element that occurs in the first position (a and c) is paired with each element that occurs in the second position (b and d). On the other hand, the set $\{\langle a,b\rangle,\ \langle c,d\rangle,\ \langle a,d\rangle,\ \langle c,b\rangle,\ \langle e,b\rangle\}$ is not self-complete, because the pair $\langle e,d \rangle$ is missing. For arities greater than 2, self-completeness is defined analogously.[1]

A set S of pairs is symmetric if and only if it meets the condition (x) (y) $[\langle x,y \rangle \in S \supset \langle y,x \rangle \in S]$; for arities greater than 2, symmetry is defined analogously (see footnote 1).

A set of n-tuples is regular if and only if its identity sequences can be specified by use of no more than its diversity sequences (or vice versa). There are a variety of ways in which a set of n-tuples can be regular. For example, a set of pairs may be regular by virtue of its identity pairs containing exactly those elements occurring in its diversity pairs (a property known as "join-reflexivity"). As another example, "irreflexive" sets—i.e., those containing no identity sequences—also count as regular. The varieties of reflexivity that can be defined for sets of n-tuples increases with n, but they are all variations on the same theme.

Departing inessentially from Goodman's usage, a complete description of a set of n-tuples in terms of its arity, self-completeness, symmetry, and regularity will be called the *relevant specification* of that set; every set of n-tuples has exactly one such description. The axioms of Goodman's theory assign complexity values to relevant specifications and thereby to sets of n-tuples falling under them. The fundamental axiom asserts that if for every set S meeting relevant specification K, there exists a set S' meeting relevant specification L such that S can be defined from S' using only first order logic with identity, then sets meeting K are at least as simple as sets meeting L.[2] Five additional axioms are stated and exploited in Goodman's Chapter III (1966), as mentioned earlier. The axioms assign complexity value 0 to sets that are structurally simplest (from the point of view of the theory), and successive integers are assigned to increasingly complex sets. The potential complexity value of a set of n-tuples grows without limit with n; for arities 1, 2, 3, and 4, it ranges from 0 to 1, 4, 15, and 59, respectively.

REPRESENTING SETS

Like all sets, the sets to which Goodman's calculus assigns integers are intangible entities, not easily presented to subjects for evaluation. To render them perceptible, several methods of representing sets pictorially were devised. In the experiments we describe, judgments of relative simplicity were

---

[1]Goodman shows how partial self-completenesses and partial symmetries can also be defined for sets of arities greater than 2. Sets of 1-tuples are degenerately self-complete and symmetric.

[2]By "first order logic with identity" is meant the logic of truth functions (conjunction, disjunction, negation, etc.), the quantifiers (universal, existential), and the equality relation.

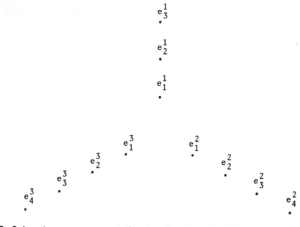

FIG. 9.1.   An arrangement of points for the pictorial representation of 3-tuples in a domain of 4 elements.

extracted from these pictures rather than from the sets themselves. This procedure commits us to a twofold theory: a competence theory, namely Goodman's, that characterizes knowledge of structural simplicity in the abstract; and a performance theory, partially embodied in our drawing methods, that characterizes the manner in which this knowledge is used in perception, memory, and so forth. We suppose that performance is related only indirectly to competence.

Our pictorial representations of sets associate each n-tuple with an n-sided polygon. Specifically, to represent a finite set of n-tuples ($n \geq 2$), a finite domain of m elements, $e_1, \ldots, e_m$, is selected. Each element e_j of the domain is associated with n points $e_j^1, \ldots, e_j^n$ on an otherwise blank page. Point e_j^i represents e_j with respect to the ith coordinate of the set of n-tuples. Figure 9.1 shows one possible arrangement of these points where $n = 3$ and $m = 4$.

In our notation, an n-tuple of elements is designated $\langle e_{j_1}, e_{j_2}, \ldots, e_{j_n} \rangle$, where each e_{j_k} is a domain element chosen for the kth position of the tuple. The elements e_{j_1} and e_{j_2}, e_{j_2} and $e_{j_3}, \ldots, e_{j_{n-1}}$ and e_{j_n}, and e_{j_n}, and e_{j_1} are said to be *adjacent*, thereby constituting *dyads* of the tuple. For each n-tuple $\langle e_{j_1}, e_{j_2}, \ldots, e_{j_n} \rangle$ in the set, an n-sided polygon is drawn on the page, with one vertex at the point $e_{j_1}^1$, the second vertex at the point $e_{j_2}^2, \ldots$, and the nth vertex at the point $e_{j_n}^n$. The result of so inserting the 3-tuple $\langle e_3, e_1, e_4 \rangle$ into Fig. 9.1 is shown in Fig. 9.2.[3] As an alternative procedure, arcs rather than lines

---

[3]Notice that the triples $\langle e_3, e_4, e_1 \rangle$, $\langle e_1, e_3, e_4 \rangle$, $\langle e_1, e_4, e_3 \rangle$, $\langle e_4, e_1, e_3 \rangle$, $\langle e_4, e_3, e_1 \rangle$ will each produce a figure identical to Fig. 9.2 in shape, but with a different orientation.

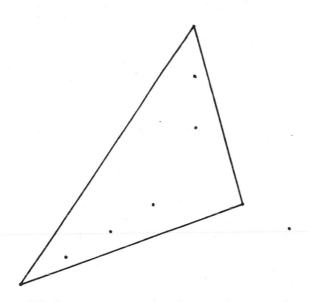

FIG. 9.2.   The representation of one 3-tuple by a drawing method based on
Fig. 9.1.

connect points in a figure; other possibilities include the connection of
identity dyads with arcs and diversity dyads with lines, or vice versa.

Clearly, the perceptual properties of pictures based on these kinds of
procedures are sensitive to the positions on the page of the points:

$$e_1^1, \ldots, e_1^n$$
$$e_2^1, \ldots, e_2^n$$
$$\cdot$$
$$\cdot$$
$$\cdot$$
$$e_m^1, \ldots, e_m^n.$$

To avoid infelicitous representations of sets, we impose four conditions on the
arrangement of these $m \times n$ points:

1. The points must segregate into n (or m) imaginary line segments of m (or
n) points apiece, where each segment contains the points listed in a column (or
row) of the matrix above. Thus, in the drawing method exemplified by Figs.
9.1 and 9.2, the points segregate into 3 segments of 4 points apiece. Spacing

between points must be uniform across all segments. As an admissible variant on this condition, the points may segregate into imaginary arcs instead of line segments.

2. The resulting segments must be positioned so that no straight line connecting points in different segments will pass through any other point.

3. Rotation through $360/n$ degrees (or $360/m$ degrees if m segments are formed) must carry the picture into itself, i.e., so as to be indistinguishable after rotation from its appearance in the original position. For example, in Fig. 9.1, the picture is carried into itself by a rotation of 120 degrees.

4. The order in which the points e_j^i appear in segments—considered from left to right, clockwise, or however else appropriate—must be consistent; for example, if in one segment, points of the ith coordinate are represented left to right in the order $e_1^i, \ldots, e_m^i$, then no other segment may order the kth coordinate as, say, e_3^k, e_1^k, e_4^k, and so on.[4] Figure 9.1 can be seen to meet this last condition by examining the subscripts on points in each of its segments.

Drawing methods of this kind can be construed as functions mapping sets into pictures. These functions are not generally one-to-one because some sets give rise to "emergent" polygons, different sides of which are deteremined by distinct n-tuples (that is, more than one set is sometimes mapped into the same picture). It simplifies later developments to exclude such sets from the domain of a given drawing method. Henceforth, drawing methods are considered to apply only to sets that can be uniquely recovered from their respective pictures. There are several enrichments of our methods that render them unequivocally one-to-one, for example, by associating each n-tuple with a polygon of unique color. Only convenience dictates use of achromatic approximations to these more faithful representations. In any event, the great majority of sets map uniquely into the pictures generated by our drawing methods.

Henceforth, a *drawing method* will be taken to be a way of arranging points that meets conditions (1)–(4), along with one of the four procedures for connecting points that was described earlier with the help of Figs. 9.1 and 9.2.[5] The effect of conditions (1)–(4) is to insure that the representations of symmetric sets exhibit perceptual "balance." Self-complete sets produce a certain "closure." Finally, different identity and diversity properties of n-tuples result in polygons of different shapes; for example, in the method

---

[4] Several details have been left implicit in this characterization of the favored class of drawing methods. It is sufficient, however, to determine whether our performance complement to Goodman's theory is roughly adequate.

[5] The four procedures are: All points connected with lines; all points connected with arcs; identity dyads connected with lines, diversity dyads with arcs; identity dyads connected with arcs, diversity dyads with lines. Note that procedures by themselves do not constitute drawing methods; an arrangement of points must be specified for a drawing method.

illustrated in Figs. 9.1 and 9.2, combinations of the type $\langle x,x,x \rangle$ will be equilateral, whereas those of the types $\langle x,x,y \rangle$, $\langle x,y,x \rangle$, and $\langle x,y,y \rangle$ will be isoceles, and those of the type $\langle x,y,z \rangle$ will be scalene.

Our theory is this: Let S_1 and S_2 be sets of the same arity, having the same finite number of members, and let $P(S_1)$ and $P(S_2)$ be the pictures associated with S_1 and S_2 by any drawing method in the sense just defined. Then, the Goodman complexity value assigned to S_1 is less than that assigned to S_2 if and only if $P(S_1)$ is perceptually simpler than $P(S_2)$; similarly, the Goodman complexity values assigned to S_1 and S_2 are equal if and only if $P(S_1)$ and $P(S_2)$ are perceptually equally complex.

The generality of this theory is limited by several ceteris paribus clauses, and it applies only to finite sets of arity greater than or equal to 2. It is possible that these restrictions can be safely relaxed, but it is the conservative version of the theory to which the current experiments are relevant.

EXPERIMENTS AND RESULTS

Experiments

Drawing Methods.   Three drawing methods were used to generate the experimental stimuli; the diagrams in Fig. 9.3 show in each case how the $n \times m$ points are arranged. In Drawing Method I, identity dyads (whether in a 2-tuple or 3-tuple) are connected with straight lines, diversity dyads with arcs. In Drawing Method II and III, a 2-tuple or 3-tuple is represented by connecting the points with straight lines. For all drawing methods, then, a 2-tuple is represented by a line (possibly curved), whereas a 3-tuple is represented by a triangle (possibly with curved sides, and possibly the degenerate case of a straight line).

Stimuli.   For each drawing method, stimuli were generated for $n = 2$ and $n = 3$ by: (1) choosing the number of n-tuples to appear in pictured sets; (2) randomly selecting relevant specifications; (3) for each such specification, choosing the number of domain elements; and (4) randomly selecting sets of n-tuples meeting the chosen relevant specifications. We now detail the decisions involved in (1) through (4), first for $n = 2$, and then for $n = 3$.

$n = 2$.   Twelve 2-tuples figured in each picture.[6] For each drawing method, one relevant specification for each of the five complexity values

---

[6]This intermediate value is a compromise between larger numbers that maximize the range of realizable relevant specifications and smaller numbers that maximize the ease of viewing the resulting pictures. Each picture contains either twelve lines (for $n = 2$), or six triangles (for $n = 3$).

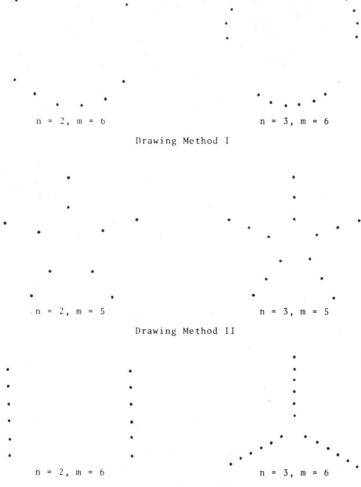

n = 2, m = 6   n = 3, m = 6

Drawing Method I

n = 2, m = 5   n = 3, m = 5

Drawing Method II

n = 2, m = 6   n = 3, m = 6

Drawing Method III

FIG. 9.3. Arrangement of points for the three drawing methods used in the experiments. (The values of m used in the stimuli depended on the relevant specifications of the sets portrayed; see text for full explanation.)

associated with $n = 2$ was chosen randomly from the class of possible relevant specifications of a set of twelve 2-tuples. In order to convert a given relevant specification into a picture, the number of domain elements (m) was chosen so as to easily accommodate that relevant specification; specifically, where not determined by the relevant specification and the number of n-tuples, this number was set equal to 12 if this neither exhausted the domain nor violated the relevant specification, and was set equal to 24 otherwise. Then, two sets of 2-tuples were randomly generated for each relevant specification so: (1) the relevant specification is met nonvacuously, i.e., with respect to symmetry and self-completeness, the antecedent of the associated conditional is true;[7] and (2) when both identity and diversity pairs are specified in the set, the proportions of each equal or exceed a fixed minimum of 25%.[8]

The experimental stimuli for sets of pairs thus consisted of six groups of five pictures, two for each drawing method; the two groups associated with a given drawing method were based on the same five relevant specifications, but different drawing methods involved different relevant specifications. Sample stimuli for each drawing method are shown in Fig. 9.4.

$n = 3.$ Six 3-tuples appeared in each picture. For each drawing method, two relevant specifications for each of the sixteen complexity values associated with $n = 3$ were chosen randomly from a reduced class of relevant specifications of sets of six 3-tuples; relevant specifications stipulating partial self-completeness or symmetry were excluded in order to facilitate random selection. For each chosen relevant specification, the number of domain elements (m) was set as just specified under $n = 2$ (substituting 6 for 12 and 12 for 24). Then, for each relevant specification, one set of 3-tuples was generated randomly so as to meet conditions comparable to (1) and (2) just specified for $n = 2$.

The experimental stimuli for sets of triples thus consisted of six groups of 16 pictures, two for each drawing method. Each group corresponds to a unique set of relevant specifications. Sample pictures for the three drawing methods are shown in Fig. 9.5. In order to remove orientational bias, the 8½ by 11 inch sheets on which the pictures were drawn were cut into circles and triangles for Drawing Method I and III, respectively.

Method.   Subjects were 93 students enrolled in psychology classes at the University of Pennsylvania. Each subject was given an envelope containing two sets of five pictures (for $n = 2$) or one set of 16 pictures (for $n = 3$). Each envelope contained pictures constructed according to only one drawing method, and the initial order of the pictures was randomized. Subjects were instructed to rank order the pictures according to complexity, assigning the lowest rank to the picture that looked "simplest and most systematic." Four subjects were dropped because they failed to complete the experiment.

---

[7]So, for example, a set such as $\{\langle a,b \rangle\}$ was never used to exemplify self-completeness, although it is, strictly speaking, self-complete.

[8]Policies (1) and (2) constitute additional *ceteris paribus* clauses in the theory formulated in the third section of the chapter.

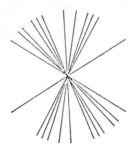 

Complexity Value = 1   Complexity Value = 4

Drawing Method I

 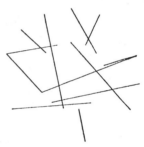

Complexity Value = 1   Complexity Value = 4

Drawing Method II

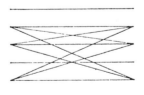 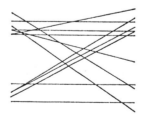

Complexity Value = 1   Complexity Value = 4

Drawing Method III

FIG. 9.4.   Sample pictures for each drawing method for $n = 2$.

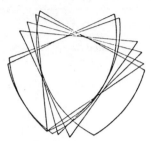 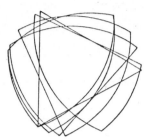

Complexity Value = 4   Complexity Value = 13

Drawing Method I

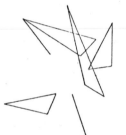 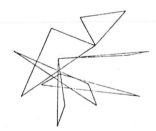

Complexity Value = 4   Complexity Value = 13

Drawing Method II

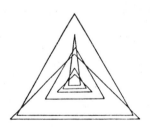 

Complexity Value = 4   Complexity Value = 13

Drawing Method III

FIG. 9.5.   Sample pictures for each drawing method for $n = 3$.

TABLE 9.1
Median Individual Rank Order Correlation Coefficients

		Rho	Number of Pictures Ranked	Number of Subjects
n = 2				
Drawing Method I	Group A	.90[a]	5	5
	Group B	.90[a]	5	
Drawing Method II	Group A	1.00[b]	5	6
	Group B	1.00[b]	5	
Drawing Method III	Group A	.85	5	6
	Group B	.80	5	
n = 3				
Drawing Method I	Group A	.48[a]	16	13
	Group B	.71[b]	16	12
Drawing Method II	Group A	.69[b]	16	11
	Group B	.51[a]	16	15
Drawing Method III	Group A	.68[b]	16	12
	Group B	.62[b]	16	9

[a] $p < .05$.
[b] $p < .01$.
Note: Comparable results were obtained in an additional experiment when the role of straight versus curved lines was reversed in the experimental stimuli of Drawing Method I for $n = 2$.

Results

For each experimental group of pictures, a Spearman rank order correlation coefficient was computed between each subject's rank ordering and the ordering of the set induced by Goodman complexity values. The medians of these individual rank order correlation coefficients across subjects are shown in Table 9.1.

An average rank order was determined for a given group of pictures by calculating the mean rank across subjects of each picture in the group, and renaming these mean ranks in order of magnitude with the first five integers

TABLE 9.2
Rank Order Correlation Coefficients Using Average Rank Orders
for Individual Groups of Pictures

		Rho	Number of Pictures Ranked	Number of Subjects
n = 2				
Drawing Method I	Group A	.98^a	5	5
	Group B	.90^a	5	
Drawing Method II	Group A	1.00^b	5	6
	Group B	1.00^b	5	
Drawing Method III	Group A	.88	5	6
	Group B	.88	5	
n = 3				
Drawing Method I	Group A	.69^b	16	13
	Group B	.76^b	16	12
Drawing Method II	Group A	.76^b	16	11
	Group B	.60^b	16	15
Drawing Method III	Group A	.66^b	16	12
	Group B	.73^b	16	9

$^a p < .05.$
$^b p < .01.$

(for *n* = 2) or sixteen integers (for *n* = 3).[9] Table 9.2 presents rank order correlation coefficients between these average rank orders and Goodman's ordering. Average rank orders and the resulting correlation coefficients were also determined for each drawing method (i.e., using the two groups of pictures associated with each method, and taking the mean of the ranks assigned to the two representations of each complexity value), and also for each arity (i.e., using all six groups of pictures); these statistics are shown in Table 9.3.

---

[9]The results are fully comparable if median ranks are used instead.

TABLE 9.3
Rank Order Correlation Coefficients Using Average Rank Orders
for Each Drawing Method and Each Arity

		Rho	Number of Pictures Ranked	Number of Subjects
$n = 2$				
Drawing Method I	Groups A & B	1.00[a]	5	5
Drawing Method II	Groups A & B	1.00[a]	5	6
Drawing Method III	Groups A & B	.88	5	6
Drawing Methods I, II, & III	All Groups	1.00[a]	5	17
$n = 3$				
Drawing Method I	Groups A & B	.85[a]	16	25
Drawing Method II	Groups A & B	.73[a]	16	26
Drawing Method III	Groups A & B	.75[a]	16	21
Drawing Methods I, II, & III	All Groups	.93[a]	16	72

[a]$p < .01$.

Coefficients of concordance were computed to assess the extent of agreement between subjects judging a given group of pictures. The obtained values ranged between .78 and .97 for sets of five pictures of 2-tuples and between .43 and .77 for sets of 16 pictures of 3-tuples. In each case, the degree of concordance is statistically reliable.

INTERPRETATION OF THE DATA

The results are impressive in their support of the proposed theory, especially because methods available in the literature for predicting the judged complexity of geometric forms—such as the number of independent turns in the outer contours of polygons (Zusne, 1970)—fare considerably worse in ordering our stimuli. As shown in Tables 9.1 through 9.3, both individual subjects' rank orders (on the average) and the average rank orders of groups of subjects correlate well with the orders predicted using Goodman complexity values.

In almost every case, the correlation based on the average rank order of a group of subjects is higher than the corresponding median individual correlation. This is because some of the variation in the subjects' ranks is random with respect to the ranks based on Goodman complexity value. By using mean ranks, this random variation cancels out. Furthermore, as mean ranks are taken over larger complexity value equivalence classes of pictures (each equivalence class containing representations of different sets of the same complexity value), the correlation between the resulting average rank order and the order by complexity value increases; for example, for 3-tuples, the correlations based on average rank orders for the six groups of pictures taken separately range from .60 to .76, whereas the correlation based on averaging across all six groups of pictures is .93.

Does this latter increase in correlation result from canceling out yet more subject variability; or, in addition to subject variability, do the true perceptual complexities of different representations of a given complexity value deviate symmetrically around the Goodman prediction? To find out, we performed an additional study in which subjects were asked to rank pictures representing different sets of the same complexity value (sometimes the sets shared the same relevant specification, sometimes not). Computation of concordance coefficients revealed that such rankings were as reliable across subjects as were the rankings of pictures differing in complexity value. So, different pictures representing the same Goodman complexity value vary systematically in their true complexity. These finer distinctions could be based either on hitherto ignored characteristics of the sets being represented (motivating an elaboration of the competence component of the theory), or on processing strategies involved in perceiving the pictures (motivating an elaboration of the performance component of the theory). At present, we do not know how the theory ought to be altered to account for the residual variance.

This issue is discussed further in Krueger (1979), which presents additional experimental data on the psychological reality of Goodman's theory. These new experiments employ standard memory paradigms and nonpictorial representations of sets.

STRUCTURAL SIMPLICITY AND
CONCEPTUAL NATURALNESS

We have hypothesized the existence of a mental mechanism that computes the structural simplicity of sets, and evidence has been presented in favor of one theory (viz. Goodman's, 1966), that describes its behavior. Such a complex mechanism would not be expected to spin idly or be engaged only by abstract line drawings. We conclude with a suggestion about the relation between structural simplicity and conceptual naturalness, a psychological dimension of considerable importance.

A concept is *(humanly) natural*[10] to the extent that: (1) it is easily learnable by children; (2) it is used in the evaluation of similarity; (3) it participates in potentially lawful (in contrast to accidental) generalizations; (4) it supports

---

[10]Or, more cautiously, "natural within a given culture." Nothing that follows depends on the extent to which experience typically determines a person's intuitions of conceptual naturalness; if cultures vary in this regard, our claims are to be taken as appropriately relativized.

analogies; and (5) it tends to be expressed succinctly in natural language. We believe that these criteria (and others of a similar nature) are roughly correlated, sufficiently so to distinguish concepts that comport with ordinary uses of human intelligence from those clearly alien to it. A central task of psychology is to characterize the continuum of conceptual naturalness in a non-question-begging way, that is, without invoking phenomena like (1) through (5) that define the problem. It would be begging the question for example, to maintain that a certain concept is unnatural because it resists simple expression in English; this stands the matter on its head.[11]

Intuitively, natural concepts are easy to grasp, whereas structurally complex sets are not; so the extensions of natural concepts would not be expected, other things being equal, to be structurally complex.[12] Chief among these "other things" is the domain of discourse, because the extension of one concept can be more complex or less complex than that of another, depending on contingent features of their respective domains. A partial order on concepts can be rescued from this variability by quantifying over domains, as follows. Let $v(C,D)$ be the Goodman complexity value of the extension of concept C in domain D.

(*) *Definition:* Concept C is *structurally at least as simple as* concept C' if and only if for all possible domains d, $v(C,d) \leq v(C',d)$. If C is structurally at least as simple as C' but not conversely, then C is *structurally simpler than C'.*

We suggest that the ordering of concepts with respect to conceptual naturalness honors the ordering established by structural simplicity; specifically:

(**) If C is structurally simpler than C', then C is conceptually more natural than C'.[13]

Hypothesis (**) is supported by such pairs of relations as *smaller than* and *smagger than.* The pair $\langle x,y \rangle$ stands in the *smagger* relation if and only if x is smaller than y, or everything is at least as big as x. It is easy to prove (see Appendix) that *smaller than* is structurally simpler than *smagger than* in the sense of (*). By (**), the former is predicted to be conceptually more natural than the latter, which is true.

---

[11]For more on the general problem of conceptual naturalness, see Osherson (1977, 1978).

[12]The *extension* of a concept is the set of things to which it applies and contrasts with the concept's *intension,* which is closer to its "meaning" or "sense."

[13]The converse of (**) is clearly false as revealed by pairs of concepts like *green* and *grue* (x is grue if and only if it is examined before time t and green, or not so examined and blue), (Goodman, 1965). The two colors cannot be ordered structurally.

Although (**) is supported by innumerable examples like these, it is threatened by odd cases that exploit the multiplicity of concepts that can share the same extension. To see this, first compare *is square* to *is self-identical*. The latter is structurally simpler in the sense of (*) than the former, yet the two concepts seem equally natural, at least roughly. This result is not too disturbing. Our naturalness judgments reflect performance as well as competence variables, and comparisons are least likely to be precise when both concepts rest at one extreme of the naturalness continuum, as here. But replace *is self-identical* with *is self-identical or frogs chuckle*. Certainly, (**) now makes a false prediction, because the enriched self-identity predicate is clearly bizarre yet structurally identical to the original.[14] Similar counterexamples can be constructed for any arity.

The conjecture (**) can be saved only by weakening it, for example, by partitioning logically coextensive concepts into equivalence classes, and, on the same basis as before, attempting to order for naturalness only the respective classes' most natural members.[15] Because *is self-identical* is more natural than the logically coextensive *is self-identical or frogs chuckle*, only the former is compared to *is square* for naturalness, not the latter. We do not pause to examine such revisions further since (**) suffices for the general point: Structural complexity likely bears a systematic relation to conceptual naturalness, although its precise role in a complete theory of such naturalness remains to be settled.

APPENDIX

Proof That *smaller than* Is Structurally Simpler Than *smagger than* in the Sense of Definition (*)

First we prove that *smaller than* is structurally at least as simple as *smagger than*, i.e., that for all domains d, $v(smaller\ than, d) \leq v(smagger\ than, d)$ (Proposition A). Then we prove that *smagger than* is not structurally at least as simple as *smaller than*, i.e., that there is a domain d' such that $v(smagger\ than, d') > v(smaller\ than, d')$ (Proposition B). Together, these proofs demonstrate that *smaller than* is structurally simpler than *smagger than* in the sense of definition (*).

---

[14]The structural identity of the two concepts follows from their being logically coextensive; the latter results from their universality, i.e., each concept applies to all things in any domain of discourse.

[15]Such equivalence classes are infinite; how is the most natural member of a given class to be determined? As noted earlier, one pretheoretical criterion of conceptual naturalness is succinct expressibility in natural language. The most natural member of a given equivalence class, therefore, ought to turn up in the finite set of reasonably succinct expressions of English (say) that pick out concepts in the class.

To render the proof comprehensible to those unfamiliar with Goodman's calculus, we briefly describe the aspects of his system that are relevant here (see Goodman, 1966, for a full account). Because *smagger than* and *smaller than* are two-place predicates, only structural properties of sets of arity two need be considered. The maximal complexity value of such a set according to the calculus is 4. The following three properties of a set render its complexity value lower than maximal: self-completeness, symmetry, and regularity. For arity two, these three properties are binarily valued, that is, a given set either has or fails to have each property; and for each such property that the set possesses, its complexity value is reduced by 1. Thus, a set of pairs that is self-complete and regular but not symmetric has a complexity value of 2, and so forth. A set of pairs receives the minimal complexity value of 0 just in case it is definable in terms of first order logic with identity alone. For example, the null set, which may be defined as $\{\langle x,y \rangle | (z) \ (z \neq z)\}$ has complexity value 0; so does the universal set, definable as $\{\langle x,y \rangle | (z) \ (z = z)\}$.

As mentioned earlier, these four structural properties—arity, self-completeness, symmetry, and regularity—are the only ones that affect the complexity value assigned to a set by Goodman's calculus. Sharing the same relevant specification is a sufficient condition for being assigned the same complexity value.

Recall that x is smagger than y if and only if x is smaller than y, or everything is at least as big as x.

Proposition A: For all domains d, $v(smaller \ than, \ d) \leq v(smagger \ than, \ d)$.

Proof: Let D be a domain. We may assume that D has at least two elements, because otherwise the extension of *smaller than* in D is null, and Proposition A is trivially true. If D has no element such that everything in D is at least as big as that element, then the extension of *smagger than* is identical to the extension of *smaller than*, also making Proposition A trivially true. So suppose that D contains some nonnull subset E of such elements. Finally, we can assume that the extension of *smaller than* is nonnull (because otherwise Proposition A is again trivially true). So let g and h be elements of D such that g is smaller than h. This implies that h is not in E (because members of E are not bigger than anything in D), and that g and h are not identical (nothing is bigger than itself).

To prove Proposition A, it is sufficient to show that:

(1) If *smagger than* is regular in D, then *smaller than* is regular in D.
(2) If *smagger than* is symmetric in D, then *smaller than* is symmetric in D.
(3) If *smagger than* is self-complete in D, then *smaller than* is self-complete in D.

Now (1) is trivially true because *smaller than* is irreflexive, hence regular, in every domain, hence in D. Also (2) is trivially true because *smagger than* cannot be symmetric in D. For g is smaller than h, hence g is smagger than h; but h is not smagger than g because h is neither smaller than g (due to the asymmetry of *smaller than*) nor a member of E (because that would contradict g being smaller than h, as noted earlier). That is, the only two ways that the pair $\langle h,g \rangle$ could stand in the *smagger* relation are blocked.

To prove (3), we show that if *smagger than* is self-complete in D, then so is *smaller than*. This is equivalent to proving that, for all x, y, w, and z in D:

If

(α) if x is smagger than y and w is smagger than z and $x \neq y$ and $w \neq z$ and $x \neq z$, then x is smagger than z

Then:

(β) if x is smaller than y and w is smaller than z and $x \neq y$ and $w \neq z$ and $x \neq z$, then x is smaller than z.

In summary, to prove (3), we prove:

(γ) for all x, y, w, and z in D, if (α) then (β).

(γ) states that any quadruple from D that fails to destroy the self-completeness of *smagger than* also fails to destroy the self-completeness of *smaller than*. In other words, any quadruple that is a counterexample to the self-completeness of *smaller than* is also a counterexample to the self-completeness of *smagger than*.

Now (γ) could be false only if (α) is true for some quadruple in D and (β) is false for that quadruple. Such a situation can arise only if the antecedent and consequent of (α) are both true, whereas (β) has true antecedent but false consequent. We do not need to consider cases in which (α)'s antecedent is false, because that would guarantee the falsity of (β)'s antecedent (because the extension of *smaller than* is included in that of *smagger than* in any domain), thereby making (β) true and hence (γ) true. We also need not consider cases in which (α)'s consequent is false, because that would render (α) false [(α)'s antecedent being true], and hence (γ) true. So we need only consider whether the antecedent and consequent of (α) can be true, whereas the antecedent of (β) is true but (β)'s consequent is false. There are two possibilities:

(i) x is not a member of E. Because x is smagger than z nonetheless, x is smaller than z, making (γ) true.

(ii) x is a member of E. Because w is smaller than z, z is not a member of E. Hence x is smaller than z; for x, being in E, is at least as small as z, and if it weren't smaller, z and x would be the same size—but then z would be in E, which contradicts our earlier statement that z is not a member of E.

This proves (γ), which proves (3), which proves Proposition A.

Proposition B: There is a domain d' such that $v(smagger\ than,\ d') > v(smaller\ than,\ d')$.

Proof: Let d' be the domain containing three spheres, s_1, s_2, and s_3, with diameters of one, two, and three feet, respectively. The extension of *smaller than* in d' is the set $\{\langle s_1,s_2\rangle, \langle s_1, s_3\rangle, \langle s_2, s_3\rangle\}$; $v(smaller\ than,\ d') = 2$ because this set is irreflexive (hence regular) and self-complete, but not symmetric. The extension of *smagger than* in d' is the set $\{\langle s_1,s_2\rangle, \langle s_1, s_3\rangle, \langle s_2, s_3\rangle, \langle s_1,s_1\rangle\}$; $v(smagger\ than,\ d') = 3$ because this set is self-complete but neither regular nor symmetric. Therefore, $v(smagger\ than,\ d') > v(smaller\ than,\ d')$.

This proves Proposition B.

REFERENCES

Goodman, N. *Fact, fiction, and forecast.* Indianapolis: Bobbs-Merrill, 1965.

Goodman, N. *The structure of appearance* (2nd ed.).Indianapolis: Bobbs-Merrill, 1966.

Krueger, J. *A theory of structural simplicity and its relevance to aspects of memory, perception, and conceptual naturalness.* Doctoral Dissertation, University of Pennsylvania, 1979.

Osherson, D. Natural connectives: A Chomskyan approach. *Journal of Mathematical Psychology,* 1977, *16*, 1–29.

Osherson, D. Three conditions on conceptual naturalness. *Cognition,* 1978, *6*, 263–289.

Zusne, L. *Visual perception of form.* Academic Press, 1970.

V MIND AND BRAIN

10 Cognitive and Neural Maps

Lynn Nadel
Dalhousie University

Concern with the problem of object perception and the rules that specify the perceptual constancies drew Hebb (1949) to the cell-assembly as a neural substrate: It had the critical property of allowing for generalization and hence category formation. Goddard (Chapter 11, this volume) shows how cell-assembly theory can be brought into line with contemporary neurophysiology and still provide a coherent account of many aspects of perception and learning. By contrast, the problem of space perception and the rules specifying the constant three-dimensional space through which we move and in which are found the objects of experience have not been clarified with this kind of object–perception-based theory (cf. Ittelson, 1973, for some discussion of why this is so). For this and other reasons, John O'Keefe and I have been led to a rather different kind of neural/cognitive assembly as the substrate for space perception and cognition: In this chapter, I trace the main outlines of our program.

We begin with an assertion about behavior: Many higher animals behave as though they have maps in their heads enabling them to navigate through, and effectively use, the various environments they encounter. The status of these "maps" is the question of interest. Tolman (1948) and more recent sympathizers (e.g., Menzel, 1978) tend to see these maps in metaphorical terms. This paper presents evidence from a variety of physiological experiments indicating that animals form internal maps, in specific neural regions, and use them in many of the ways Tolman envisioned. More details of the studies we discuss, plus some of the subsequent speculations, can be found in O'Keefe and Nadel (1978).

MAPS IN THE BRAIN

Early work by O'Keefe and Dostrovsky (1971) set the stage for this notion. They described single neurons in the hippocampus of the unanesthetized freely moving rat, which appeared to be activated whenever the animal was in a particular location in its test environment. An example of such a unit, taken from a later paper (O'Keefe, 1976), is given in Fig. 10.1. In the early work it was essential to be skeptical about the precise correlates of single neuron activity, but later research, including several independent replications, has ruled out most of the possible alternative explanations of the activity patterns of these "place" units in the hippocampus (see Best & Ranck, 1975; Hill, 1978; O'Keefe, 1976; O'Keefe & Conway, 1978; Olton, Branch, & Best, 1978). One might have thought, for instance, that these neurons fired whenever the rat made a certain movement; but, identical movements activate or fail to activate a place neuron depending on *where* in the environment they are made. The neuron fires regardless of the nature of the animal's movements in that place. Similarly, one might have thought that some specific combination of apparatus or room cues necessarily triggered neuron activity; but, O'Keefe and Conway (1978) have shown that this is also not the case, at least not in any simple fashion. They used a restricted test environment, composed of a plus-maze inside a curtained area, with a set of cues attached to the curtains. Neurons recorded in this kind of environment fire whenever the animal is located in a specific relation to these cues. Figure 10.2 shows that removal of

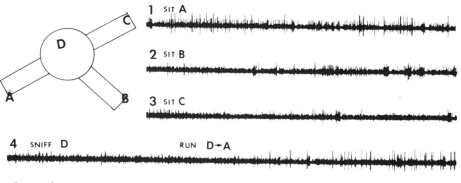

FIG. 10.1.   Recordings taken with microelectrode implanted in the hippo-campus of a freely moving rat. Each vertical line, or "spike," denotes a single action potential in a neuron. The large spikes, prominent in row 1, are from a "place" unit. This neuron fired maximally whenever the rat was located such that its head was in the hatched area in maze arm A. Row 5 was recorded with the room darkened and a new physical arm substituted for the usual arm A: The place unit's maintained activity demonstrates that neither visual nor olfactory inputs are essential to its activation (from O'Keefe, 1976).

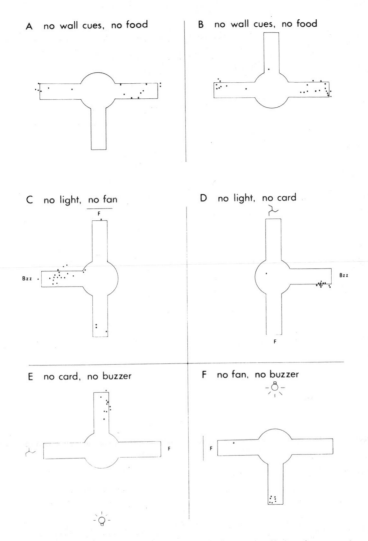

FIG. 10.2. Data from a study of place units in a controlled environment (see text). Each dot corresponds to a single spike from the neuron and to the rat's location at the time it occured. Traces A and B indicate that in the absence of the interior wall cues, the only source of heterogeneous stimulation within the curtains, the unit fires without regard to the rat's location. Any two of the four cues used in this study provided sufficient information to define this unit's place field. Note that this unit always fires on the arm nearest the buzzer, or where the buzzer would have been (O'Keefe & Nadel, 1978).

any two of these cues fails to disrupt this firing pattern. This suggested to us that what these neurons code for is *place,* as overdefined by all of the static cues in the test situation. Any small set of landmarks or reference stimuli in the situation is sufficient to activate a place neuron, and no particular stimulus appears necessary for this to occur.

In addition to these place neurons, two other kinds of cells have been identified in the hippocampus of the rat. The first is a variant of the place cells, with an interesting additional property. These neurons fire maximally whenever the rat is in a location and: (1) does not find what is normally there; or (2) does not perceive what normally stands in a certain relation to that location; or (3) when something that is not normally there is unexpectedly found. That is, these units are activated primarily by discrepancies between what prior experience in an environment causes the animal to expect and what actually occurs. We have assumed that these cells, which we call *misplace* neurons, are activated by novelty and themselves trigger a set of reactions that center around exploration, during which information about the new contingencies is incorporated into the animal's internalized representation of its environment.

The final class of cells constitutes a completely separate category, with the neurons manifesting firing rates and burst patterns quite different from those seen in the place and misplace neurons (Ranck, 1973). An understanding of their function requires some background information. It has long been known that under certain circumstances the electroencephalogram (EEG) recorded from the hippocampus demonstrates a regular sinusoidal waveform called *theta,* or rhythmic slow activity (RS) (Green & Arduini, 1954); an example of this is shown in Fig. 10.3. The third class of neurons alluded to

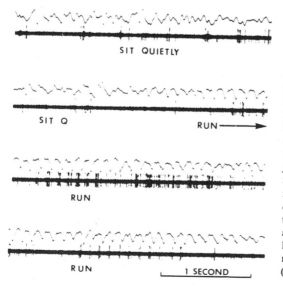

SIT QUIETLY

SIT Q   RUN ⟶

RUN

RUN   1 SECOND

FIG. 10.3. Recordings taken with a microelectrode in the hippocampus of a freely moving rat. The upper trace on each row is low-frequency, massed neural activity, whereas the lower trace is high-frequency neural spike activity; both were recorded from the same electrode but subjected to different filtering and amplication. When the rat begins to run, the low-frequency EEG trace demonstrates the onset of RSA, or theta rhythm. For much, though not all, of this time, individual cells in the hippocampus fire in a constant relation to the phase of RSA (O'Keefe, unpublished).

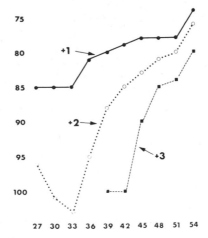

FIG. 10.4. Data from a study on the relation between distance jumped (abscissa) and hippocampal theta rhythm (the *period* of which is on the ordinate). The three lines map this relation for the first three hippocampal RSA waves following jump take-off. In this rat, there was little relationship below 33 cm jumps, then a strong relationship, such that increased distance was associated with decreased theta period, e.g., increased frequency.

earlier shows a phase-locked relation to this theta activity, as also shown in Fig. 10.3. A satisfactory analysis of the function of these units must account for the precise behavioral conditions during which theta activity occurs. Vanderwolf (1969) initially suggested that RSA occurred during voluntary movement, and this characterization does seem to capture much of the data, though it leaves one with the not inconsiderable problem of going beyond an intuitive feeling for what is voluntary to an operationally useful definition.

We have approached this issue from a somewhat different perspective, taking a lead from the anecdotal observation by Vanderwolf, Bland, and Whishaw (1973) that the frequency of RSA during jumping was a function of the distance jumped. Assuming that the hippocampus was involved in spatial mapping, we reasoned that it would need information about distances in the external environment. Figure 10.4 shows the results of a study (Morris, Black, & O'Keefe, 1976), which explored the possibility that RSA conveys distance information, presumably in the form of corollary discharges from a central movement programming system. In this study, rats were first trained to jump various distances to grab onto a ledge that took them off the (electrifiable) grid floor. At times the rats had extra weights strapped to their bodies to increase the force needed to jump a given distance. Changing weights had no effect on theta frequency during jumping. However, as seen in Fig., 10.4 the frequency of theta just after the initiation of the jump varied in a nearly linear fashion above a certain distance with the distance to be jumped. The weight control condition indicated that a variety of changes associated with jumps of increased distance could not have been responsible for the regular shifts in RSA frequency, including such things as force and the acceleration of the body (cf. O'Keefe & Nadel, 1978, pp. 180–182). We concluded that the frequency of hippocampal RSA is related in some way to the distance that a given movement would translocate the animal in space. The story is actually more complicated than this, in that there appears to be two separate forms of theta activity, only one of which is initiated by movement (Vanderwolf, 1975). However, these data on jumping enabled us to give a name to the class of neurons related to movement-generated RSA—we call them *displace* neurons—as well as to incorporate within our model of spatial mapping some source of information about distance.

This collection of elements in the hippocampus—place cells, misplace cells, and displace cells conveying distance information—add up to the bits and pieces of a spatial mapping system. Insofar as can be determined, the maps formed therein are not isomorphic to the real world in any simple fashion: That is, adjacent neurons do not seem to code adjacent locations in a given environment. We initially wondered, as did others, if there were enough neurons in the hippocampus to code all of the (potential) locations an animal might visit. However, Ranck (1977) and O'Keefe & Conway (1978) have now shown that any given place neuron might participate in the mapping of several different environments. In addition, it is certain that the hippocampus itself is but the core structure in the spatial mapping system: Its input and output structures, including at least the subiculum and septum, undoubtedly play some role in this system as well.

The initial schematic version of the neural basis of the spatial (cognitive) mapping system, the wiring diagram for the bits and pieces noted previously (Nadel & O'Keefe, 1974; O'Keefe & Nadel, 1978), has been broadened but basically unchanged by these later data. There is little doubt that the highly specific, though tentative, schemes outlined by O'Keefe and Nadel (1978) are wrong in detail, but we feel safe proceeding with the molar assumption that the hippocampus is centrally involved in spatial–cognitive mapping.

WHAT DO YOU DO WITH A MAP?

What does it mean for an animal to have a mapping system of the type described earlier? We think it means that rats (and other animals) form internal representations of the spatial disposition of things in their environment. These maps are created in the course of exploration, which itself is triggered from the hippocampus by the absence of a map for the current situation or by some discrepancy between an existing representation and the current external manifestation. Hill (1978) has shown that hippocampal place neurons acquire their spatial "field" almost immediately upon initial exposure to an environment, in accordance with our assumption that maps are, and must be, rapidly established. This means that they quickly become available for several important functions. We would emphasize the following:

1. *Place Recognition.* Animals always know where they are; indeed, they need to know. When in a strange place, exploration takes precedence over other forms of appetitive-consummatory behavior. When in a familiar place (as identified by the retrieval/activation of the appropriate map), animals are continually predicting *what* will be experienced *where*. This process carries on largely unbidden, directs attention away from biologically nonsignificant things and events, and is exposed only when something unanticipated happens. Thus, cognitive maps keep track of the environment, allowing the animal to skip over information it knows and does not seek in favor of information it seeks or does not know. As a corollary to recognizing a place, animals can "tag" places as safe or dangerous, good or bad. By this means, recognition can lead rapidly to adaptive behavior—escape from a dangerous place if possible, or movement into a safe area (one that possibly contains some reward).

2. *Navigation.* Higher animals move efficiently within the environment, avoid danger and various obstacles, track the location of other group members, and gather food and water, whether distributed by nature or by an experimenter (Menzel, 1978). Some species navigate effectively across vast reaches of space, making use of a myriad of information sources while depending on no one source. Such examples indicate that a central feature of all navigational capacity is its flexibility—that is, its independence of specific routes or reference landmarks. This flexibility reflects the nature of the spatial maps upon which navigation is based: There is no information in the maps about the specific behaviors or responses originally used during their construction, and there is considerable redundancy in the cues defining places. The animal's spatial map, like a road map, offers a choice of ways and means of travel.

3. *Context Coding.* A place is defined by all of its static elements—what many have referred to as the background or situational cues. Things that come and go, dynamic elements such as CSs and USs, occur within the spatial frame, or place, established by these stable referents. What animals learn about these dynamic elements can often be restricted or referenced to this context. Thus, the long-term inhibitory effects of repetitive exposure to a dynamic stimulus are context-specific. For example, a stimulus exposed in one place will lose its salience, or associability, only in that context (e.g., Lubow, Rifkin, & Alek, 1976; Shalter, 1978). Associations formed between several dynamic stimuli can also show context specificity (Sheafor, 1975), though "generalization decrement" of this sort is rarely complete. Very little is known at present about the precise ways in which context coding functions in animal learning, and this is reflected in the absence of any satisfactory treatment of the issue in contemporary learning theory. We assume that cognitive maps are essential for coding events into spatial contexts, and hence

that an analysis of mapping should shed considerable light on this latter problem.

However, it is important to note that the cognitive mapping system is *not* involved in every kind of learning. Maps are not necessary for learning about the specific features of particular stimuli—their size, shape, texture, color, or even biological significance. They are also not responsible for learning based on interoceptive sources of information; for example, the kinesthetically based learning studied extensively in the course of the place versus response controversy of the 1940s. These kinds of learning and the internal representations resulting from them can function independently of the mapping system. The main thrust of the distinction to be made here is that between (spatial) context-specific coding and context-independent coding. The first gives rise to the cognitive maps just described, the second to categories and concepts, those aspects of knowledge that are trans-situational.

Evidence linking the hippocampus and its spatial mapping neurons to most of the functions outlined earlier (place recognition, exploration, navigation, context coding) is plentiful. Rats with lesions in this structure consistently fail to explore, and show profound deficits in tasks requiring navigation, such as complex spatial mazes (e.g., Kimble, 1963; see O'Keefe & Nadel, 1978, for other references and further discussion). On the other hand, such rats can learn mazes based on: (1) kinesthetic feedback (e.g., position habits on the T-maze [Means & Douglas, 1970]); (2) simple associations between cues and their consequences (e.g., simultaneous discrimination learing, such as visual brightness, or pattern [see O'Keefe & Nadel, 1978, Table A–17 for documentation]) and (3) sequential habits requiring the stringing together of several acts in specified temporal order (e.g., pressing several levers in a patterned sequence [Jackson & Strong, 1969]).

A study we have conducted (O'Keefe, Nadel, Keightley, & Kill, 1975) explored the role of the hippocampus in two kinds of learning: one based on navigation and hence requiring a mapping system, and the other based on stimuli independent of location in space. Rats were trained on an elevated circular maze, which had eight equally spaced water-wells sunk into it. Water was delivered by the experimenter when the rat made a correct response. Two conditions were established by which the thirsty rats could learn the particular well to approach in order to get water. In the CUE condition a small microscope light was put next to the maze, illuminating the region just around the correct well. This light, and hence the correct well, was moved about from trial to trial so that reward was not related to location in the room. In the PLACE condition, the correct well could be identified solely by its position in the room. There were no cues systematically related to the correct well other than those at a remove from the maze. The light which signaled the correct well in the CUE condition was also available in the PLACE condition, but its movements about the maze from trial to trial were unrelated to reward.

Separate groups of control rats and rats with lesions in the fornix (a major input–output path of the hippocampus) were tested on the two versions of the task. Control rats learned both versions at nearly the same rate (about 10 trials to criterion), suggesting that these tasks were of comparable difficulty. The rats with lesions, on the other hand, learned the CUE task very rapidly (less than 3 trials to criterion), but failed utterly on the PLACE task: All but 1 of the 7 rats in this group failed to reach criterion within 55 trials. Further details on the procedure and interpretation of this study can be found in O'Keefe et al. (1975). The basic result, a selective loss in place learning, has been repeated in other labs (Olton, 1977; Winson, 1978). We have attempted to cast the many and various effects of hippocampal lesions within the spatial mapping framework in several places (Black, Nadel, & O'Keefe, 1977; Nadel, O'Keefe, & Black, 1975; O'Keefe & Nadel, 1978; O'Keefe, Nadel & Willner, 1979), and do not repeat these arguments here. One clear implication of this study worth emphasizing is that there is an important distinction between learning to go to a place and learning to approach a specific cue notwithstanding Restle's (1957) assumption that place learning is nothing more than learning based on distal cues (see Nadel, 1979, for further discussion of this issue in its appropriate historical context). It seem certain that the brain can tell the difference between places and cues. Places are defined by cues, but they take on a quasi-independent life of their own within the richly redundant network of the various fixed elements in the animal's environment.

The evidence previously described is consistent with the view that rats form representations (of considerable variety), generate strategies and expectancies, explore, and learn about events and the contexts within which they occur. We have every reason to assume that humans too can form and use representations, generate strategies, explore, navigate, and so on.

MAPS IN THE HUMAN MIND

The foregoing considerations might lead one to expect that the hippocampus in humans is also involved in spatial mapping and exploration and that disruption of its function should lead to a loss of these abilities. Indeed, it is the case that spatial disorientation and lack of curiosity are common features of the syndrome produced by such neural damage.

But, this seriously distorts chronology. We have known about the effects of hippocampal damage in humans for some time. Scoville and Milner (1957) demonstrated that such damage, in a patient operated for relief epilepsy, caused a profound amnesia, including both anterograde and retrograde components. The boundaries of this defect have not yet been accurately delineated. Much of the research on hippocampal function in infrahumans was sparked by the desire to establish parallels to human amnesia in the laboratory—and most of these early attempts failed. Among the possible reasons for this failure, three seem most plausible: (1) there might be genuine species differences in hippocampal function, as suggested by Winson (1972) for the theta activity; (2) appropriate tests of memory failure have, perhaps, not been carried out in animals, either because we don't yet understand the precise nature of the human defect or because such tests are simply not possible; and (3) there is something special about memory as it relates to language. This latter point reminds us that the hippocampus is a bilateral structure: Data exist on the effects of damage to the hippocampus of both the language-dominant and spatial-dominant hemispheres (e.g., Milner, 1971). As one might expect, lesions in the hippocampus of the language hemisphere typically cause verbal defects, whereas comparable damage in the non-language hemisphere causes nonverbal defects.

We reject as inelegant the possibility that major species differences are the cause of this apparent discrepancy. In order to draw a firmer connection between the human and infrahuman work we need to digress into a discussion of amnesia.[1] We conclude that there is, in fact, no strong discrepancy between these lines of research and that the cognitive mapping theory offers a medium for bringing them closer together. These conclusions, of course, rest on certain assumptions, and it is to these that we now turn.

One prominent line of research and analysis in amnesia has been the attempt to specify the selective nature of the memory defect. It has been clear for some time that not all learning becomes impossible in amnesia. Claparede (cited in Talland, 1965) greeted a patient with a pin in his hand that stuck the patient; on a subsequent meeting the patient refused to shake hands but could not say why. More recently, amnesics have been shown to learn a variety of motor skills (Cermak, Lewis, Butters & Goodglass, 1973, Corkin, 1968; Talland, 1965), associations and discriminations (Gaffan, 1972; Sidman, Stoddard, & Mohr, 1968), and rules, such as those embodied in a mathematical sequence (Kinsbourne & Wood, 1975), or in a mirror-reading

---

[1] We refer here to the studies on patients with a variety of etiologies, not all of which include obvious damage to the hippocampus (though its immediate afferent or efferent structures might be damaged). Current knowledge indicates that this simplifying assumption is probably risky, if not altogether incorrect. Amnesia resulting from chronic alcoholism (the Korsakoff syndrome) is different from amnesia caused by temporal lobe surgery; there are additional defects in the Korsakoff patients that suggest more widespread damage. None of the arguments in the present paper rest on data generated solely in these latter kinds of patients. We reject, though we cannot give the reasons here, the argument raised by Horel (1978) that the damage critical to the amnesic syndrome is not in the hippocampus at all, but rather in the temporal stalk.

task (Cohen & Squire, 1979). In addition to these and other (Brooks & Baddeley, 1976) indications of preserved memory function, several studies by Warrington and Weiskrantz (1968, 1970) seemed to suggest that amnesic patients were getting more into storage than they could successfully retrieve. That is, there appeared to be a gap between what was available and what was accessible. These authors proposed that amnesia involved faulty retrieval due to excessive interference.

Later work (Squire, Wetzel, & Slater, 1978; Woods & Piercy, 1974) has confirmed that the availability–accessibility distinction is equally true of normal subjects (cf. Tulving & Pearlstone, 1966) and that there is no strong reason to suppose that amnesia involves any special retrieval difficulties or that it can be explained by appeals to excessive interference problems alone (cf. Warrington & Weiskrantz, 1978). Though few would now accept that a pure retrieval defect underlies amnesia, this view did spark several interesting and revealing studies. In attempts to improve accessibility of memories for amnesic patients, the effects of various forms of input organization on memory performance have been assessed. For example, it has been shown that amnesic patients benefit from the clustering of words within categories in list learning (Baddeley & Warrington, 1973), from the use of phonetically and semantically related words as the stimuli and responses in paired associates learning (Winocur & Weiskrant, 1976), and from the provision of salient cues, which help the subject distinguish one paired associates list from another (Winocur & Kinsbourne, 1978). However, they do not benefit from instructions to use imagery (Baddeley & Warrington, 1973), though they apparently have no defect in generating or scanning images (Kapur, 1978). This failure is particularly striking in view of the acknowledged power of imagery as a mnemonic aid in normal subjects.

Two studies with temporal lobe resection patients, in whom the hippocampus had been damaged, confirm this picture. Jones (1974) showed that H. M., the bilaterally lesioned patient, could not benefit at all from the use of imagery in a paired associates task. In Jones-Gotman and Milner (1978), patients with unilateral right temporal lobe resection failed to benefit normally from the use of imagery: This defective utilization of imagery was positively related to the extent of hippocampal removal. These patients did benefit from the use of a verbal (sentence) mediator, in an entirely normal fashion.

It appears that amnesics can generate, scan, and manipulate images but cannot use them as conduits for improved memory. Imagery takes on a special importance in view of these results, as it appears to involve something selectively defective with amnesic patients. The aspect of imagery that I focus on here is the spatiality of it. The "method of loci," as first described by Simonides (cf. Yates, 1966), is explicitly spatial. In this technique, subjects improve memory by putting to-be-remembered items into some place or spatial context. Retrieval is effected simply by "going" to that place in thought, which is the formal equivalent of the rat's spatial map predicting what will be encountered where. Two recent studies suggest that other imaginal techniques also establish contexts within which to-be-remembered items are located and that recall of the context makes recall of its contents quite likely (Peterson & Jacob, 1978; Winograd & Lynn, 1979).

The properties of imaginal techniques are similar to those attributed earlier in this chapter to cognitive maps; two studies of spatial learning in rats confirm this highly suggestive similarity (Maki, Brokofsky, & Berg, 1979; Roberts, 1979). Events occurring within separate contexts are efficiently recalled in those contexts and minimally confused between contexts, though the events themselves might be highly similar. The mental maps we have of our home town, our neighborhood, and our house are all examples of the kinds of spatial contexts within which events occur, can be coded internally, and can subsequently be effectively retrieved or recalled: Studies by Smith, Glenberg, and Bjork (1978) and Bellezza and Reddy (1978) indicate that the power of the method of loci might lie in its ability to take advantage of this natural state of affairs.

Our mental maps, however, are not images—they cannot be "imagined" in their entirety, not unless one takes an unusual perspective. From such abstract maps, on the other hand, segments can be generated for utilization. New information can be appended to these maps—information about the spatial relations of new things experienced in the familiar context. A description of how information might be incorporated into the rat's cognitive map will facilitate our discussion of the way in which a mapping system might function in the construction of both spatial and verbal maps.

With specific reference to spatial maps, information is derived from an interaction between two sources of input. Highly analyzed sensory inputs are "placed" into the map according to a *coding strategy* input that derives from distance information, as outlined earlier in our analysis of the EEG activity of the hippocampus. Specifically, environmental objects (or, the internal representation thereof) are initially sited in given parts of the map on the basis of the hippocampal RSA generated by the movements that took the animal from one of these objects to the other. The specific siting of representations of objects A and B in map locations α and β means that they are at a certain distince from each other in the environment. Had they been at a different distance, the movements leading from one to the other would have generated a different RSA that would then have resulted in storage in different hippocampal sites. Thus, the relation between distance in the real world and distance as represented in the internal map is constantly preserved by the prewired RSA-distance mechanism. This coding strategy guarantees that inputs to the rat (and right, human) hippocampus are arrayed in the form of a spatial map.

If we assume that the hippocampus in our left hemisphere does more or less the same thing as its mate in the right, then verbal maps could be formed by the interaction of inputs specifying certain entities (objects, events, entire contexts) and coding strategies, which capture the nature of the semantic relations between these entities. Such maps could provide the means by which related information, as in the sentences of a paragraph, parts of a story, or episodes from an epic, would be brought together in a format that takes advantage of the organization inherent in their relatedness; that is, the fact that they all refer to the same conceptual frame of reference (see Reichman, 1978, for some intriguing discussion of this issue). When the shared frame is either lacking from the material or absent from the observer's capacities, as in amnesia, memory function will deteriorate.

These verbal maps have the advantages associated with all maps: They are unbounded, have multiple access routes, and can be used in ways that make them largely independent of specific reference stimuli (lexical items) or routes (syntactic frames). The *rule* in spatial mapping transforms distance moved or to be moved in the external world into an electrical coding strategy that imbues the resulting map with its accurate spatiality. The rules in verbal mapping must be somewhat different, but one would hope minimally so. Some recent work by Jackendoff (1976, 1978) indicates one way in which certain properties of the physical and spatial world could serve as the basis for these rules and hence provide the framework and the means for verbal mapping. Objects, locations, and events related to one another in terms of certain semantic primitives are the elements in this system. These primitives, which refer to the status of things in locations (BE and STAY), to movement between locations (GO), and to cause–effect relations (CAUSE and LET), could play the role in verbal mapping filled by distance (and perhaps direction) in spatial mapping. That is, they would specify the (semantic) relations that hold among things, just as the distance-coded hippocampal RSA specifies the (spatial) relations that hold among objects in the mapped environment. Thus, Jackendoff argues that mapping in the verbal domain is based on the same rules and operations used in mapping the perceptual domain. O'Keefe and Nadel (1978) provide a means by which his model could be couched in cognitive mapping terms. As with the fine details of the neural map, the precise form of these verbal maps remains largely a guess, but it seems feasible to proceed with the assumption that they are built in the human left hippocampus. Amnesics should, according to this veiw, demonstrate a lack of verbal mapping, much as they show a lack of spatial mapping. The remainder of this section focuses on some initial attempts to demonstrate this kind of defect in an amnesic patient.

During the course of a year's research with L. Squire, I studied the focal stab wound patient N. A. (see Squire & Slater, 1978; Squire, 1979; Teuber, Milner, & Vaughan, 1968, for discussion of this amnesic patient). N. A.'s brain damage seems limited to the left hemisphere (and to the dorsomedial nucleus of the thalamus on that side), his memory defect is primarily verbal, and he appears to be much like the left temporal lobectomy patients tested by Milner and her colleagues (cf. Milner, 1971). His performance on a paired associates test is very poor; N. A. recalls no more than 3 of 10 associates after three training trials.

In one of our studies with N. A. and his matched control subjects, we set up a "list discrimination" task with sentences as the to-be-remembered items. In this study, subjects read two lists of 12 sentences each, separated by a 3 min interval (LISTS 1 and 2). Retention was tested 5 min later by presenting 36 sentences (LISTS 1 and 2, plus a new LIST 3) in random order. Subjects first had to indicate, for each sentence, if it was old or new, and then, if it was judged as old, which LIST it had been on. Given that the two sentence lists were presented in the same physical environment, in the presence of the same experimenter, there appear to be only two kinds of information the subjects could use to make successful list attributions. First, they could make *temporal context,* or recency, judgments—deciding which list a sentence was on in terms of how recently they judged it to have been heard. Second, they could make *associative context* judgments—deciding list membership by somehow remembering that certain sentences went together. By itself, this strategy could not work, as subjects might be able to group the same-list sentences together without knowing *which* list came first or second.

Figure 10.5 shows that N. A. performed below normal levels on both recognition and context (list attribution) judgments. Although it might seem that N. A. was particularly impaired on the context task, this does not appear to be the case. We tested control subjects at a variety of retention intervals, seeking a point on the normal forgetting curve where recognition would match that seen in N. A.. For our controls this occured somewhere between 40 and 90 min after presentation of the second list. With recognition performance thus degraded, that is, with a diminished corpus of sentences to associate, normal subjects also failed on the context measure. Thus, N. A.'s failure in this task seems explicable in terms of his generally defective memory for sentences; the same appears true of subjects tested during the amnesic phase of recovery from electroconvulsive (ECT) shock therapy (Squire, Nadel, & Slater, 1979). There do not appear to be selective defects in the ability of amnesic subjects to use the forms of context available in this study.

One of the striking features of the data is the rather poor performance on the context task by control subjects. With a 5-min retention interval context, judgments were correct only 66% of the time, barely better than chance. In an attempt to improve upon this performance, lists consisting of three sets of 4 related sentences were compiled. These sets established semantic contexts within which sentences from the same list could be recognized and associated. The use of related sentences led to a marked improvement in control subjects

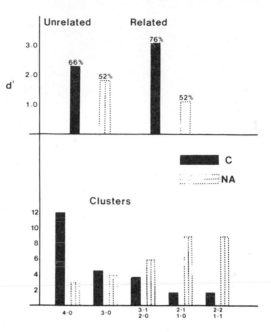

FIG. 10.5.   TOP: memory strength (d′) and list attribution performance for N. A. and control subjects using either related or unrelated sentences, as described in the text. BOTTOM: Clustering of related sentences in terms of attributions by subjects to the same list of those related sentences judged as old. When all four related sentences were recognized as old and attributed to the same list, this gave rise to a 4–0 for that set.

in both recognition and list attribution, as shown in Fig. 10.5 but paradoxically led to poorer recognition performance in N. A., leaving his context judgments at chance. It was possible to measure in this study the extent to which subjects put related sentences together, independent of assigning them to the correct list. Figure 10.5 shows that the control subjects generally attributed related sentences to the same list, though this was not inevitable. One control subject showed the interesting pattern of good clustering of related sentences with chance performance on the list attribution task, indicating that these functions are indeed separable. As the figure shows, N. A. was more or less random in terms of clustering related sentences, indicating that he was at least defective, if not altogether lacking, in the ability to form and/or use integrated semantic contexts.

These preliminary data are consistent with the view that amnesia involves a loss of the ability to put together verbal semantic maps.[2] It is our view that the profound loss of memory capacity seen in amnesic patients reflects the extent to which this cognitive system is involved in verbal memory processes. Information coded for its spatial (or semantic) context of occurrence will, by virtue of that encoding, be easier to retrieve: A map provides many independent retrieval routes, as discussed earlier.

---

[2]To be fair, this is not the only interpretation of these data. One would like to test control subjects at a variety of retention intervals and manipulate other variables in testing N. A. before concluding that there was a selective defect here.

It is intriguing that related sentences in our study facilitated normal performance but actually made N. A.'s recognition performance worse. One might have said that N. A. was unusually susceptible to interference from related materials. This would be accurate description, and its general presence in amnesic performance formed the basis for one recent model of amnesia, as noted already (Warrington & Weiskrantz, 1970). The data just presented suggest that this symptom could be the indirect product of a more deep-seated failure. Semantic maps, by linking together related events or event descriptions provide the means by which otherwise confusingly similar acquisitions can be kept in separate order. Without the disambiguating context they provide, amnesic patients, like rats with hippocampal lesions, appear reduced to behaving in contextually inappropriate ways.

GAPS IN THE MAPS

It is an advantage of maps that they retain their utility even though dotted with uncharted areas. Three relatively unexplored regions bear mention and some discussion in the final section of this chapter:

1. *The Learning–Performance Distinction.* Cognitive map theory requires a separation between what is learned and what is performed and hence calls for the specification of map utilization as well as formation. Guthrie's influential "lost in thought at the choice point" criticism of Tolman's cognitive theory was aimed at this problem. Although it is less heretical today to allow for a distinction between learning and performance, the rules by which behavior is generated from cognitive maps remain to be spelled out with precision. Some of what the mapping system does gets done without conscious thought or plan (e.g., the tracking of novelty), but other functions, such as deciding the best route from place A to place B, seem to require conscious control. The way in which behavior is generated from cognitive maps, and the physiological mechanisms underlying this transcription, are prominent candidates for future research.

2. *Memory Stages.* What aspects of memory function require hippocampal participation? The discrepancy between animal lesion data and human clinical observations is most obvious in this domain. Amnesic patients, incapable of learning most new things, generally have adequate working memory unless they are disrupted, and have apparent access to most of what they learned prior to disease onset (cf. Milner, 1966). This split between anterograde and retrograde effects has suggested to many investigators that the hippocampal role is somehow limited to the stages during which memory transfers or is "transformed" from some transient short-term format to a permanent long-term storage system. Though adequate definition

of this "consolidation" function has not been achieved at any level, the idea persists that the hippocampus is some sort of catalyst, or temporary-memory register, necessary for learning but not for retention. Both Olton (in press) and Wickelgren (1979) have proposed models of this type, as did Marr (1971) some years ago.

Three current areas of investigation suggest to us that this approach, with respect to both hippocampal function and the amnesic syndrome, is probably misguided. First, this view predicts that hippocampal lesions in animals will fail to produce deficits in the retention of preoperatively acquired information, much as amnesic patients often show little apparent retrograde loss. However, defects in cognitive mapping tasks such as complex spatial mazes are typically seen, both in post-operative learning (e.g., Kimble & Dannen, 1977) *and* in post-operative retention (e.g., Thomas, 1971; Thompson, 1974; Sinnamon, Freniere, & Kootz, 1978).[3] These data suggest a role in memory storage for the hippocampus. Second, neurophysiological data from studies of synaptic plasticity in the hippocampus, as described by Goddard (Chapter 11, this volume), demonstrate that both transient and long-term changes can be induced at the same synapses; this argues for both short- and long-term memory functions within the hippocampus.

Third and finally, the conception of working memory most recently applied to the hippocampus (cf. Olton, 1977) has been called into question by several recent results. Olton has suggested that the spatial working memory function of the hippocampus can be likened to the working memory concept studied in human list learning research, or in the operant task frequently used with pigeons and monkeys known as "delayed matching to sample" or DMTS. According to Olton, this working memory can be thought of as a list of positions in an environment defined by stimuli at or near those positions. Rats use their hippocampal working memory to keep track of those positions they have recently visited, so as to avoid them in the future in a food-gathering task, or approach them when food can only be found in particular positions. Whereas these appear to be the kinds of functions that the spatial mapping system can subserve, the characteristics of this spatial working memory system do not correspond to those postulated by Olton. Maki et al. (1979) demonstrated that spatial working memory is unlike other kinds of working memory because it is strongly resistant to interference from competing tasks, even ones that appear highly related to the contents of "working memory" at the time. The work of Suzuki, Augerinos, and Black (in press) shows that the

---

[3]Several recent studies have shown that rats with certain selective hippocampal lesions *can* relearn spatial mazes (Jarrard, 1978; Winson, 1978). Our position on such data is that relearning is accomplished by means of alternative strategies after operation. This can only be tested by probe trial procedures both before and after operation to demonstrate what kind of learning strategies the rats are using.

entities in the spatial working memory system are *places*, defined by the relations among cues in the environment, and not elements in a list as Olton supposed. Finally, Roberts (1979) demonstrated that this working memory system has no obvious capacity limitation, calling into question altogether the legitimacy of the working memory label.

In sum, there are reasons to question the view that the hippocampal cognitive mapping system functions as a temporary memory buffer of some sort. However, the split between anterograde and retrograde defects in amnesic patients that originally fostered this view remains to be explained. Our preference at present, vaguely stated, is: What looks like the "transfer" of information from one neural/cognitive system to another is more aptly characterized as the "recoding" of information in another, spatial-context independent, system.

3. *The Nature of Context*. If there can be said to be an emerging consensus on hippocampal function, it is that this structure and its immediate neighbors are somehow involved in *context* effects. Context is an overused word, applied in many situations, and not without considerable theoretical problems. We do consider spatial maps to be important in providing contextual processing and storage capacities, as noted earlier, but see the need for considerable caution here lest this notion approach the vacuousness of others applied in the past (cf. Nadel & O'Keefe, 1974). Nonetheless, it seems clear that whatever context is, the hippocampus has something to do with it.

The most important qualifier is that there are many kinds of context— internal (as in hormonal or motivational), cultural, social, temporal, spatial, associative, phonetic, semantic, and so on. The list is as long as one's patience to enumerate the kinds of frameworks within which elements can be arranged; these frameworks themselves contributing something to the interpretation of the elements. Those investigators who have applied the contextual handle to hippocampal function (Hirsh, 1974; Solomon, 1979; Wickelgren, 1979; Winocur & Kinsbourne, 1978; Winocur & Olds, 1978) have generally failed to distinguish between these different kinds of context in their models. In contrast to this approach, we have sought to restrict the contextual role of the hippocampus to the spatial or semantic contexts discussed in this chapter. (see O'Keefe & Nadel, 1978; O'Keefe, Nadel & Willner, 1979). The data from amnesic patients demonstrate no particular failure at temporal or associative context coding (Squire, Nadel, & Slater, 1979; Winocur & Kinsbourne, 1978) but do raise the possibility of defects in semantic context processing. Considerably more data are required before this suggestion can be asserted with any degree of certainty. What can and will be asserted, however, is that closer study of the pure language capacities of amnesic patients would strongly improve our chances of coming to a clearer understanding of the precise form of verbal context in which the hippocampus plays a role.

   More immediately approachable, perhaps, is the search for a theory of spatial context effects in learning—what is the spatial context, how is it defined and internally represented by the animal, how does it influence or interact with the things (stimuli) occuring within it, and how does it bear on the associations formed among these stimuli when various contingencies (temporal and other) are arranged? According to our view, places or spatial contexts can be defined by the stimuli that they are paradoxically thought to "contain." That is, the container, or space, is defined by the contents, or elements, that fill it. Although this hierarchical relation is in the spirit of the "vertical chunking" discussed by Wickelgren (1979) in his stimulating review paper, our current preference is to eschew his, and other, versions of the theory that assign to the hippocampus a broad range of contextual functions. A context is like a set of rules specifying the relations of interest among a group of elements by structuring the framework within which these elements are cast. One might say that it is by virtue of the framework, or context, that these elements are seen to be related in this way at all. The spatial frame helps the organism establish the subjective, three-dimensional, continuous environment in which we act and live, and within which we must find our clues to adaptive behavior. To a considerably greater extent than many have recently allowed, learning, memory, and performance are influenced by the places where things are located or where events transpire.

   In *The Italians*, Barzini poses the question: Can psychology be mixed up with geography? Advanced organisms need to map spaces that go beyond immediate apprehension, beyond the here and now, and hence must become geographers if they are to do all the things mobile, social species do. One of the earliest reactions to the current resurgence of interest in spatial mapping was to assume that rats, after all, are highly spatial animals, living in burrows, and that their spatial mapping capacity is some special adaptation to be expected in such a species (cf. Bolles, 1978). However, the research of Peters (1973) in wolves, Menzel (1978) in chimps, and O'Keefe (in press) in rabbits, as well as many recent investigations in humans, all attest to the generality of the spatial mapping function, both behaviorally and physiologically. It must be left to future work to determine the precise physiological basis of the mapping system and its exact role in behavior, but it is likely that this will become central to our understanding of normal learning and memory processes.

ACKNOWLEDGMENTS

During the writing of this manuscript, I was supported by grants from the Natural Sciences and Engineering Research Council of Canada, the Dalhousie University Development Fund, and the Human Factors Programme, NATO. Much of what is written here is based on collaborative work with John O'Keefe during 6 years in England at the Department of Anatomy, University College London, where we were supported by the MRC and SRC of the United Kingdom, as well as the Wellcome Trust. My thanks to John for the use of some of his unpublished data and for all the contributions he has so obviously made to the ideas in this chapter, or at least to the good ones. Special thanks go also to Larry Squire, first for his generous and unconditional support, second for providing access to the amnesic patient, N. A., and finally, for graciously tolerating an opposing viewpoint. The interpretations put on N. A.'s data are mine; the caution thrown to the wind is Larry's.

Several members of a cognitive seminar at Dalhousie have made important improvements in this paper, forcing me to clarify it so that they could at least understand it, if not agree with it. The additional comments of other members of the seminar, B. Earhard, M. Ozier, J. Willner, and J. Day in particular, aside from the special thanks to J. Barresi, P. Juscyzk, and R. Klein, must be recorded. Finally, the support, criticism, and financial help of G. Goddard are noted; his help throughout this enterprise to both John and myself must be acknowledged.

REFERENCES

Baddeley, A. D., & Warrington, E. K. Memory coding and amnesia. *Neuropsychologia*, 1973, *11*, 159–165.

Bellezza, F. S., & Reddy, B. G. Mnemonic devices and natural memory. *Bulletin of the Psychonomic Society*, 1978, *11*, 277–280.

Best, P. J., & Ranck, J. B., Jr. Reliability of the relationship between unit activity and behavior in the rat. *Neuroscience Abstracts*, 1975, *1*, 538.

Black, A. H., Nadel, L., & O'Keefe, J. Hippocampal function in avoidance learning and punishment. *Psychological Bulletin*, 1977, *84*, 1107–1129.

Bolles, R. C. *Learning Theory* (2nd ed.). New York: Holt, Rinehart & Winston, 1978.

Brooks, D. N., & Baddeley, A. D. What can amnesic patients learn? *Neuropsychologia*, 1976, *14*, 623–624.

Cermak, L. S., Lewis, R., Butters, N., & Goodglass, H. Role of verbal mediation in performance of motor tasks by Korsakoff patients. *Perceptual and Motor Skills*, 1973, *37*, 259–262.

Cohen, N., & Squire, L. R. *Acquisition of motor and verbal skill in the amnesic syndrome.* Paper read at the International Neuropsychological Society meetings. New York, February 1979.

Corkin, S. Acquisition of motor skill after bilateral medial temporal-lobe excision. *Neuropsychologia*, 1968, *6*, 255–265.

Gaffan, D. Loss of recognition memory in rats with lesions of the fornix. *Neuropsychologia*, 1972, *10*, 327–341.

Green, J. D., & Arduini, A. Hippocampal electrical activity in arousal. *Journal of Neurophysiology*, 1954, *17*, 533–557.

Hebb, D. O. *The organization of behavior.* New York: Wiley-Interscience, 1949.

Hill, A. J. First occurrence of hippocampal spatial firing in a new environment. *Experimental Neurology*, 1978, *62*, 282–297.

Hirsh, R. The hippocampus and contextual retrieval of information from memory: A theory. *Behavioral Biology*, 1974, *12*, 421–444.

Horel, J. A. The neuroanatomy of amnesia. A critique of the hippocampal memory hypothesis. *Brain*, 1978, *101*, 403–445.

Ittelson, W. H. (Ed.). *Environmental cognition.* New York: Seminar Press, 1973.

Jackendoff, R. Toward an explanatory semantic representation. *Linguistic Inquiry*, 1976, *7*, 89–150.

Jackendoff, R. Grammar as evidence for conceptual structure. In M. Halle, J. Bresnan, & G. A. Miller (Eds.), *Linguistic theory and psychological reality*. Cambridge, Mass.: MIT Press, 1978.

Jackson, W. J., & Strong, P. N., Jr. Differential effects of hippocampal lesions upon sequential tasks and maze learning by the rat. *Journal of Comparative and Physiological Psychology*, 1969, *68*, 442–450.

Jarrard, L. E. Selective hippocampal lesions: Differential effects on performance by rats of a spatial task with preoperative versus postoperative training. *Journal of Comparative and Psyiological Psychology*, 1978, *92*, 1119–1127.

Jones, M. K. Imagery as a mnemonic aid after left temporal lobectomy: Contrast between material-specific and generalized memory disorders. *Neuropsychologia*, 1974, *12*, 21–30.

Jones-Gotman, M., & Milner, B. Right temporal-lobe contribution to image-mediated verbal learning. *Neuropsychologia*, 1978, *16*, 61–71.

Kapur, N. Visual imagery capacity of alcoholic Korsakoff patients. *Neuropsychologia*, 1978, *16*, 517–519.

Kimble, D. P. The effects of bilateral hippocampal lesions in rats. *Journal of Comparative and Physiological Psychology*, 1963, *56*, 273–283.

Kimble, D. P., & Dannen, E. Persistent spatial maze-learning deficits in hippocampal-lesioned rats across a 7-week postoperative period. *Physiological Psychology*, 1977, *5*, 409–413.

Kinsbourne, M., & Wood, F. Short-term memory and the amnesic syndrome. In D. Deutsch & J. A. Deutsch (Eds.), *Short-term memory*. New York: Academic Press, 1975.

Lubow, R. E., Rifkin, B., & Alek, M. The context effect: The relationship between stimulus preexposure and environmental preexposure determines subsequent learning. *Journal of Experimental Psychology. Animal Behavior Processes*, 1976, *2*, 38–47.

Maki, W. S., Brokofsky, S., & Berg, B. Spatial memory in rats: Resistance to retroactive inference. *Animal Learning and Behavior*, 1979, *7*, 25–30.

Marr, D. Simple memory: A theory for archicortex. *Philosophical Transactions of the Royal Society* (Series B), 1971, *262*, 23–80.

Means, L. W., & Douglas, R. J. Effects of hippocampal lesions on cue utilization in spatial discrimination in rats. *Journal of Comparative and Physiological Psychology*, 1970, *73*, 254–260.

Menzel, E. W. Cognitive mapping in chimpanzees. In S. H. Hulse, H. Fowler, & W. K. Honig (Eds.), *Cognitive processes in animal behavior*. Hillsdale, N.J.: Lawrence Erlbaum Associates, 1978.

Milner, B. Amnesia following operation on the temporal lobes. In C. W. M. Whitty & O. L. Zangwill (Eds.), *Amnesia*. London: Butterworth, 1966.

Milner, B. Interhemispheric differences and psychological processes. *British Medical Bulletin*, 1971, *27*, 272–277.

Morris, R. G. M., Black, A. H., & O'Keefe, J. Hippocampal EEG during a ballistic movement. *Neuroscience Letters*, 1976, *3*, 102. (Abstract).

Nadel, L. *Cognitive maps: At the choice point again.* Paper read at American Psychological Association meetings. New York City, September, 1979.

Nadel, L., & O'Keefe, J. The hippocampus in pieces and patches: An essay on modes of explanation in physiological psychology. In R. Bellairs & E. G. Gray (Eds.), *Essays on the Nervous System: A Festschrift for Prof. J. Z. Young*. Oxford: The Claredon Press, 1974.

Nadel, L., O'Keefe, J., & Black, A. H. Slam on the brakes: A critique of Altman, Brunner and Bayer's response inhibition model of hippocampal function. *Behavioral Biology*, 1975, *14*, 151–162.

O'Keefe, J. Place units in the hippocampus of the freely moving rat. *Experimental Neurology*, 1976, *51*, 78–109.

O'Keefe, J. A review of the hippocampal place cells. *Reviews in Neurobiology*, in press.

O'Keefe, J., & Conway, D. Hippocampal place units in the freely moving rat: Why they fire when they fire. *Experimental Brain Research,* 1978, *31,* 573–590.

O'Keefe, J., & Dostrovsky, J. The hippocampus as a spatial map. Preliminary evidence from unit activity in the freely-moving rat. *Brain Research,* 1971, *34,* 171–175.

O'Keefe, J., & Nadel, L. Maps in the brain. *New Scientist,* 1974, *62,* 749–751.

O'Keefe, J., & Nadel, L. *The hippocampus as a cognitive map,* Oxford: The Claredon Press, 1978.

O'Keefe, J., Nadel, L., Keightley, D., & Kill, D. Fornix lesions selectively abolish place learning in the rat. *Experimental Neurology,* 1975, *48,* 152–166.

O'Keefe, J., Nadel, L., & Willner, J. Tuning out irrelevancy? Comments on Solomon's temporal mapping view of hippocampus. *Psychological Bulletin,* 1979, *86,* 1280–1289.

Olton, D. S. Spatial memory. *Scientific American,* 1977, *236,* 82–98.

Olton, D. S. *Hippocampal function and working memory. The Behavioral & Brain Sciences,* in press.

Olton, D. S., Branch, M., & Best, P. J. Spatial correlates of hippocampal unit activity. *Experimental Neurology,* 1978, *58,* 387–409.

Peters, R. Cognitive maps in wolves and men. In W. F. E. Preiser (Ed.), *Environmental design research,* (Vol. 2). 1973.

Petersen, R. C., & Jacob, S. H. Evidence for the role of contexts in imagery and recall. *American Journal of Psychology,* 1978, *91,* 305–311.

Ranck, J. B., Jr. Studies on single neurons in dorsal hippocampal formation and septum in unrestrained rats. *Experimental Neurology,* 1973, *41,* 461–555.

Ranck, J. B., Jr. *Spatial correlates of firing of single neurons in septal nuclei, hippocampus, and entorhinal cortex.* Paper read at Society for Neuroscience meetings, Anaheim, Calif., November 1977.

Reichman, R. Conversational coherency. *Cognitive Science,* 1978, *2,* 283–327.

Restle, F. Discrimination of cues in mazes: A resolution of the place-vs-response question. *Psychological Review,* 1957, *64,* 217–228.

Roberts, W. A. Spatial memory in the rat on a hierarchical maze. *Learning and Motivation,* 1979, *10,* 117–140.

Scoville, W. B., & Milner, B. Loss of recent memory after bilateral hippocampal lesion. *Journal of Neurology, Neurosurgery and Psychiatry,* 1957, *20,* 11–21.

Shalter, M. D. Effect of spatial context on the mobbing reaction of pied flycatchers to a predator model. *Animal Behaviour,* 1978, *26,* 1219–1221.

Sheafor, P. J. "Pseudoconditioned" jaw movements of the rabbit reflected associations conditioned to contextual background cues. *Journal of Experimental Psychology: Animal Behavior Processes,* 1975, *104,* 245–260.

Sidman, M., Stoddard, L., & Mohr, J. Some additional quantitative observations of immediate memory in a patient with bilateral hippocampal lesions. *Neuropsychologia,* 1968, *6,* 245–254.

Sinnamon, H. M., Freniere, S., & Kootz, J. Rat hippocampus and memory for places of changing significance. *Journal of Comparative and Physiological Psychology,* 1978, *92,* 142–155.

Smith, S. M., Glenberg, A., & Bjork, R. A. Environmental context and human memory. *Memory and Cognition,* 1978, *6,* 342–353.

Solomon, P. R. Misplaced data? The hippocampus in classical conditioning of the rabbit's nictitating membrane response: Temporal versus spatial information processing theories of hippocampal function. *Psychological Bulletin,* 1979, *86.*

Squire, L. R. *Diencephalic amnesia: Dorsal thalamic lesion in a noted case of human memory pathology.* Paper read at the International Neuropsychology Society Meetings, New York, February 1979.

Squire, L. R., Nadel, L., & Slater, P. C. *Anterograde amnesia and memory for contextual information.* Paper read at the Society for Neuroscience Meetings, Atlanta, Georgia, November 1979.

Squire, L. R., & Slater, P. C. Anterograde and retrograde memory impairment in chronic amnesia. *Neuropsychologia,* 1978, *16,* 313–322.

Squire, L. R., Wetzel, D., & Slater, P. C. Anterograde amnesia following ECT: An analysis of the beneficial effects of partial information. *Neuropsychologia,* 1978, *16,* 339–347.

Suzuki, S., Augerinos, G., & Black, A. H. Stimulus control of spatial behavior on the eight arm maze in rats. *Learning and Motivation,* in press.

Talland, G. *Deranged memory.* New York: Academic Press, 1965.

Teuber, H. L., Milner, B., & Vaughan, H. G., Jr. Persistent anterograde amnesia after stab wound of the basal brain. *Neuropsychologia,* 1968, *6,* 267–282.

Thomas, G. J. Maze retention by rats with hippocampal lesions and with fornicotomies. *Journal of Comparative and Physiological Psychology,* 1971, *75,* 41–49.

Thompson, R. Localization of the "maze memory system" in the white rat. *Physiological Psychology,* 1974, *2,* 1–17.

Tolman, E. C. Cognitive maps in rats and men. *Psychological Review,* 1948, *55,* 189–208.

Tulving, E., & Pearlstone, Z. Availability versus accessibility of information in memory for words. *Journal of Verbal Learning and Verbal Behavior,* 1966, *5,* 381–391.

Vanderwolf, C. H. Hippocampal electrical activity and voluntary movement in the rat. *Electroencephalography and Clinical Neurophysiology,* 1969, *26,* 407–418.

Vanderwolf, C. H. Neocortical and hippocampal activation in relation to behavior: Effects of atropine, eserine, phenothiazines and amphetamine. *Journal of Comparative and Physiological Psychology,* 1975, *88,* 300–323.

Vanderwolf, C. H., Bland, B. H., & Whishaw, I. Q. Diencephalic hippocampal and neocortical mechanisms in voluntary movement. In J. D. Maser (Ed.), *Efferent organization and the integration of behavior.* New York: Academic Press, 1973.

Warrington, E. K., & Weiskrantz, L. A study of learning and retention in amnesic patients. *Neuropsychologia,* 1968, *6,* 283–291.

Warrington, E. K., & Weiskrantz, L. Amnesic syndrome: Consolidation or retrieval? *Nature,* 1970, *228,* 628–630.

Warrington, E. K., & Weiskrantz, L. Further analysis of the prior learning effect of amnesic patients. *Neuropsychologia,* 1978, *16,* 169–177.

Wickelgren, W. A. Chunking and consolidation: A theoretical synthesis of semantic networks, configuring in conditioning, S–R versus cognitive learning, normal forgetting, the amnesic syndrome, and the hippocampal arousal system. *Psychological Review,* 1979, *86,* 44–60.

Winocur, G., & Kinsbourne, M. Contextual cueing as an aid to Korsakoff amnesics. *Neuropsychologia,* 1978, *16,* 671–682.

Winocur, G., & Olds, J. Effects of context manipulation on memory and reversal learning in rats with hippocampal lesions. *Journal of Comparative and Physiological Psychology,* 1978, *92,* 312–321.

Winocur, G., & Weiskrantz, L. An investigation of paired-associate learning in amnesic patients. *Neuropsychologia,* 1976, *14,* 97–110.

Winograd, E., & Lynn, D. S. Role of contextual imagery in associative recall. *Memory and Cognition,* 1979, *7,* 29–34.

Winson, J. Inter-species differences in the occurrence of theta. *Behavioral Biology,* 1972, *7,* 479–487.

Winson, J. Loss of hippocampal theta rhythm results in spatial memory deficits in the rat. *Science,* 1978, *201,* 160–163.

Woods, R. T., & Piercy, M. A similarity between amnesic memory and normal forgetting. *Neuropsychologia,* 1974, *12,* 437–445.

Yates, F. A. *The art of memory,* London: Routeledge & Kegan Paul, 1966.

11 Component Properties of the Memory Machine: Hebb Revisited

Graham V. Goddard
Dalhousie University

> When from a long distant past nothing subsists, after the people are dead, after the things are broken and scattered, still, alone, more fragile, but with more vitality, more unsubstantial, more persistent, more faithful, the smell and taste of things remain poised a long time, like souls, ready to remind us, waiting and hoping for their moment, amid the ruins of all the rest; and bear unfaltering, in the tiny and almost impalpable drop of their essence, the vast structure of recollection.
>
> —Marcel Proust

To many of us, the essence of Hebb's genius is found in Chapters 4 and 5 of the 1949 statement of his cell-assembly theory, *Organization of Behavior*. His theory attempted to explain psychological reality in terms of available knowledge of the anatomy and physiology of the nervous system. To the extent that it was strictly mechanistic, shunning vague analogy and rejecting dualism, while attempting great breadth of application, Hebb's theory had no predecessor and has had no peer. Since 1949, Hebb's contributions include insight and comment on almost every segment of psychology, always it seems, flowing naturally from his original neuropsychological theory. Many aspects of the theory were not based on hard physiological evidence. Hebb postulated a set of physiological assumptions that were necessary for the theory, but which could not be tested with the physiological methods of the day.

Developments in neuroscience over the past three decades have provided knowledge and methodology that now permit direct test of some of Hebb's main postulates. I describe here the relevant new knowledge and suggest how theoretical implications with significance for cognitive psychology may be generated by viewing this new knowledge from a Hebbian perspective. I cite evidence that certain types of neuronal activity result in at least two fundamentally different types of change in synapses. They have radically different time courses of decay and obey different rules for their formation. I argue that these properties must impose certain characteristic patterns of behavior upon any neuronal network containing such synapses. I then suggest how Hebbian cell-assembly theory in particular is affected by these properties.

THE THEORY

Let me first describe the essential features of Hebb's original theory, accepting Milner's revision, which includes inhibition (Milner, 1957). The brain is made up of millions of interconnected neurons. The most common type of connection between them is the chemical synapse. Each neuron sends its output signal, which may be excitatory or inhibitory, from the terminals of its branching axon across many such synapses. Likewise, each neuron receives input signals from many synapses distributed along its dendrites and cell body. We now know that many neurons send over ten thousand outputs and receive more than a hundred thousand inputs. A neuron that connects to another neuron does not do so at random, but in a structured and complex way. The total set of neuronal pathways involve convergent and divergent feed-forward connections as well as convergent and divergent feed-back connections. The possible number of open and closed loop circuits within this network is immense.

As a first approximation, a neuron will discharge whenever the sum of excitation it receives is greater than the sum of inhibition. The impulse travels from the initial segment to most if not all of the axon terminals, releasing a transmitter substance across the synapses and affecting each of the many postsynaptic neurons. In Hebb's theory, each psychologically significant event, such as a sensation, percept, expectation, memory, emotion, or thought is neither more nor less than the flow of activity in a set of interconnected neurons. Emphasis is placed on positive feedback and reverberation of activity in re-entrant loops called cell assemblies. Fig. 11.1 (reproduced from Hebb, 1949) illustrates the complexity of temporal and spatial distribution that such a cell-assembly would assume in a three-dimensional brain.

In Hebb's theory, one percept differs from another if activity flows through different cell assemblies. By virtue of its branching structure, any one neuron might participate in many different cell assemblies. Thus, when the inputs to one neuron cause it to become active, it tends to excite or inhibit a number of

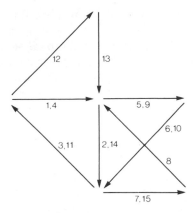

FIG. 11.1. Arrows represent a simple "assembly" of neural pathways or open multiple chains firing according to the numbers on each (the pathway "1, 4" fires first and fourth, and so on), illustrating the possibility of an "alternating" reverberation that would not extinguish as readily as that in a simple closed circuit (Hebb, 1949).

other neurons. Whether or not they become active depends in part on inputs received from other sources, and in part on the strength of the synapses in question. Which neurons are thus brought to a state of activity will determine which cell assemblies are brought into play.

In order to provide a basis for learning, Hebb assumed that the strength of a synapse can be modified. He postulated an increase in strength whenever a synapse conducts excitation at just the time when the postsynaptic neuron discharges. As explained in his second footnote of Chapter 4 (Hebb, 1949), the required conjunction provides the basis for association: If an input to a cell occurs reliably at the same time as others, together they will be sufficient to activate the cell. As a consequence, the particular input coincides with the cell's activation and is strengthened. This strengthening by association means that, at a later date, the input in question could activate the cell without the assistance of all the usually occurring associates.

Behind this argument lies an important concept: Each neuron is a choice point in the network of the brain. When active, it tends to excite many other neurons, some more strongly than others. Which of these excited neurons actually become active will depend partly on the strength of the exciting synapses and partly on the sum of other inputs being received at the time. The factors determining which cell assemblies come into play at any moment in life are thus fourfold: The ongoing activity of neurons carried forward from the immediate past, the incoming sensory excitation arising from both the internal milieu and the external environment, the "hard wired" anatomical structure of the brain, and the "soft wired" relative strengths of synapses. The promise of Hebb's theory is that an understanding of the hard wiring will provide explanations for gestalt properties and the psychology of the Continental Rationalists, and an understanding of synaptic plasticity will provide explanations for memory and the psychology of the British Empiricists. My comments will be relevant, if at all, to the latter issue; but first, the evidence.

PHYSIOLOGICAL EVIDENCE

Bliss and Lømo (1973) were the first to show unequivocally that long-lasting changes in the strength of a synapse can occur in the brain of an adult mammal. They used a technique, which is standard in neurophysiology for demonstrating a well-known short-lasting phenomenon of increased synaptic conductance, called post-tetanic potentiation. In this method, a preliminary test pulse of electricity, less than 1 msec in duration, is delivered to a nerve or pathway (axons), and the magnitude of response in the area to which the axons project is measured in terms of voltage change (evoked potential), which corresponds to the depolarization of the post-synaptic membranes by the transmitter released from the terminals of the activated axons. Depending on the electrode configuration and the anatomy of the system under study, the response may be recorded from within one cell or as an average of many.

Bliss and Lømo (1973) used an electrode configuration that recorded the average response of many cells in the fascia dentata of the hippocampus (see Fig. 11.2). This technique allows stable recording over very long periods of time. The test pulse is normally delivered once every few seconds. After a stable baseline of response to the test pulse has been established, a train of pulses at higher frequency is applied, driving the system very hard. The test pulses are then resumed, once every few seconds, and the magnitude of response is expressed as the percent increase over the response to the preliminary test pulse. The time course of decay back to original baseline is also measured.

As known from many previous studies of post-tetanic potentiation, the response to the test pulse is markedly increased shortly after repetitive

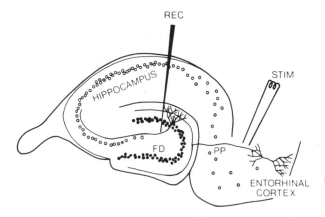

FIG. 11.2. Schematic section through hippocampus showing electrode configuration used in many of the studies described in the text. FD—granule cells of fascia dentata; pp—perforant path; stim—stimulation electrode; rec—recording electrode.

activation and returns to normal within a time course of some several minutes, depending partly on the system under study, and partly on how hard and for how long the system has been driven. Post-tetanic potentiation has been observed in many different neural systems. It has been studied in greatest detail where it is most accessible for study, the neuromuscular junction. Wherever it has been studied, the mechanism of this short-lasting change appears to be presynaptic (i.e., in the axon reaching the synapse, not in the cell on the other side), the axon terminal releasing more transmitter substance per depolarization for a period of time after it has been highly active.

The new information discovered by Bliss and Lømo (1973) was that responses recorded in the rabbit hippocampus to test pulses on the incoming perforant path may remain elevated for as long as is practical to measure them (in that study, about 16 hours). Because this long-lasting increase in synaptic transmission differs from post-tetanic potentiation, it has been called by a new name, "enhancement" (McNaughton, 1977).[1] Bliss and Gardner-Medwin (1973) used awake rabbits with chronically implanted electrodes to extend the observation period and report examples of enhancement lasting many days. Enhancement has since been observed in rats, still present in some cases after 2 months, (Douglas & Goddard, 1975), and in the squirrel monkey (Goddard & Douglas, 1976). Barnes (1977, 1979) has reported that enhancement decays within a few days unless the high-frequency stimulation is repeated a few times, in which case it can last much longer.

The factors necessary and sufficient to produce lasting alterations in synaptic strength are under investigation in several different laboratories (see Bliss, 1979, for review)[2]. Although minor controversy and confusion has arisen over some of the details, the main phenomenon of enhancement is no longer in question and has been shown to occur in the hippocampus at more than one type of excitatory synapse.

In a fine-grained analysis of the time course of the changes in synaptic strength that follow high-frequency activation of the perforant path, McNaughton (1978) has found that both post-tetanic potentiation and enhancement can co-exist in the same system. In fact, two processes are probably too few to adequately describe the changes over time that occur within these synapses. For the arguments to be developed later, it is sufficient to distinguish between the short-term changes (summarily referred to here as potentiation) and the long-term changes (enhancement). Of prime im-

---

[1]Bliss, and other authors, have used the term "long-term potentiation."

[2]The reader who is interested in the molecular mechanisms that underlie these effects is referred to studies in which similar effects are observed in slices of hippocampal tissue that have been removed from the brain and maintained in an appropriately moist and oxygenated environment (Alger & Teyler, 1976; Anderson, Sundberg, & Sveen, 1977; Dudek, Deadwyler, Cotman & Lynch, 1976; Dunwiddie & Lynch, 1978; Lynch, Dunwiddie, & Gribkoff, 1977; Schwartzkroin & Wester, 1975; Yamamoto, 1970).

portance is evidence that potentiation and enhancement are generated by very different rules of nervous system activity.

Both potentiation and enhancement are generated when axons leading to the synapses in question discharge repetitively at a moderate to high rate. A complete description of the parameters has not been worked out, but one condition that results in both potentiation and enhancement is a brief train of some half dozen impulses at about 400 Hz (Douglas, 1977). Neurons in many different parts of the nervous system have been shown capable of discharging in such bursts when activated strongly (Calvin, 1974; Ranck, 1973) implying that the conditions for potentiation and enhancement may occur in the normal life of a normal brain.

Enhancement approaches asymptote when the high-frequency stimulation is repeated many times (McNaughton, Douglas, & Goddard, 1978). Enhanced to their limit, however, the synapses retain their ability to show further short-term potentiation (McNaughton, 1978).

An important condition for enhancement, which is not required for potentiation, is that the high-frequency stimulation must be delivered to a sufficient number of axons converging to the area (McNaughton, et al., 1978). In other words, cooperative action is necessary before enhancement is seen at any of the synapses. When the enhancement occurs, it is seen at, and only at, the synapses exposed to the high-frequency inputs (McNaughton & Barnes, 1977). By varying the number of perforant path fibers activated by the high-frequency stimulation, it was found that the threshold number of inputs for inducing enhancement is remarkably close to the threshold number for activating cell discharge (McNaughton et al., 1978). This condition is reminiscent of Hebb's postulate that synapses change only when they are active at the time of post-synaptic cell firing.

However, by imposing inhibition to prevent cell discharge at the critical time, it is possible to show that enhancement does not depend on cell firing in the way that Hebb thought it might, at least not in the hippocampal system under study (Douglas, 1978a, 1978b; McNaughton et al., 1978). This failure to confirm the exact form of the Hebb hypothesis, however, is far less critical to his general theory than might have been expected. As noted earlier, Hebb's postulate that synapses are strengthened when their action coincides with postsynaptic cell firing was the mechanism by which he made synaptic change dependent on the association of activity between several inputs. But Hebb's postulate is rendered unnecessary by the emprically determined rule that enhancement is based on cooperative action of convergent inputs. The same theoretical associative properties of cell-assemblies are achieved in both cases. The only significant difference is that, unlike the Hebbian synapse, enhancement may sometimes result from appropriate convergent activity, even in the absence of cell discharge. At the theoretical level, this minor difference might have implications for learning in the absence of an overt response.

Although enhancement is not prevented by inhibition strong enough to prevent cell discharge, it can be aborted by high-frequency input from the inhibitory pathway (Douglas, 1978a, 1978b). High-frequency stimulation of the inhibitory commissural path prevented the enhancement that otherwise resulted from high-frequency stimulation of the perforant path. Potentiation, however, was not affected. We do not know why a single inhibitory input fails to affect enhancement when high-frequency input from the same pathway can prevent it. The finding is interestingly symmetrical to the finding that a single excitatory impulse from many fibers can discharge cells en masse and have no lasting effect, whereas high-frequency activation of the same fibers can cause enhancement.

The shape of the curve describing decay of potentiation over time is shown in Fig. 11.3. Two curves have been drawn: one to show potentiation on an occasion when enhancement is also induced, and one to show potentiation on an occasion when potentiation occurs alone. The latter can happen when too few fibers engage in high-frequency activity, or when concurrent high-frequency inhibition is present, or when the synapses in question have been enhanced to asymptote on a previous occasion. These curves are drawn from

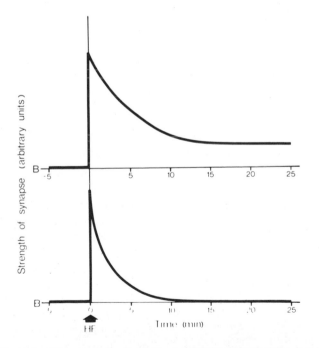

FIG. 11.3. Time course of decay of synaptic strength following high-frequency (HF) stimulation. In the upper curve, synaptic strength does not return to baseline (B) indicating enhancement was induced by the HF. In the lower curve, synaptic strength does return to baseline, indicating that potentiation only was induced on this occasion.

the data obtained in the hippocampus of anesthetized rats (Douglas, 1978a; McNaughton, 1977; McNaughton, 1978; McNaughton et al., 1978), and the time scale should be taken to indicate only a crude approximation of what might be expected elsewhere.

NETWORK IMPLICATIONS

It is assumed that in any brain or neural network, each excitatory neuron acts as a complex choice point where entering activity may exit as activation of some but not all of the many neurons to which it projects. Which of those neurons are activated will depend partly on synaptic strength and partly on momentary converging inputs from all other anatomically possible sources. Figure 11.4 simplifies this complex situation to a neuron A which has excitatory connection to only two other neurons: B and C. When an event occurs in which A discharges with high frequency, and when the context of that event involves activity of D and E, then B will be excited by the joint action of A and D, whereas C will remain inactive due to excitation from A and inhibition from E.

In addition to the immediate outcome, B active and C silent, the synapses would be left in a modified state. Synapse A–B would be enhanced because the high-frequency excitation received by neuron B from both A and D would

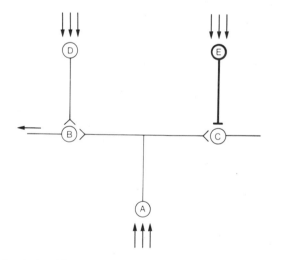

FIG. 11.4.   A simplified choice point in a network of neurons in which neuron A has excitatory synaptic connection to neurons B and C. Neuron D has excitatory synaptic connection to B, whereas neuron E has inhibitory connection to C. When A, D, and E are all active, B is activated whereas C remains inactive. If A became active at high frequency, synapses A–B and A–C would both be potentiated (short term), whereas only the A–B synapse and not the A–C synapse would be enhanced (long term).

cooperate to exceed the enhancement threshold. Neuron C, on the other hand, receives high-frequency input from A that is not concurrent with other excitatory inputs, only with the inhibition from D. These conditions are not adequate for enhancement of the $A-C$ synapse. As explained earlier, however, potentiation is likely to be a presynaptic phenomenon that would occur at *all* terminals of a highly active axon, and therefore would occur at $A-C$ just as readily as at $A-B$. Such potentiation in the presence of concurrent inhibition has been demonstrated by Douglas (1978a, 1978b). Thus, enhancement would occur only at the $A-B$ synapse, whereas potentiation would occur at both the $A-B$ and $A-C$ synapses. Clearly, enhancement is a very selective process, whereas potentiation is quite unselective.

Because enhancement is durable and potentiation fades, a probe stimulus that excites A will have different consequences in the network at different times after the potentiation-enhancement experience. Obviously, if the other inputs (D and E) were the same, the outcome (activation of B, not C) would also be the same, regardless of time. But if the D and E inputs were not present, but perhaps some other random inputs to B and C, then the probability of activating B or C, or both, would depend more heavily on the relative strengths of the $A-B$ and the $A-C$ synapses. In the short term, because potentiation can be very powerful and because both $A-B$ and $A-C$ are potentiated, A might activate B, C, or both. Activation of B would be somewhat favored because $A-B$ is enhanced as well as potentiated, whereas $A-C$ is potentiated only. In the long term, however, the outcome would clearly favor the activation of B only. This is because the enhancement at $A-B$ would persist whereas the potentiation at both would have decayed away. It is clear, therefore, that a choice between B and C cannnot be made on the basis of potentiation but only on the basis of enhancement.

The preceding paragraph has described the situation only in a naive network where enhancement is still possible. It is important to keep in mind that repeated enhancement of a synapse can drive that synapse to some asymptotic level. This might happen at $A-B$ on occasions such as the one just described. But at this very same choice point, enhancement might occur at $A-C$ on other occasions when A is very active but when the context involves excitatory inputs to neuron C. Eventually, both $A-B$ and $A-C$ could reach asymptote. Such a situation would then give equal probabilities of B or C as the outcome of activity in A, regardless of recent experience. Any network theory of the brain, it seems to me, should incorporate these attributes.

APPLICATION TO HEBB'S THEORY

It is clearly wrong to assume that all neurons of the brain are of like type, or that all intercellular communication is synaptic, or that all synapses will show properties of potentiation and enhancement, just as it is clearly wrong to view the mind as a tabula rasa to be given its entire form by experience. I stress only the plastic elements here because these are the only aspects of Hebb's theory about which I have anything new to say. Serious philosophical difficulties are encountered when trying to relate the working of the mind to the working of neurons, Hebb notwithstanding. Physiological psychology is an act of faith; it is the illogical assertion that to proceed with faulty assumptions is better than to do nothing at all and that, as knowledge is acquired, the imponderable problems will disappear. In this section I examine how the preceding descriptions of physiology might apply to psychology. This exercise requires the adoption of the remaining untested assumptions and general perspective of Hebb's theory.

Assume that the simplified situation represented in Fig. 11.4 is not only a choice between activation of neurons B and C, but is a contributing factor to the choice between activation of competing[3] cell assemblies. If we assume also that the high-frequency activation of A, D, and E (which activates B) is an episode of experience, then it follows that synapse $A-B$ will subsequently tend to excite a cell assembly leading to behavior that we would call correct remembering, whereas $A-C$ will tend to excite cell-assemblies leading to behavior that we would call erroneous remembering.

If this episode of experience were to occur in a naive brain, $A-B$ would be enhanced and potentiated, whereas $A-C$ would only be potentiated. A short-term memory probe, which tended to activate neuron A would favor outcome B, correct remembering, because enhancement and potentiation would add together to make $A-B$ more effective than $A-C$, which was merely potentiated. Similarly, a long-term memory probe that tended to activate neuron A would favor outcome B, correct remembering, because potentiation would have faded from both $A-B$ and $A-C$, leaving only the enhancement at $A-B$.

But all brains are not naive. Neither are they equally naive in all parts. I described earlier how both the $A-B$ and the $A-C$ synapses of Fig. 11.4 might have been enhanced on separate occasions to their respective asymptotic levels. If an episode of experience were to occur in a brain that had been habitually exposed to the constitutent stimulus conditions, the commonly used synapses would have little capacity for further enhancement. Thus, in our example, $A-B$ and $A-C$ would be equally potentiated by the episode, but neither would be additionally enhanced by it. A short-term memory probe that activates A will tend to activate B and C with equal strength, implying that an error is as likely as correct remembering.

---

[3]The whole question of competition between cell assemblies, or the "ecology" of patterned activity in nerve nets, is too complex to be dealt with at this time. I merely assume here that cell assemblies can be active and that, when active, they exclude others from activity. I also assume that they have a limited duration of activity and, by the processes described here, influence which cell assemblies are likely to become active upon their cessation.

Yet, short-term memory for familiar material is known to be very accurate. How then can a short-term memory probe that tends to activate *A* select appropriately between *B* and *C?* Clearly, the answer must lie in terms of the context. I assume that the *neural* context is the sum of all other excitatory and inhibitory influences on the neurons of the cell assemblies in question (e.g., *D* and *E* in Fig. 11.4) and, whereas this neural context is not strictly isomorphic with the *environmental* context of the behaving organism, it will be strongly affected by that environmental context. It is obvious that the sooner the memory probe is given after the episode of experience, the less the environment and neural context will have changed. The more similar the neural context is to that existing at the time of the episode of experience, the more it will facilitate accurate remembering.

The role of synaptic potentiation in short-term memory is to selectively strengthen all synapses of the previously active neurons. This will facilitate activation of a set of cell assemblies that is very much larger than the subset that was active during the episode of experience, but very much smaller than the set of all possible cell assemblies. This relatively diffuse form of priming, together with guidance from the neural context, is sufficient, I assume, to account for the accuracy of short-term memory. The property of diffuse priming, it seems to me, bears a striking resemblance to spreading activation theory as reviewed by Collins and Loftus (1975).

When considering long-term memory, and the effects of enhancement, it is convenient to think in terms of a complex network where activity from the sense organs directly affects only the most peripheral parts. Cell assemblies in the more peripheral parts of the net would tend to relate closely to sensory events, whereas cell assemblies in the more central parts would not have direct sensory components but would relate to particular conjunctions of activity from sets of peripheral cell assemblies. A formal similarity exists between the distinction of physical depth of cell assemblies in a network and the psychological levels-of-processing metaphor where peripheral can be interpreted as physical (e.g., acoustic) level and depth as semantic level (Craik & Lockhart, 1972).

The developmental sequence expected in a large complex brain of this type would be for commonly experienced sensory events to "structure" the peripheral areas first. Activity in more central areas will occur at all ages, but the patterns of activity that they receive will change as the peripheral areas become structured. When the central areas start to receive commonly recurring patterns of input from the periphery, they too will start to become more structured. The mechanism of structuring that I refer to here is simply the strengthening of certain cell assemblies by enhancement of their component synapses according to the rules described earlier. The more familiar a certain set of inputs becomes, the more closely will the component synapses of the relevant peripheral cell assemblies approach asymptotic levels of enhancement. The more this happens, the more stereotyped will be the output of those cell assemblies. The more stereotyped the output, the more suitable will be the conditions for association in central areas with stereotyped outputs from other peripheral cell assemblies.

But at the same time, the opportunity for new enhancement in synapses of the peripheral cell assemblies is diminished. An episode of experience comprised of familiar elements will involve activity in commonly used peripheral cell assemblies where the component synapses are fully enhanced. Only if an unusual sensory detail occurs will the possibility for new enhancement be present. Therefore, long-term memory of an episode cannot be based on differential enhancement of synapses in the peripheral cell assemblies.

As in the case of short-term memory, the context will be an important contributor to which cell assemblies are likely to be activated. But the delayed remembering of an episode that was comprised of familiar material can only be facilitated or degraded by the context. The context can only "set the stage" in Bransford and Franks' terms (1976); it cannot retrieve the items. The remembering of such an episode would have to be based on differential enhancement that can only result from some unusual attribute of the experience. If this unusual attribute was not provided by an unusual sensory feature, then the only loci in the netork where the differential enhancement of synapses is still possible are in the more central areas. That is, a central cell assembly, associated with the meaning of the particular configuration of familiar elements, is the only place where new learning might have occurred. Remembering, therefore, would be based on meaning, i.e., the semantic properties of the episode.

Presumably, the peripheral cell assemblies that were active at the time that the central assembly was formed could again be co-active with the central assembly and not interfere with it. In fact, they should facilitate it. But so also would certain other peripheral cell assemblies that happen to have excitatory connections with the central assembly. Other peripheral cell assemblies would be expected to interfere if they have inhibitory connections, either directly or indirectly, to the central assembly. Thus, a restricted set of peripheral assemblies are expected to have reciprocal excitatory connection with the central assembly, among which only a subset were active at the time that the synapses of the central assembly were enhanced. The peripheral cell-assemblies that most facilitate activity in the central assembly are the ones most likely to become active during the remembering, regardless of whether they were *actually* active during the original experience.[4]

Sensory details, therefore, comprise part of the remembering by being compatible with the meaning of the episode. The only other mechanism by

---

[4]The elementary neural mechanism by which this interactive capture and mutual support may occur are complex, but not mysterious. I presume it involves the same principles of facilitatory feedback and lateral inhibition as proposed by Milner to cause figure ground separation and the

which one peripheral cell might be activated in preference to another would be summation with some part of the ongoing neural context. Thus, it is clear that remembering after a long delay may correctly identify the meaning of the episode of experience, yet incorporate erroneous sensory detail that is compatible with the remembered meaning. These theoretical attributes may account for the fallibility of eyewitness evidence in which plausible, but erroneous details are "remembered" quite often with great conviction (Bartlett, 1932; Buckhout, 1974).[5]

The important statement here is that the type of error to be expected when testing for long-term memory of familiar material is different from the type of error expected when testing short-term memory. I explained earlier that good short-term memory of familiar material in an adult brain is made possible by a combination of potentiation at all synapses of the recently active neurons and persistence of a very similar neural context. But errors will occur. And when they occur, they will most likely involve activation of cell assemblies that were primed by synaptic potentiation. The sensory feature that is shared by two words that sound alike will activate peripheral neurons common to cell assemblies representing both words. The synapses between the common neurons and each of the cell assemblies will be left in a potentiated state, regardless of which particular cell assembly was activated. When an error is made in short-term memory, therefore, it is likely to be based on the potentiated synapses leading from previously active neurons to a nonactive cell assembly, and, thus, might involve the activation of an acoustically similar word, regardless of its meaning.

Long-term memory on the other hand is based on a probe that has been delayed until potentiation has faded. Potentiation-based errors originating in the periphery of the net, therefore, are less likely. Because the remembering must be based on activation of a cell assembly in parts of the brain where differential enhancement was possible (i.e., central areas representing semantic properties), errors, when they occur, are likely to involve the actvation of dissimilar sensory detail that does not conflict with the meaning of the experience.

The foregoing account, or point of view, has shown how both short- and long-term memory of an item *when correct* can involve one and the same set

---

emergence of "attention" in visual shape recognition (Milner, 1974, pp. 532, 533). The only added assumption is that a process involving the same organizational principles in the sensory cortex could be started by activity in pathways to and from a central part of the network as readily as it is by activity in pathways to and from a sense organ.

[5]"It looks as if what is said to be reproduction is, far more generally than is commonly admitted, really a construction, serving to justify whatever impression may have been left by the original. It is this 'impression,' rarely defined with much exactitude, which most readily persists. So long as the details which can be built up around it are such that they would give it a 'reasonable' setting, most of us are fairly content, and are apt to think that what we build we have literally retained [F. C. Bartlett, 1932, p. 176]."

of cell assemblies as originally understood by Hebb. Only when an error occurs will short- and long-term memory appear to differ. This difference will involve signals going astray in different areas (periphery or depth) of the nerve net, depending on quite simple properties of potentiation and enhancement. This account is mechanically much simpler than the idea that items of experience are entered in a short-term memory file in one part of the brain and later transferred to some other file for more permanent storage.

An act of remembrance, whether it be of short-term memory or of long-term memory, whether it be recognition, cued recall, or spontaneous rehearsal, will involve the activation of many cell assemblies in both the periphery and in the more central areas of the brain. To be successful, the act of remembrance must involve activation of cell assemblies that can be co-active without interfering with, or inhibiting, one another. It is this property, I think, that provides an answer to the interesting paradox of infantile amnesia. As pointed out by Schachtel (1947) (see also Campbell & Spear, 1972), the experiences of early life are profoundly important to the psychological development of animal and man, yet specific events from this early life cannot be remembered in adulthood. I have argued here that, in early life, the peripheral areas of the brain are being progressively structured by experience, and as a consequence, the more central areas eventually start receiving stereotyped inputs. Presumably, the patterns of activity in central areas prior to this peripheral structuring would involve enhancement of central assemblies corresponding to what we might call infantile cognitive structures. These would have to be the basis for later remembering. However, as cell assemblies in the peripheral areas are built up and become more structured, it is likely that many of them will be incompatible with those of the infantile cognitive structure. Infanitile amnesia, therefore, would be explained not in terms of the loss of any enhanced synapses, or central cell assemblies, but in terms of the incompatibility of those infantile assemblies with the highly structured set of peripheral assemblies that would exist in the mature brain.

VERIFICATION STUDIES

Thus, we have seen that Hebb's theory provides us with an approach to the understanding of memory, if granted the premise that synapses can be modified. And we have seen evidence that synapses are modified in appropriate ways. But what evidence have we that such modification of synapses does, in fact, relate to the establishment of memory? Direct evidence is lacking. Barnes (1977, 1979) has completed a series of experiments that establish both a correlation and an experimental dependency between spatial learning and enhancement of synapses in the hippocampus of rats. Spontaneous alternation behavior in a T-maze, acquisition of a complex circular maze choice habit, and enhancement of perforant path synapses were all compared between a group of sensescent and a group of mature adult rats. The senescent rats were slower to acquire the correct choice in the complex maze and showed less durable synaptic enhancement following repeated high-frequency stimulation of the perforant path. Within both the senescent group and the younger animals, significant positive correlations were found between the measures of maze performance and synaptic enhancement. T-maze spontaneous alternation (a putative measure of spatial memory) was significantly impaired in the senescent rats following the physiological enhancement of many perforant path synapses, whereas the younger animals were able to absorb the treatment without significant effects on their T-maze alternation behavior. Barnes interprets these results to mean that the lifetime experiences of the old animals have yielded a proportion of enhanced synapses in the hippocampus that may be very useful for guiding behavior in situations the animal is likely to encounter again, but a proportion that leaves only a few for the learning of new tasks. When these few are inappropriately enhanced by physiological experimentation, too few remain for distinguishing between a novel and a previously chosen arm of a T-maze. Therefore, the data are in general confirmatory. But they are still indirect and are open to more than one interpretation.

FINAL COMMENT

Some of the physiological predictions made by Hebb have been confirmed. I have modified other postulates of his theory according to the evidence. The major change has been to relate short-term memory to potentiation instead of to the reverberation of activity in closed loops. This particular change not only fits the available physiological information, but avoids a conceptual dilemma that was encountered by Hebb's earlier theory: Namely, if short-term "holding" is based on reverberation of activity in cell assemblies, and if perception and awareness are also based on activity in cell assemblies, why are we not simultaneously conscious of all items that are stored or primed in short-term memory? The same problem is also encountered when Hebb considers thought. In Chapter 2 in this volume, Hebb points out that reverberation of activity in cell-assemblies would very quickly lead to a form of noise and proposes that the very large number of inhibitory neurons of the brain serve to promptly terminate activity in a cell-assembly "once it has served its function of exciting the next one." In the formulation presented here, I have shown how the network properties of potentiation would serve a priming function that does not depend ongoing activity. Only those aspects of short-term memory that remain in consciousness should involve active reverberation.

It is a tribute to Hebb that, even though some of his postulates concerning synaptic mechanism were wrong, it is only by adopting his theoretical perspective that I have been able to see how the newly discovered details of synaptic plasticity have any importance at all.

ACKNOWLEDGMENTS

This work was supported by a Killam Senior Scholarship awarded to me by the Canada Council and by grant number A0365 awarded to me by the Natural Sciences and Engineering Research Council of Canada.

REFERENCES

Alger, B. E., & Teyler, T. J. Long-term and short-term plasticity in CA1, CA3 and dentate regions of the rat hippocampal slice. *Brain Research,* 1976, *110,* 463–480.

Andersen, P., Sundberg, S. H., & Sveen, O. Specific long-lasting potentiation of synaptic transmission in hippocampal slices. *Nature,* 1977, *266,* 736–737.

Barnes, C. A. *Memory deficits associated with senescence: A neurophysiological and behavioral study in the rat.* Unpublished doctoral dissertation, Carleton University, 1977.

Barnes, C. A. Memory deficits associated with senescence: A neurophysiological and behavioral study in the rat. *Journal of Comparative and Physiological Psychology,* 1979, *93,* 74–104.

Bartlett, F. C. Remembering: A study in experimental and social psychology. Cambridge: *Cambridge University Press,* 1932.

Bliss, T. V. P. Synaptic plasticity in the hippocampus. *Trends in Neurosciences,* 1979, *2,* 42–45.

Bliss, T. V. P., & Gardner-Medwin, A. Long-lasting potentiation of synaptic transmission in the dentate area of unanesthetized rabbit following stimulation of the perforant path. *Journal of Physiology,* 1973, *232,* 357–374.

Bliss, T. V. P., Lømo, T. Long-lasting potentiation of synaptic transmission in the dentate area of the anaesthetized rabbit following stimulation of the perforant path. *Journal of Physiology,* 1973, *232,* 331–356.

Bransford, J. D., & Franks, J. J. Toward a framework for understanding learning. In G. Bower (Ed.), *The Psychology of Learning and Motivation.* Academic Press: New York, 1976, *10,* 93–127.

Buckhout, R. Eyewitness testimony. *Scientific American,* 1974, *231,* 23–31.

Calvin, W. H. Three modes of repetitive firing and the role of threshold time course between spikes. *Brain Research,* 1974, *69,* 341–346.

Campbell, B. A., & Spear, N. E. Ontogeny of memory. *Psychological Review,* 1972, *79,* 215–236.

Collins, A. M., & Loftus, E. F. A spreading-activation theory of semantic processing. *Psychological Review,* 1975, *82,* 407–428.

Craik, F. I. M., & Lockhart, R. S. Levels of processing: A framework for memory research. *Journal of Verbal Learning and Verbal Behavior,* 1972, *11,* 671–684.

Douglas, R. M. Long-lasting synaptic potentiation in the rat dentate gyrus following brief high-frequency stimulation. *Brain Research,* 1977, *126,* 361–365.

Douglas, R. M. *The conditional nature of synaptic modification in the fascia dentata of the rat.* Unpublished doctoral dissertation, Dalhousie University, 1978. (a)

Douglas, R. M. Heterosynaptic control over synaptic modification in the dentate gyrus. *Eighth Annual Meeting, Society for Neuroscience,* St. Louis, Mo. November 1978. (b)

Douglas, R. M., & Goddard, G. V. Long-term potentiation of the perforant path-granule cell synapse in the rat hippocampus. *Brain Research,* 1975, *86,* 205–215.

Dudek, F. E., Deadwyler, S., Cotman, C., & Lynch, G. Intracellular responses from granule cell layer in slices of rat hippocampus: perforant path synapse. *Journal of Neurophysiology,* 1976, *39,* 384–393.

Dunwiddie, T., & Lynch, G. Long-term potentiation and depression of synaptic responses in the rat hippocampus: Localization and frequency dependency. *Journal of Physiology,* 1978, *276,* 353–367.

Goddard, G. V., & Douglas, R. M. Does the engram of kindling model the engram of normal long-term memory? In J. A. Wada (Ed.), *Kindling.* New York: Raven Press, 1976.

Hebb, D. O. *Organization of behavior.* New York: John Wiley & Sons, 1949.

Lynch, G. S., Dunwiddie, T., & Gribkoff, V. K. Heterosynaptic depression: A postsynaptic correlate of long-term potentiation. *Nature,* 1977, *266,* 737–739.

NcNaughton, B. L. Dissociation of short- and long-lasting modification of synaptic efficacy at the terminals of the perforant path. *Seventh Annual Meeting, Society for Neuroscience,* California, November 1977.

McNaughton, B. L. *The dynamics of synaptic modulation in the medial and lateral components of the perforant pathway to the fascia dentata in the rat.* Unpublished doctoral dissertation, Dalhousie University, 1978.

McNaughton, B. L., & Barnes, C. A. Physiological identification and analysis of dentate granule cell responses to stimulation of the medial and lateral perforant pathways in the rat. *Journal of Comparative Neurology,* 1977, *175,* 439–454.

McNaughton, B. L., Douglas, R. M., & Goddard, G. V. Synaptic enhancement in fascia dentata: Cooperativity among co-active afferents. *Brain Research,* 1978, *157,* 277–293.

Milner, P. M. The cell assembly: Mark II. *Psychological Review,* 1957, *64,* 242–252.

Milner, P. M. A model for visual shape recognition. *Psychological Review,* 1974, *81,* 521–535.

Ranck, J. B., Jr. Studies on single neurons in dorsal hippocampal formation and septum in unrestrained rats, Part I. Behavioral correlates and firing repertoires. *Experimental Neurology,* 1973, *41,* 461–531.

Schachtel, E. G. On memory and childhood amnesia. *Psychiatry,* 1947, *10,* 1–26.

Schwartzkroin, P. A., & Wester, K. Long-lasting facilitation of a synaptic potential following tetanization in the *in vitro* hippocampal slice. *Brain Research,* 1975, *89,* 107–119.

Yamamoto, C. Synaptic transmission between mossy fiber and hippocampal neurons studied *in vitro* in thin brain sections. *Proceedings of the Japan Academy,* 1970, *46,* 1041–1045.

Author Index

Subject Index